Chicago is eating it up!

Reviews and Raves for A Cook's Guide to Chicago

"Pocius leaves few baking stones unturned . . . This handy reference book documents area shops for those seeking kitchen tools, unusual ingredients, cooking classes and, maybe best of all, bargains."

—*Chicago Tribune*

". . . Just what we all have needed . . . We use it as a reference in almost every one of our World Kitchen cooking classes. I learned right away that I need one copy in my kitchen and one in my car."

—*Judith Dunbar Hines, Director, Culinary Arts & Events, City of Chicago Department of Cultural Affairs*

"The chef/food writer has done her homework, and she offers nicely detailed listings of ethnic and gourmet grocers, equipment suppliers, cooking schools and much more."

—*Chicago Sun-Times*

"Pocius manages to combine humor with expertise for double the enjoyment."

—*Alice Van Housen, Local Palate*

". . . [A] great guide for having your own mini-vacation to some of Chicago's most interesting ethnic neighborhoods and their markets."

—*Dana Benigno, Chef/Owner, chicagocooks.com*

"From abalone to the spiced palm oil known as zomi, this zesty compendium of local sources for international cuisine provides a valuable resource for those in search of ethnic supermarkets, gourmet shops, chef's equipment stores, food clubs and organizations and even bookstores."

—*The Daily Southtown*

" . . . [A] tell-all guide for finding the best exotic foods, spices and cooking supplies in the city and suburbs."

—*Chicago Life*

A Cook's Guide to Chicago

Where to find everything you need and lots of things you didn't know you did

by Marilyn Pocius

Second Edition

LAKE CLAREMONT PRESS
www.lakeclaremont.com
Chicago

A Cook's Guide to Chicago, 2nd Edition
by Marilyn Pocius

Published February, 2006, by:

4650 North Rockwell Street
Chicago, Illinois 60625
773/583-7800
lcp@lakeclaremont.com
www.lakeclaremont.com

Publisher's Cataloging-in-Publication Data

Pocius, Marilyn.
   A cook's guide to Chicago : where to find everything you need and lots of things you didn't know you did / by Marilyn Pocius. – 2nd ed.
   p. cm.
   Includes bibliographical reference and index.
   "Includes original recipes, sources for professional equipment, and lists of the best ethnic markets."
   LCCN: 2005922959
   SBN: 1-893121-47-X

   1. Grocery shopping--Illinois--Chicago--Directories.
   2. Ethnic markets--Illinois--Chicago--Directories.
   3. Cookery--Illinois--Chicago--Equipment and supplies--Directories.   I. Title

   TX356.P63 2002   381'.456413'002577311

Printed in the United States of America by United Graphics, an employee-owned company based in Mattoon, Illinois.

09 08 07 06   10 9 8 7 6 5 4 3 2 1

For my two Genevieves

Thanks for making life delicious.

(bamboo shoots)

Publisher's Credits
Cover design by Timothy Kocher. Interior design and layout by
Sue Petersen and Todd Petersen. Scans by Marilyn Pocius. Editing
by Laura R. Gabler. Proofreading by Sharon Woodhouse, Elizabeth
Daniel, and Karen Formanski. Index by Sharon Woodhouse.

Contents

Acknowledgments vii

Introduction xi
How to Use This Book xi

Gourmet 1
Herbs and Spices 9
Meat, Poultry, and Game 19
Fish and Seafood 27
Produce 35
Equipment 45
Health Food and Nuts 61
Kosher Food 67
Cooking Schools, Groups, and Books 73

Latin America 81
    Tips on Tropical Tubers .101
Eastern Europe 107
Germany, Ireland, and Scandinavia 125
Italy 129
Greece, Turkey, and the Balkans 145
The Middle East 157
Africa and the Caribbean 171
India and Pakistan 181

China 201

Southeast Asia 219

   Knowing Your Noodles 233

Japan, Korea, and the Philippines 239

Multiethnic Stores 257

A Drink with That?

   Coffee and Tea 266

   Brewing and Winemaking .267

   Wine Stores 267

Delicious Day Trips 271

Leftovers

   Bibliography 276

   Indexes 281

      Recipe Index 281

      Stores, Clubs, and Organizations Index 284

      Equipment Index 289

      Ingredient Index 294

About the Author 335

Acknowledgments

Genna, thank you for putting up with dawn excursions to Maxwell Street, breakfasts of halvah puri, and plenty of experimental dinners. I truly appreciate all the demos you've helped with and coolers you've schlepped. You are—what's the word?—raw.

Thanks to my mom, who is still teaching me plenty at the age of 87 and whose wit and wisdom I appreciate more every year.

The whole Pocius clan deserves a round of applause. Thanks to Judy, for your humor and common sense; Paul, for your humor, intelligence, and occasional lack of common sense; and Tom and Mike, for being fun, strong, and willing to help with anything from flipping pennycakes to grinding poppy seeds.

Julie Gibson-Lay, thanks for all the hard work, good times, and inspiration you provided; and thanks to Chris and Cecil, for bequeathing me so much of your time.

I'd be lost without my support group: Andrée Tracey, Charlie Propsom, Gracie and Gregg Weiss, Maria Murzyn, and Nancy and Doug Deuchler. The gang at Publications International has helped in more ways than they know: Thanks to Susan Garard (the best boss), Marvella Bowen, Karen Jensen, Jane Lindeman, Ruth Siegel, and the rest. The friends and foodie folk I'm still learning from are too numerous to mention. Special thanks to Mary Ann Sochacki, Metta Miller, Bob Blumer, Ruth Clark, and Virginia Mekkelson.

Lake Claremont Press has been helpful, understanding, and accessible. I'm lucky to have you as my publisher.

Finally, an enormous thank-you goes to the scores of anonymous people I met along the way, from so many different backgrounds and countries. Thanks for answering my questions and sharing your cultures. Food is a pathway to understanding and a universal language. Peace.

A Cook's Guide to Chicago

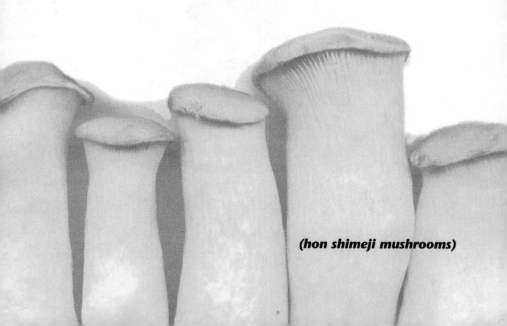

(hon shimeji mushrooms)

(pomegranate)

Introduction to the Second Edition

Since the publication of the first edition of *Cook's Guide* in 2002 (not that long ago in wine-years), a lot has changed. Chicago has become a more sophisticated food town in every way. There are new world-class restaurants, world-famous chefs, cooking schools, and markets catering to the cognoscenti. For once, my timing was right, and I've enjoyed being a part of this foodie frenzy.

This book began as a simple idea: Tell home cooks where to go to get the ingredients and equipment they need or want. It quickly evolved into something more. It seems like every week I find another wonderful recipe, exotic fruit, or ethnic market to try out. Living in Chicago is like having a big, gorgeous pantry chock-full of flavors waiting to be tasted.

The journey has brought me nose to nose with the infamous durian (it doesn't taste as bad as it smells) and alerted me to some things I never want to eat (water bugs and eyeball tacos). Mainly it has added savor and delight to my life in a zillion ways. My taste buds will never settle for ordinary again. I didn't know I couldn't live without mushroom soy sauce, pomegranate concentrate, or guava paste until I found them.

Whether you just want to find semolina flour to make pasta or you want to explore a new cuisine every week, this book's mission is to help you find your way and have a tasty trip. Wherever you may wander, I wish you a life filled with flavor.

How to Use This Book

When I started my research, I had visions of listing every store where each ingredient could be found. Hah! Too many variables. Things are in season or not. They are there one time and not the next, and besides, there are just too darn many. So ingredients are listed in chapters based on rather arbitrary categories. Some will be obvious—if you need truffle oil, look for a gourmet store; sushi rice will be found in a Japanese market. But there are a lot of delightful in-betweens. For instance, an Asian store is a great place to buy fresh fish, and a farmers market may offer fresh Asian greens. Where possible, I've cross-referenced stores and provided suggestions on alternatives. The index is designed to be specific enough to help you find a particular ingredient or piece of equipment.

The "Top Ten Ingredients" listings for ethnic stores are there to demystify your shopping experience. They point out items that are unusually delicious and that fit into most cooking styles. They should help give focus to your shopping trip and keep you from being overwhelmed with the new and the strange. (Of course, being somewhat overwhelmed IS part of the fun.)

If you're looking for a particular ethnic ingredient, I suggest you browse the general category in addition to checking the index. You may discover another name for what you want, a possible substitution, or a new ingredient to try. Spelling on labels of ethnic products is inconsistent at best and often hilarious. It can be particularly inventive and confusing when translations are from alphabets different from ours.

What I hope you also discover is the joy of the chase. Finding exotic stuff like durian fruit and sea slugs and silk squash right here in the city is exhilarating. Visiting ethnic markets can quickly become habit forming. They're so much juicier than a regulation American supermarket with all its frozen dinners and shrink-wrap. Sure, ethnic markets smell a little peculiar sometimes, but so does food. Remember the first good whiff you got of garlic?

Another thing to remember is that ethnic cuisines have their own convenience products. Many of them are good. Try a jar of Thai curry paste or Mexican mole sauce. It's not the same as making it from scratch, but I assure you, even some decent restaurants use these things, and it's an easy way to expand your weeknight repertoire.

Happy shopping!

Disclaimers

While every attempt was made to include a good cross-section of sources, this book makes no claim at being definitive. Retail establishments close and change with great rapidity, so call before you go or you risk disappointment. No stores were asked whether they wanted to be listed. The choices of what should be included or omitted were based on my personal judgment and may seem arbitrary and idiosyncratic to some readers. It's because they are.

The recipes and tips were invented by the author unless it is otherwise indicated, and inspiration came from many cookbooks and friends who cook. The opinions expressed are mine, all mine. Most stores were visited only once or twice, so your experience may be very different.

Don't blame me if you eat something you shouldn't. I did on occasion, but it was never a problem, because I tasted things in small quantities if I was unsure. Be aware that in many cultures, food is medicine. Some things, especially herbs, teas, and drinks, can be potent (and taste bad).

Gourmet

(smoked salmon, cheese, capers, and cornichons)

Gourmet Ingredients

Gourmet has become an old-fashioned sounding word. These days the term is *foodie*. The stores that specialize in gourmet products have changed a lot, too. Remember those tiny places with dusty jars of esoteric sauces you paid too much for and never used? Instead, we now enjoy bustling marketplaces that offer cheese, wine, bread, charcuterie, and plenty of service without the hoity-toity attitude.

Chicago is catching up with New York. We don't have a Dean & DeLuca yet, but our gourmet stores carry all the high-end products along with Midwestern specialties. There are even two shops specializing in cheese (finally!) included here. This is a list of some of the kinds of things you'll find.

caper berries
capers
caviar
cheese, imported and
 artisanal
chocolate, high cocoa content, imported
cornichons
crème fraîche
European (high-fat)
 butter
marcona almonds

mustards: imported and/or flavored with green peppercorns, fruits, or herbs
oils—
 grapeseed oils: plain
  and flavored
 nut oils: hazelnut,
  pistachio, walnut
 olive oils: unfiltered,
  pressed with fruit
  (lemon, tangerine),
  flavored with herbs
pâtés
prosciutto
smoked fish and seafood
tapenades: olive, artichoke,
 red pepper, sun-dried
 tomato
terrines and mousses
truffle oil
truffle powder and
 paste
truffles
vinegars: aged balsamic,
 sherry, fruit and herb flavored, fancy wine vinegar
 (Cabernet, Merlot)

Gourmet Stores

The Artisan Cellar

222 Merchandise Mart Plaza
Suite 116
312/527-5810
See "A Drink with That?"
chapter (p. 268).

Binny's Beverage Depot

3000 N. Clark St.
773/935-9400

213 W. Grand Ave.
312/332-0012
www.binnys.com

Binny's is a chain of wine and liquor stores (16 stores in the greater Chicagoland area), but the two stores listed also carry a variety of gourmet items and have an extensive selection of **cheeses**, too. The Clark Street store is the Ivanhoe Castle Binny's, complete with wine cellar "catacombs."

The stores carry a huge selection of cheeses, plus **olive oils, jams, gourmet ice cream**, and the line of **Dahlia Exotic Flavoring Pastes**. You can buy little bottles of **truffle oil** for less than $10 (good if you're just trying it out) and also **imported truffles, truffle paste**, and **truffle cream**. Local producers are well represented by **Frontera's line** of salsas and Mexican foods, as well as **caviar** from **Carolyn Collins Caviar** (see p. 34). She distributes American sturgeon caviar, plus flavored whitefish caviar (pepper, citron), salmon caviar, and **tobikko** (Japanese flying fish roe). A deli features cured meats (**pancetta, soprasetta**) and almost a dozen **pâtés** and **terrines** sold by the pound.

Chalet Wine and Cheese

40 E. Delaware Pl.
312/787-8555

Chalet has been around for decades. Most of the space is devoted to wine and some very interesting liquor, including **300-year-old cognacs** and an extensive choice of **good rum, tequila, and liqueurs**. They also have an excellent assortment of **cheese** and knowledgeable sales folk to assist you. They stock **pâtés** and cute little **cornichons** to go with them. Oh, yeah, **caviar**, too, plus lots of sauces and condiments. There's **truffle oil, porcini paste**, pine nut and pistachio oil, and the newly popular olive oil pressed with citrus. They carry both Italian and Californian versions. There are spices, balsamic vinegars, sherry vinegars, and flavored vinegars of all kinds. Lots of pasta, too, including striped, sombrero shaped, and squid ink.

The Cheese Stands Alone

4547 N. Western Ave.
773/293-3870

This small shop is all about cheese—they carry more than 100 varieties from the United States and around the globe. One can't live by cheese alone (though, heaven knows, I've tried), so they do also carry bread, prosciutto, and some other gourmet items.

Foodstuffs

2106 Central St.
Evanston
847/328-7704

338 Park Ave.
Glencoe
847/835-5105

1456 Waukegan Rd.
Glenview
847/832-9999

255 Westminster Rd.
Lake Forest
847/234-6600
www.foodstuffs.com

Foodstuffs offers an assortment of mouth-watering goodies. They do a brisk take-out business in sandwiches and salads. The Evanston store also has a wide variety of condiments, oils, vinegars, and other gourmet ingredients, both imported and domestic. You'll find products from many restaurant lines, including Vong and Frontera. There is a small assortment of Asian and Middle Eastern specialties, like Thai curry paste and tahini, plus a dizzying array of tapenades, soup mixes, imported pasta, mustard, and more. You can purchase Foodstuffs' frozen appetizers (egg rolls, quiche, phyllo bites), prepared sushi, and ready-to-cook seasoned and breaded fish and meat. Foodstuffs has a butcher shop and a selection of cheeses as well.

Fox & Obel Food Market

401 E. Illinois St.
312/410-7301
www.fox-obel.com

Opened in 2001, this 22,000-square-foot premium food market offers much beyond the usual condiments, oils, and vinegars. There are **meats and fish smoked on premises**, a bakery, a **dry-aging room for beef**, and a produce department. A dairy case offers **European-style high-fat butter** and **crème fraîche**. There is a huge selection of oils and ethnic specialties from around the world. They take great pride in their **cheese department**, where everything is fresh-cut, not shrink-wrapped. The butcher shop carries **foie gras**, prime meat, and specialty cuts, and the fish department displays **whole fish on ice** and then fillets to order. Fox & Obel is committed to a high level of service, so if you're looking for something special, ask if they'll stock it. They even promised me they'd try to get fresh wasabi. Fox & Obel has a café and prepared food, too.

Pastoral

2945 N. Broadway St.
773/472-4781
www.pastoralartisan.com

Cheese is the thing here, and Pastoral is the exclusive retail outlet for some **artisanal varieties** that are usually offered only in restaurants. Wine, **pâtés**, **sausages**, **olives**, and bread from **Evanston's Bennison's Bakery** are also available.

Sam's Wine and Spirits/Marcey Street Market

1720 N. Marcey St.
312/664-4394
www.samswine.com

If you've lived in the city any length of time, you know Sam's. It was one of the first serious—and seriously affordable—wine places. The huge warehouse is loaded with wine and very hip clerks, and there's a gourmet section called the Marcey Street Market in the rear of the store. The **cheese** selection is huge and well priced. In addition to the chefs' lines of sauces and condiments (such as **Vong**, **Bobby Flay**, and **Rick Bayless**), there is a collection of **vinegars**, among them **aged balsamic** and **sherry**. They also stock **gourmet salts**, including **Fleur de Sel** from France and **Malden** from England, **dried mushrooms**, **canned San Marzano tomatoes**, and an item I'd been looking for everywhere—**smoked paprika**.

Schaefer's Wines, Foods and Spirits
9965 Gross Point Rd.
Skokie
847/673-5711
See "A Drink with That?" chapter (p. 270).

Trader Joe's
1840 N. Clybourn Ave.
312/274-9733

3745 N. Lincoln Ave.
773/248-4920

17 W. Rand Rd.
Arlington Heights
847/506-0752

122 Ogden Ave.
Downers Grove
630/241-1662

680 Roosevelt Rd.
Glen Ellyn
630/858-5077

1407 Waukegan Rd.
Glenview
847/657-7821

25 N. La Grange Rd.
La Grange
708/579-0838

735 Main St.
Lake Zurich
847/550-7827

44 W. Gartner
Naperville
630/355-4389

577 Waukegan Rd.
Northbrook
847/498-9076

14924 S. La Grange Rd.
Orland Park
708/349-9021
www.traderjoes.com

Trader Joe's originated in California as a great place to buy cheap wine. It has become a phenomenon. TJ's isn't like anyplace else. They are a full-service wine and grocery, but they also carry more than 800 private label items. Trader Joe's imports from all over the world and has products made to their specs. The quality is top-notch, and the prices are amazingly low. Selection is somewhat Californian, with lots of **salsa**, **dried fruits and nuts** (great **dried wild blueberries**), **organic items**, and a fair number of frozen prepared dishes, including some frozen "bowl" dinners with an Asian or Indian theme. There's nothing tremendously esoteric, but you'll find good buys on sauces, vinegars, and the like. There is a small selection of mostly organic produce, too. They import excellent **frozen seafood** and **Australian lamb**. Once you get hooked on TJ's, you have to go back for more of your favorites. I'm totally dependent on their **marcona almonds**, tuna burgers, frozen French green beans, and frozen berries. Oh, yeah, they also have lots of **cereals and cookies made with NO hydrogenated fats**.

To add to the California feel, the staff wears Hawaiian shirts and is a little too friendly.

Trotter's To Go
1337 W. Fullerton Ave.
773/868-6510
www.charlietrotters.com/togo

Charlie Trotter's latest endeavor offers carryout foods prepared to the exquisite Trotter specifications. They also carry a high-end collection of gourmet condiments and ingredients. You'll find **artisanal cheeses, grains, forbidden rice, organic soba noodles, soy sauces**, and many different **chefs' lines** of products, alongside Charlie's. They have a small refrigerated case with the most gorgeous **white anchovies** I've ever seen. There are **expensive aged vinegars**, of course, and a small but unique assortment of cooking equipment, including **wasabi graters** and beautiful, expensive **mandolines**. You can

watch chefs at work in an open kitchen and find suggestions on pairings for a variety of wines.

And don't forget:

Marshall Field's Marketplace
Multiple locations

Many Field's stores devote an entire floor to food and cooking equipment. They carry all the name brands, like **Calphalon, Wüsthof**, and **KitchenAid**, not to mention condiments, pasta, sauces, cookbooks, and dishes, too. I tend to forget this wonderful resource for cooks even exists until I wander into Field's looking for something else. Prices can even be good when there's a sale.

Treasure Island
Multiple locations

Yeah, it's a supermarket, but what a supermarket! They have **fresh chanterelles, Belgian chocolates**, and quite a decent selection of **ethnic ingredients**. The butcher shop is comprehensive. In stock last time I was there were **Niman Ranch pork, foie gras**, and **smoked duck**, as well as **fresh duck breasts**.

Whole Foods
Multiple locations

Very similar to Treasure Island only with more emphasis on **organic and health food**, Whole Foods also runs a butcher shop and fish department dedicated to personal service. They will order what you want with advance notice, and they **dry age meat** on premises. The produce department is well stocked with **organic greens**, as well as less common things, like **blood oranges** and **fiddlehead ferns**, in season.

Chocolate

Blommer Chocolate Company
600 W. Kinzie St.
312/266-7700
www.blommerstore.com

If you work in the South Loop, you're probably acquainted with Blommer by the wonderful aroma of chocolate wafting through the air. They are one of the largest producers of **bulk chocolate** in the country. The tiny retail store sells **baking chocolate** in handy chunks or discs for easy melting. Blommer also offers **high-fat Dutch cocoa**, as well as many **chocolate-covered goodies**. Doesn't **dark chocolate–covered ginger** sound divine?

PRODUCED IN SPAIN

FREE FROM ANY OBJECTIONABLE OR ANIMAL MATTER

WELL KNOWN AND PURE

THE GATHERING OF SAFFRON

REGISTERED TRADE MARK

Herbs and Spices

(saffron box, crystallized ginger, sea salt, and salt cellars)

Herbs and Spices

Nothing improves your cooking quicker than using better, fresher (and more!) herbs and spices. Chicago is lucky enough to have quite a number of shops that specialize in just that.

Most dried herbs and spices retain their flavor for only about a year. Some have volatile oils that dissipate even faster. Go through your spice cupboard, open every jar, and sniff. If it smells like nothing, it is. Toss it and buy new.

Many things (**cayenne**, **chiles**, **poppy seed**, **sesame seed**) keep their oomph longer if stored in the freezer. And the whole form of a spice lasts much longer, so grind whole **peppercorns**, **allspice**, **cardamom**, and **nutmeg** as needed.

Store herbs and spices in airtight jars or bags away from heat and light. (In other words, don't keep spices in a rack over the stove!)

All the stores listed will have the basics (**dried oregano**, **basil**, **ginger**, **cinnamon**, etc.), so I'm only mentioning the less common ones. If you've always bought your herbs and spices at the grocery store, try purchasing them at a specialty shop, where things are fresher. The difference in flavor is substantial.

When looking for herbs for an ethnic recipe, you're best off picking them up at the same store where you buy the rest of your ingredients. They'll probably be both fresher and cheaper.

ajowan (carom)
Aleppo pepper
annatto seeds (achiote)
cardamom, whole green and/or decorticated (without the shell)
chipotle powder
epazote
fenugreek
galangal
ginger, crystallized
grains of paradise
gumbo filé (sassafras)
juniper berries
kala jeera (black cumin)
kalonji (charnuska, nigella)
mace
mahleb, mahlab (sour cherry pits)
saffron
smoked paprika
star anise
sumac
turmeric
whole allspice
whole nutmeg
whole vanilla beans

Some Fresh-Ground Pepper??

green peppercorns

pink peppercorns

Sarawak peppercorns

Szechuan peppercorns (fagara)

Tellicherry peppercorns

white peppercorns

Remember the first time you had a waiter grind fresh pepper on your salad with that huge pepper mill? Or was it Julia Child who first convinced you fresh ground was a whole lot better? Well, here's some more info, so you can be an even bigger pepper snob.

Black peppercorns are not all the same. The ones with the most developed flavor have been allowed to ripen longer on the vine, so they tend to be bigger. **Tellicherry** are considered the biggest and best Indian peppercorns. But **Sarawak peppercorns** from Borneo also have their fans (including me). They are dried a different way and have a mellower, richer dimension.

Green peppercorns are the immature version of the same plant and taste much milder. **White peppercorns** are the old folks of the family. They are left to ripen the longest on the vine (so they're pricier). Then their outer shell is removed. They're preferred in most Asian cuisines and other recipes where specks of black don't look appetizing. What about **pink peppercorns** and **Szechuan peppercorns**, you ask? They are not real peppercorns at all, since they come from totally different plants, and only have the name because they have the same shape.

Salt Gets an Extreme Makeover

Salt used to be considered the most banal of seasonings. Funny, just when you start taking something for granted, it goes and gets trendy. Designer sea salts that cost $2 an ounce and on up are hot these days.

Are they worth their salt? Isn't it just sodium chloride? Yes and no.

I purchased my first container of fleur de sel in a French supermarket decades ago, when I couldn't afford it. (Come to think of it, I still can't.) It came in a really cute container and had the name of the paludier (salt harvester) on it. The flavor

Cracking Nutmeg

If you've only experienced dusty powdered nutmeg from a supermarket jar, freshly grated nutmeg will blow you away. No special equipment is required. Just rub a whole nutmeg against the small holes on your box grater. The aroma is fantastic—tropical, mysterious, sweet, and pungent. Try it in any cream sauce, with spinach, or on a baked sweet potato. Wow!

Flavored Coffee

1. **Vanilla coffee**. Cut a piece of fresh vanilla bean into a 1-inch length and split it open. Toss it into the coffee filter with the ground coffee and brew as usual.

2. **Cardamom coffee**. In parts of the Middle East, people believe that coffee can sap your masculinity unless cardamom is added. I don't know about that, but it tastes good. Crush 2 whole green cardamom pods and put in with the ground beans and brew.

3. **Cinnamon coffee**. Add a cinnamon stick to the brewing basket. You can retrieve and reuse the stick a few times before it loses flavor.

Herbs and Spices

was almost sweet and minerally, and the texture was crunchy but irregular, so the level of saltiness changed as you tasted. I still buy fleur de sel, though it never tastes quite as good as it did that first time. Salt can come from the ground (rock salt) or the water (sea salt). Ordinary table salt is extracted by machines in factories. Fleur de sel, on the other hand, is harvested by hand from salt ponds in France. There are many different ways to extract the chemical from the carrier. Although all salt is sodium chloride, it can taste wildly different depending on where it came from and what other minerals and impurities came along for the trip. A gourmet salt like fleur de sel is what is called a finishing salt. It's intended for use almost as a garnish, not to be thrown into the pasta water.

These days there seems to be a new, and more expensive, salt available every week, such as **Sicilian Trapani salt**, **Korean bamboo salt**, **pink Peruvian salt**, and **Danish smoked salt**. You can't possibly sample them all, so here are a few of the ones worth knowing:

Fleur de sel (flower of salt). Imported from France. The name refers to the process of gathering the salt "bloom." This is the one to try on something simple, like tomatoes or black bread with sweet butter.

Hawaiian red sea salt. The red (pinkish orange, really) comes from a natural red clay (called alaea), rich in iron oxide, that is added to the salt.

Hawaiian black sea salt. Very strong and very salty, this salt has lava and activated charcoal added to it. It looks lovely sprinkled on light colored food, like pale fish fillets or hard-cooked eggs.

Kosher salt. See "Kosher" chapter (p. 70).

Malden sea salt. Made off the southern coast of England by traditional methods, this is the salt preferred by many hip London chefs.

Sel gris (gray salt). This moist, unrefined French sea salt gets its pinkish gray color from the clay in the salt flats where it is harvested.

Black salt (kala namak). This odiferous salt is used in many Indian snacks and is part of the blend called chaat masala. It is actually pink in color once ground and smells like sulfur. It is an unrefined rock salt.

Herb and Spice Stores

Fox & Obel Food Market

401 E. Illinois St.
312/410-7301
See "Gourmet" chapter (p. 4).

Penzeys Spices

235 S. Washington St.
Naperville
630/355-7677

1138 W. Lake St.
Oak Park
708/848-7772
800/741-7787
www.penzeys.com

The premier mail-order source for fresh, excellent spices now has retail stores in the Chicago area. If you've never received Penzeys catalog, call right now and get on their mailing list. They offer just about every spice and dried herb, even some of the less common ones, like **juniper berries** and **charnushka**. They also carry **four kinds of ground cinnamon** and **seven different peppercorns**. The differences can be a revelation. For instance, what we think of as cinnamon is actually cassia; real cinnamon is sweeter and milder tasting without that hot bite. The retail stores offer everything that's in the catalog. You can purchase herbs and spices in jars or preweighed plastic bags. It is perfectly possible to spend 30 minutes just wandering around sniffing things.

The Home Economist

906 S. Northwest Hwy.
Barrington
847/382-4202

419 N. La Grange Rd.
La Grange Park
708/352-1514

Church Point Plaza
9159 Gross Point Rd.
Skokie
847/674-7252

6382 Cass Ave.
Westmont
630/852-0214

J.B. Sanfilippo & Sons Thrift Stores

300 E. Touhy
Des Plaines
847/298-1510

1717 Arthur St.
Elk Grove Village
847/871-6662

This chain of stores, owned by Fisher Nuts (J.B. Sanfilippo & Sons), carries mostly **bulk bins of ingredients**. They offer a bit of a hodgepodge: **candies**, **nuts**, **lentils**, and **snack mixes**, as well as **spices** of all kinds, too (although not as extensive a selection as found at Penzeys or The Spice House). Most things are sold by the ounce. You will find some otherwise hard-to-locate items, especially in the area of **baking supplies**. This is a good place to go for **gum arabic**, **baker's ammonia**, **citric acid**, **paste food colors**, **extracts way beyond vanilla** (e.g., kona coffee, rum), **TVP** (texturized vegetable protein), **MSG**, **fructose**, **alum**, **sanding sugar**, and other **decorating sprinkles and sugars**. I haven't visited the thrift stores, but I suspect their selections are more limited.

The Spice House
1512 N. Wells St.
312/274-0378

1941 Central St.
Evanston
847/328-3711
www.thespicehouse.com

In Evanston since 1997, the Spice House now has a thriving business in Old Town as well. These charming old-fashioned stores sell dried herbs and spices in bulk. They also grind and blend their own spices and offer nifty gift boxes based on **ethnic Chicago blends**, among other things. The staff is friendly, patient, and extremely knowledgeable. There are sample jars of everything for you to sniff, and lots of information is posted.

The Spice House usually carries a few items that Penzey's doesn't, such as **fennel pollen**, **Tahitian vanilla beans**, **Aleppo pepper**, and **Hawaiian red sea salt**.

The Spice Merchant and Tea Room
108 W. Park
Elmhurst
630/941-7288
www.spicemerchant-tea-room.com

This suburban store sells a decent selection of dried herbs and spices in bulk. They don't carry some of the more esoteric things, but they do have **bulk teas** for sale and a cozy tea shop where you can sample their wares.

Fresh Herbs

Most supermarkets sell fresh herbs in the produce section. They are a great convenience; however, they are pricey, not always fresh, and mostly hydroponically grown, which makes them rather bland tasting.

The best way to have fresh herbs available is to grow them yourself. Even without a backyard it's fairly easy to keep pots of rosemary, oregano, chives, and basil going. That way you don't have to buy an entire package of something just for a few sprigs. The other advantage to growing your own is that you can try some of the more exotic things, like borage, lemon verbena, sorrel, and lavender, to name a few of my favorites.

See also the listings in the "Southeast Asia" chapter (p. 226), since those stores stock a selection of fresh herbs all year-round. In fact, the Argyle Street shops are the place to find out-of-season basil that is fresh and not too expensive.

Here are a few gardening stores that carry a selection of the more unusual culinary herbs. Check newspapers in May for yearly events, like the Chicago Botanic Gardens herb sale and the Oak Park Conservatory herb sale.

It's All in the Family

Penzey's is owned and operated by Bill Penzey; the Spice House, by his sister Patty Penzey-Erd and her husband. They compete with each other. Mom and Dad Penzey started things off with a retail business in Wisconsin years ago. Bill continued and built a mail-order business with a growing number of retail outlets. Patty built a retail business that sells some mail order, too. Many of their products are identical. Must make for some spicy family gatherings.

Fertile Garden
1650 W. Diversey Ave.
773/929-9330

Gethsemane Garden Center
5739 N. Clark St.
773/878-5915

Pesche's
170 River Rd.
Des Plaines
847/299-1300

Ted's Greenhouse
16930 S. 84th Ave.
Tinley Park
708/532-3575

Platt Hill Nursery
222 W. Lake St.
Bloomingdale
630/529-9394

Saving Summer

I'll spare you yet another recipe for pesto, but did you know you can make pesto with many other leafy herbs besides basil? Parsley and cilantro work particularly well and can be frozen in pesto form to preserve their flavor through a long, leafless winter. Just chop them up in a food processor and add enough oil to hold them together. Freeze in an ice cube tray to make herb cubes and use wherever you'd use the fresh herb.

Herb butter is easy to make, too. Chop by hand or machine almost any herb or combination of herbs (2 or 3 tablespoons will do the trick) and add to a stick of softened butter. Mash it together in a bowl, shape it into a log using plastic wrap, then wrap and freeze. You can serve your herb butter log on a special occasion or just cut off a piece anytime to add great flavor to everything from muffins to steak.

You can even dry herbs in your microwave. Please proceed cautiously, as I have started a few (minor) fires trying out this technique. Place herbs in a single layer between two paper towels. You can leave herbs on the stem, as they will crumble off more easily when dried. Nuke for no more than a minute to start. Peek in and poke the herbs to see how they're doing. Then proceed in 20-second increments until the herbs are dry enough to crumble between your fingers. Store in a glass jar until you're ready to use. Like store-bought dried herbs, their shelf life is limited to a year or less.

Herbs and Spices

Saffron-Pistachio Biscotti

(Makes about 3 dozen biscotti)

These Italian-style cookies were inspired by the flavors of my favorite Indian ice cream.

2 generous pinches saffron (about 30 threads)
1 T. hot water
2 C. flour
2 tsp. baking powder
½ tsp. salt
1 stick (4 oz.) butter, softened
⅔ C. sugar
2 eggs
1-¼ C. unsalted, shelled pistachios, toasted

Crumble the saffron threads into hot water to dissolve. Sift together the flour, baking powder, and salt. Cream the butter and sugar until fluffy with an electric mixer. Mix in the saffron and water. Beat in the eggs one at a time. Add the flour mixture a little at a time. Gently mix in the pistachios. Refrigerate the dough for an hour for easier handling.

Preheat the oven to 350°. On a floured surface, form the dough into logs that are about 3 inches in diameter and not quite as long as your baking sheets. Flatten the logs slightly and transfer them to greased or parchment-lined baking sheets. Place them about 4 inches apart, since they will spread. Bake 20 to 25 minutes, until they are slightly golden and firm to the touch.

Lower the oven temperature to 325°. Let the logs cool and remove to a cutting board. With a serrated knife, cut the logs into slices that are about ¾ of an inch thick. Arrange the slices on a baking sheet and bake another 15 to 20 minutes, until they are dried out and the cut sides color slightly. Store in an airtight container.

Herbs and Spices

Meat, Poultry, and Game

(veal and lamb chops)

Meat, Poultry, and Game

Your local butcher shop is to be cherished. These days even decent beef (choice grade) is hard to come by at the supermarket. It is beyond the scope of this book to seek out all the good local butchers. Part of what makes them good is the relationship you establish with the men or women who work there. Then not only will they order whatever you need, they'll make sure it's the best.

If you can't find a local source or don't have time to look, talk to the person behind the scenes at your big anonymous chain store. Ring that bell or buzzer and ask for what you want. There are sometimes real butchers in the back of the store who are quite delighted to give you personal service. Sometimes.

The stores included here are specialists and worth seeking out when you require an out-of-the-ordinary cut, quantity, or kind of meat or fish.

Ethnic stores are also good places to buy meat, so check the listings in the appropriate chapter, especially if you want **variety meats** (offal) or a cut that's frequently used in a particular cuisine.

For **fresh ham**, **pork belly**, **smoked butt**, **pig trotters**, or just about any other part of a pig, go to one of the Polish or Mexican markets.

Skirt steak, which has become trendy and expensive, is still a bargain at Latin American butchers. You'll also find the more usual cuts of beef, and the markets frequently offer **choice grade**. Many of the bigger ones also sell **barbacoa** and **carnitas** on the weekends. These deli specialties are already cooked and seasoned, and are tasty and handy fillings for tacos or enchiladas. Carnitas means "little meats" and is pork slow cooked until it is meltingly tender. Barbacoa is barbecued beef. (O.K., full disclosure here, barbacoa is traditionally made from a cow's head, but don't be scared, there are no tell-tale indications, such as eyeballs.)

For **lamb**, try any of the Devon Avenue meat markets listed in the "India and Pakistan" chapter (pp. 190–194). They offer good prices and will cut to order.

Veal shanks for **osso bucco** and other veal cuts, like breast and shoulder, are usually available at Italian markets.

Multiethnic stores usually have a wide selection of meat and decent butchers, too, so check that chapter (pp. 258–264).

20

Meat, Poultry, and Game Stores

Chicago Game and Gourmet

350 N. Ogden Ave.
312/455-1800
(wholesale)

These guys sell to high-end restaurants and do not have a retail store. They're listed here, however, because they are still a good resource. If you need **poussin**, **wild boar**, **foie gras**, **buffalo**, **ostrich**, or **high-quality venison**, call them. They may be able to sell to you directly if the quantity fits their wholesale specs. (For instance, some **game birds** are sold individually shrink-wrapped for the restaurant market, and you might be able to purchase them direct.) At the very least, they will be able to steer you to one of the retail establishments they deal with (**Whole Foods**, p. 8, is one), where you can get what you need.

City Noor Meat Market

4718 N. Kedzie Ave.
773/267-9166

This full-service meat market is on the busy Kedzie shopping strip, across from **Andy's** (p.

41). They primarily serve a Middle Eastern clientele but cater to many other ethnicities too. And they have everything, such as **lamb** (including **baby lamb**), **goat**, **chicken**, **beef**, and **homemade sausages**.

Columbus Meat Market

906 W. Randolph St.
312/829-2480

This is one of the Randolph Street wholesalers also open to the public. They carry **prime and choice beef**, but for prime you need to order a whole loin, which they will then butcher into the cuts you want. What a smart way to stock your freezer! They can also order anything, and I do mean anything. I asked about **caul fat** (the fat netting they're always wrapping around things on *Iron Chef*) and was told it would be no problem. "We even get **bull penis** for a restaurant that uses it in an authentic Jamaican soup."

Farm Meat Market

4810 N. Kedzie Ave.
773/588-1266

Like City Noor, listed earlier, Farm Meat is in the Kedzie-Lawrence shopping neighborhood and is a Middle Eastern–oriented shop. They are also full-service and carry **baby lamb** and **goat**, in addition to regular cuts.

Gepperth's Meat Market

1964 N. Halsted St.
773/549-3883

Gepperth's is one of the oldest, most respected full-line butcher shops in the city. They will even **age beef** for you upon request. They carry **Hudson Valley foie gras** but prefer a day's notice.

Halsted Packing

445 N. Halsted St.
312/421-5147

Peek through the windows into the back room of this place and you'll spot hanging carcasses. Halsted Packing slaughters their own meat, some of it on the premises. The staff looks like central-casting butchers—tough guys with bloody aprons and accents (Greek and/or Spanish?). Call ahead with your order since they specialize in **custom cuts** and don't have a case full of precut meats.

Harrison's Poultry Farm, Inc.

1201 Waukegan Rd.
Glenview
847/724-0132

This far north suburban place has been owned by the same family (Zimmerman) since the 1940s. They used to slaughter poultry on the premises. They no longer do that but still sell their own birds, raised in Georgia. **Poultry** is delivered daily to the retail outlet and is excellent quality. While it is not certified organic, I was assured that their poultry is **grain raised without antibiotics or hormones**. They also offer **preseasoned chicken breasts** and an **assortment of seasonings** and such. The **eggs** are extremely fresh and tasty, too.

Jerry & John's Quality Meats

3706 Dempster St.
Skokie
847/677-9360

Jerry & John's is a real old-fashioned butcher shop and a true treasure. Meat is **choice or prime** and they will help you plan quantities, choose the right cut, find a recipe—heck, they'll practically come home with you and cook it! They also carry **Harrison poultry and** eggs. While their **duck** and some other items are frozen, they did have a decent price on **duck breasts** last time I was there. There are some frozen prepared items as well.

Nicholas Quality Meats
908 W. Randolph St.
312/563-0145

Though primarily wholesale, this market is open to the public and offers good prices on **beef** and **pork**. They also carry **rabbit**, **smoked meats**, and **shrimp**.

Olympic Meat Packers
810 W. Randolph St.
312/666-2222

This wholesale-retail operation specializes in package deals and posts different collections of meats on the walls. The package deals start at about $50 and include some of everything: **beef** (**short ribs**, **T-bones**, **ground beef**) and **pork** (ribs, pork chops), as well as **sausage** and even **tamales** and **pizza puffs**. You choose the assortment that suits your budget, tastes, and freezer capacity.

Paulina Market
3501 N. Lincoln Ave.
773/248-6272

Paulina Market began as an old-time German neighborhood butcher shop and still carries many **homemade sausage** and **German specialties**, as well as **choice-grade meats**. They are service oriented and will **age beef** if you ask. This is one of the butcher shops at which food stylists purchase their meat. (**Gepperth's**, p. 22, is another.) Paulina Market obtained a specialty turkey for me once for an article I was writing. The breed was a species of wild turkey although it was farm raised in Canada—best turkey I ever cooked.

Peoria Packing
1300 W. Lake St.
312/738-1800

A great place to buy pork, Peoria Packing is a wholesale business that has a store open to the public. You wear throwaway plastic gloves while checking out aisles of gorgeous cuts of meat on ice. They have every part of the pig, including whole, **skin-on fresh ham**, **ribs** of every kind, plus **trotters**, **chitterlings**, etc. **Beef** (including **liver**, **skirt steak**, and **whole pieces of round**) is also stocked. A butcher is on

Meat, Poultry, and Game

23

premises to trim or further break down your purchase into smaller cuts. They also offer a good selection of **smoked meats**. Check their frequent ads in the *Chicago Sun-Times* food section for specials.

Schmeisser's Meats

7649 N. Milwaukee Ave.
Niles
847/967-8995

Schmeisser's has been making **sausage in the German tradition** and butchering meat for over 50 years. If the door is open, peek into the back of the shop, where they take apart **primal cuts**, **smoke meats**, and generally do old-fashioned, macho butcher things. **Prime aged steaks** as well as any other cut of meat you desire are cut to order by the friendly staff. Schmeisser's sausages are famous and include **six kinds of bratwurst**, **Italian**, **knackwurst**, **chorizo**, and a truly delicious spicy **thuringer**, which is excellent grilled. They prepare many **lunch meats** as well, including more kinds of **liver sausage** than you could ever dream of (if you dream of liver sausage . . . some of us do). Oh, yes, there's **smoked goose**, too. Bring cash. Credit cards are not accepted, although there is an on-premise ATM.

Live Poultry

Yes, you can find it in the city. My friend Mary Ann, in fact, ended up raising a chicken in her apartment. She took pity on the runt of the flock in the window of a Ukrainian Village store. "Cheep," as the chicken was called, even provided Mary Ann with eggs for a while.

I think it is respectful to remember that the meat we eat was once alive. It does not grow in plastic-wrapped Styrofoam trays. Live poultry stores can be reminders of some of the unpleasant things that go along with being a carnivore, however, so don't shop in one if you are squeamish.

On the other hand, the chickens in these stores are no worse off than those at factory farms. Certainly the meat is much fresher and the taste difference is noticeable.

These stores are also a good place to get **fresh quail**, **goose**, and **duck**, which you usually only find frozen, if at all, elsewhere.

Chicago Live Poultry
2611 S. Ridgeway Ave.
773/542-9451

6421 N. Western Ave.
773/381-1000

Here you can get **chicken**, **quail**, **turkey**, **ducks**, and **rabbits**, all butchered to order. The South Side store is near the Mexican Little Village neighborhood; the North Side shop is just off Devon in the Indian-Pakistani area. The stores have the same name; I don't know whether they have the same owner.

John's Live Poultry and Egg Market
5955 W. Fullerton Ave.
773/622-2813

John's specializes in phone orders and has been providing freshly slaughtered **Thanksgiving turkeys** for decades. They also sell **chickens**, **geese**, **quail**, and their **eggs**. According to the clerk, most of the animals are raised on farms in Indiana.

Meat, Poultry, and Game

25

Fish and Seafood

(grouper from Isaacson L and Stein Fish Co.)

Fish and Seafood

The fishmongers listed in this section are experts. Count on them to get you **impeccably fresh, high-quality seafood** and also to provide information. They can tell you where the fish came from, when it arrived, how to cook it, and sometimes even how it was caught and by whom. This is an important benefit when you're purchasing shellfish and you want to be confident that it came from unpolluted waters or when you're planning to serve something out of the ordinary, like **monkfish**, for the first time and you need information on handling it. If I were looking for fresh oysters or soft-shell crabs, I'd want to buy them from one of these experts.

On the other hand, ethnic markets, particularly Asian ones, have a wide assortment and low prices, so check the listings in the "Southeast Asia" (p. 226), "China" (p. 208), and "Japan, Korea, and the Philippines" (p. 249) chapters, especially:

Chicago Food Corporation (p. 251)

International Club (p. 214)

Mitsuwa Marketplace (p. 249)

For **caviar**, a gourmet shop is sometimes a good source. Russian specialty stores (**Three Sisters**, p. 118) also often carry caviar and sometimes at good prices. You can even find some types of caviar in the refrigerated case of multiethnic supermarkets (**Marketplace on Oakton**, p. 260), although it is usually salmon roe or whitefish and not beluga that is available. Call **Collins Caviar** (p. 30) in nearby Michigan City to order freshly processed American caviars.

Smoked fish can be found in many of the Eastern European and Russian (p. 111–119) markets, especially:

Three Sisters Delicatessen (p. 118)

Wally's International Market (p. 118)

Whole Foods (p. 8) and **Treasure Island** (p. 7) stores also carry an excellent selection of fresh seafood and will order things for you with advance notice.

Trout Meunière

(Serves 4)

Sounds fancy, but you won't believe how simple this is. It works with whole trout or fillets of any delicate white fish. Sole Meunière is a French classic. I have seen it on chichi menus for big bucks, and there's really nothing to it.

½ C. flour

salt and pepper

½ tsp. thyme

2 to 4 T. unsalted butter, more if needed

4 whole trout, or about 2 lb. trout or sole fillets or other mild white fish

2 lemons

fresh parsley, chopped

Spread out the flour on a platter and mix in the seasonings. Heat enough butter in a sauté pan (or pans) to thoroughly coat the bottom. Roll the fish in the seasoned flour, shake off excess, and fry until brown and crisp (about 5 minutes for skinny fillets, 5 to 7 minutes a side for whole trout).

Remove and keep warm. Pour off any burnt butter. Add another 2 tablespoons to the pan; when it froths, squeeze in the lemon, swirl around, and pour over the fish. Sprinkle with parsley. Serve with buttered noodles topped with poppy seeds.

Fish and Seafood

29

Seafood Stores

Burhop's Seafood

1413 Waukegan Rd.
Glenview
847/901-4014

14 N. Grant Sq.
Hinsdale
630/887-4700

One of the first and best, Burhop's has been around since the 1930s. They have changed locations and no longer operate a store in the city. Cooking tips and recipes are happily provided, and Burhop's will happily order most anything you want. You can also pick up **sauces**, **breading**, and accompaniments for your seafood dinner. Preprepared and ready-to-cook items are available, too. There are often **free cooking classes** as well.

Captain Alex Seafood

8874 N. Milwaukee Ave.
Niles
847/803-8833

Friendly staff who know their stuff sell pretty much anything you could want at Captain Alex. There are boards posted with lists of fish, whether they're available fresh or frozen, and the prices. Some fresh fish is displayed on ice, but a lot is warehoused in the back since this is also a wholesale operation. A self-serve refrigerated case holds take-home items that are ready to cook, like **crab cakes** and **battered fish fillets**.

Collins Caviar

800/715-4034
www.collinscaviar.com
(See p. 34.)
Call to place your order.

Di Cola's Seafood

10754 S. Western Ave.
773/238-7071

South Siders have relied on Di Cola's since the 1930s. They carry prepared, to-go food in addition to a complete selection of **seafood that they will fillet** or cut to your specifications.

Dirk's Fish and Gourmet Shop

2070 N. Clybourn Ave.
773/404-3475
www.dirksfish.com

Dirk opened his shop after 28 years with Burhop's, and the experience shows. This place consistently gets raves for fresh fish and great customer service. There are so many kinds of fresh fish, you'll feel like you're living on the coast. **Sushi-grade fish** is a specialty. They offer frequent sushi classes, and sell **nori** and **sushi rolling mats**, too. Dirk's has **caviar**, of course, and also offers **gourmet sauces**, **marinades**, and lots of ready-to-cook items made on the premises. There are **bisques**, **gumbos**, **seafood salads**, **spreads**, and **crab cakes**, natch. Dirk will honor your fishiest requests for unusual items or preparations. Equipment, such as **cedar planks**, **oyster knives**, and the like, are also available.

The Fish Guy Market

4423 N. Elston Ave.
773/283-7400
www.fishguy.com

Bill Dugan, the proprietor, is charming, personable, and passionate about seafood. If he's there when you are, be sure to chat him up. He supplies some of the premier Chicago restaurants, like Charlie Trotter's and the Ritz-Carlton. While the store is relatively small, he carries a wide variety and will get you pretty much anything you want. He will happily give you cooking advice as well. When I visited he had **monkfish, scallops in the shell, skate**, and **caviar**, among other things. Part of the place is a deli that offers prepared items, including some very **classy seafood salads**. A small selection of relevant equipment, like **oyster knives** and **cedar planks** to cook on, are also offered.

Food Harbor

1421 W. Lake St.
Addison
630/629-1700
See "Multiethnic" chapter (p. 259).

Good Morgan Kosher Fish Market

2948 W. Devon Ave.
773/764-8115
See "Kosher" chapter (p. 69).

Hagen's Fish Market
5635 W. Montrose Ave.
773/283-1944

A family business since 1946, Hagen's offers an array of fresh and frozen seafood, as well as prepared items, including **fried shrimp and calamari**. Their real specialty, though, is seafood they smoke themselves, such as **smoked sable, salmon, chubs, whitefish, sturgeon, and shrimp**. They'll even **smoke your own catch** for you.

Isaacson L and Stein Fish Co.
800 W. Fulton Market
312/421-2444

In this place you feel like you're in a fishing village, buying off the dock. Isaacson's is a wholesaler, but they let retail customers walk around and look at, sniff, and touch (wearing gloves) displays of all kinds of **fish on ice**. They claim to carry **250 kinds**. They almost always have **monkfish, many kinds of grouper**, **oysters**, **scallops**, and **skate**. While you get eye to eye with dinner, you can read signs that tell you where each fish came from. Choose the fish you want, bag it, and give it to one of the guys wearing a rubber apron and boots and have him clean it. They will also fillet, cut a big fish into steaks—whatever you like. On Saturdays they charge for some of these services, and it is CROWDED. The staff is always friendly and patient with questions and seems to enjoy the stunned look on new customers' faces. Prices are excellent, and there's even free parking in front or in a lot across the street.

Mercato del Pesce
2623 N. Harlem Ave.
773/622-7503

This **fish market, Italian-style**, is right across the street from Caputo's. It's small but quite lively. Especially at holiday time you need to arrive early and take a number to get served from the lovely array of fish, **shrimp**, **squid**, **scallops with their shells**, **clams**, and **mussels**. On my last visit, they had octopi that were practically big enough to be featured in Jules Verne's *20,000 Leagues Under the Sea*. A freezer case is crammed with **frozen squid rings, shrimp, scallops**, and more. Prices are quite good, too.

Roberts Fish

2916 W. Devon Ave.
773/761-3424
See "Kosher" chapter (p. 71).

Rubino's Seafood

735 W. Lake St.
312/258-0020 or 0021

This Fulton Market–area wholesaler **specializes in shellfish** and will sell to retail customers. There is no sales area. You enter an office through hanging strips of plastic and order from a product and price list posted on the wall. Merchandise is warehoused in the back. It would be a good place to investigate if you were serving shrimp cocktail to a huge party. Call first to get minimums and place your order. They're not geared for walk-ins but are perfectly friendly.

Sea Ranch

518 Dempster St.
Evanston
847/492-8340

3217 Lake St.
Wilmette
847/256-4404

These small but beautiful fish markets specialize in **sushi-grade fish** and also do a huge business in **carryout sushi**. As you would expect, freshness is impeccable. The Wilmette store is also conveniently located across the parking lot from the **Sea Ranch Market** (p. 250), so you can do all your Japanese shopping with one stop.

Sea World Food Market

1130 W. Argyle St.
773/334-5335

This store serves the Southeast Asian Argyle crowd. The place has been around for many years. It's spookily empty looking, with an aquarium and service counter toward the rear. You will find good prices on **live fish and lobsters**. Not much English is spoken.

Supreme Lobster and Seafood Company

220 E. North Ave.
Villa Park
630/834-FISH
www.supremelobster.com

This suburban wholesaler also operates a retail store. In addition to **fresh fish, live lobster, oysters, and clams**, you'll find a huge selection of frozen seafood and shelves filled with **breading, cocktail sauces**, and such. Visit the Web site for a 10 percent off coupon.

Roe, Roe, Roe Your Boat

Caviar, fish eggs, roe—whatever you call them, they are luxury ingredients, but there's more than one way to roe. To enjoy caviar, you needn't spend a bundle on the imported sturgeon kind.

Collins Caviar (www.collinscaviar.com), of Michigan City, Indiana, offers plain and flavored American caviar. Elegant choices include **wasabi tobikko, caviar citron** (with vodka), **smoked golden caviar**, and **Hackelback sturgeon caviar. Mother-of-pearl caviar spoons** are sold, too.

Tobikko. I think of these as Japanese pop rocks. They are often dyed bright orange and used in California rolls and other sushi. They don't have a lot of flavor, but they have plenty of texture and are very affordable. Collins Caviar creates Caribbean Caviar by flavoring tobikko with habanero peppers.

Salmon roe. This big (¼-inch diameter) red caviar, which is served as sushi (ikura), is also tasty on its own or as a luxurious garnish for an omelet.

Lumpfish caviar. These are the tiny black fish eggs you'll find in jarred (cheap) caviar in the grocery store.

Whitefish caviar (American golden). With slightly larger eggs than lumpfish, this can be very tasty. If you don't like the heavy deep-sea flavor of sturgeon caviar, you may actually prefer it. Collins offers it in mango, ginger, and other flavors.

Produce

(bounty from the farmers market)

Farmers Markets

Chicago is finally catching up with New York in offering locally grown produce to home cooks. Even with a short growing season, there are more wonderful vegetables and fruits to be found than we dreamed of as city kids who thought peas came in cans. As more restaurants commit themselves to cooking with the seasons and using fresh local ingredients, we home cooks benefit from the availability of **specialty greens, fresh herbs, heirloom tomatoes, exotic eggplant and squash varieties**, and other perishable wonders that have to be enjoyed close to where they grow.

Every summer there are neighborhood markets as well as three or four downtown, sponsored by the city. To find them, check the city's Web site (www.cityofchicago.org) or call the Department of Consumer Affairs at 773/489-4180.

Green City Market (www.chicagogreencitymarket.org) is a mostly organic market that is run as a private, not-for-profit organization. Supported by local chefs and committed to supporting sustainable agriculture, Green City Market sells **meat, poultry**, and **cheese**, in addition to fruits and veggies. They also sponsor **cooking demonstrations** and frequent fundraising events that feature celebrity chefs preparing the market's offerings. In 2005 the market was held on Wednesdays and Saturdays, 7 A.M. to 1:30 P.M., in Lincoln Park north of LaSalle Street along the path between 1750 N. Clark Street and Stockton Drive. They also hold three or four winter markets in November and December at the Lincoln Park Zoo Lion House.

Community-Supported Agriculture

Another way to enjoy our local bounty is to buy a share in an actual farm's harvest for the season. This is called **subscription farming** or CSA, community-supported agriculture. If you sign on, produce is delivered to a drop-off spot near your house, usually on a weekly basis for the season. There are various kinds of shares, so you can plan when and how much you receive (or find someone to share your share). You can even extend your subscription with some farms to receive deliveries of **winter storage vegetables** in November and December.

For information on farms that deliver in your area, check these Web sites: **Biodynamic Farming and Gardening Association** (www.biodynamics.com/usda/) and **Sustainable Agriculture Research and Education (SARE)** (www.sare.org).

Two local farms that participate are **Angelic Organics** (www.angelicorganics.com or 815/389-3106) and **Prairie Crossing** (www.prairiecrossing.com or 847/548-4030).

Pick-Your-Own Farms

A city person's excuse to get out in the country for a day. U-pick farms in the area have strawberries in the spring, pumpkins in the winter, and lots more in between. Some of them also feature hayrides, tractor rides, and gift shops. Check **Illinois Fresh** (www.urbanext.uiuc.edu/fresh/), a University of Illinois Extension Web site, for listings of farms and what produce is available when.

For information on organic produce as well as organic meat, poultry, and eggs, visit **The Organic Food Network** (www.organicfoodnetwork.net). This organization offers a publication called *The Guide to Eating Organic in and Around Chicago*, which lists organic farms, co-ops, mail-order sources, annual events, and more.

Andrée's Swiss Chard and Pasta

(Serves 4 to 6)

8 strips of bacon (optional)

3 cloves garlic, chopped

2 bunches Swiss chard, washed and chopped

3 T. olive oil

I lb. fusilli (or other short pasta), cooked

1 T. Dijon mustard

2 T. white wine vinegar

¼ C. grated Parmesan cheese

¼ C. pine nuts, preferably toasted

Fry the bacon until crisp. Drain and crumble, then set aside. Sauté the garlic and chard in olive oil until tender-crisp. Whisk together the mustard and vinegar in the bottom of a large bowl. Stir in the pasta, then add the cooked chard, cheese, and bacon. Toss well and top with pine nuts.

Serve hot or at room temperature.

Produce

We Be Jammin'

If you're like me, you overbuy fruit. It's very seductive at the farmers market, so you bring home too much and it rots. Jam is the answer. The quickest way to make it is in the microwave. I'll spare you a lecture about low-pectin and high-pectin fruits. It doesn't matter much, as long as you don't mind runny preserves. If it's too gooey to spread on toast, you've made fruit sauce!

You need:

2 to 4 C. chopped fruit (strawberries, rhubarb, raspberries, plums, etc., or a mixture)

1 to 2 C. sugar (depending on the fruit and your taste)

1 to 2 tsp. lemon juice (optional)

a humongous Pyrex measuring cup—8 cups is perfect (if you don't have one, a microwave-safe casserole or soufflé dish will do; the container must be at least twice as big as the quantity of fruit, since it will boil and bubble over)

Saran Wrap, a wooden spoon, and clean jars (right out of the dishwasher) to put the jam in

Here's how:

1- Prepare the fruit. Wash and cut into bite-size pieces. If you are using stone fruit, like apricots or plums, leave the pits in the mix till after cooking. They add thickening and flavor.

2- Mix in the sugar. If the fruit is dryish, squash it some with a potato masher or another blunt instrument. You want a bit of juice to start things off. Pour the mixture into your Pyrex (or other microwave-safe) container.

Produce

3- Securely cover your container with Saran Wrap. No vents. No cheap plastic wrap. Nuke on high power for 4 to 8 minutes. Watch through the microwave window. After about 4 minutes, the jam will bubble wildly, climb to the top, and start sneaking around the wrap to drool on your microwave. How quickly this happens depends on all kinds of things: your microwave, the fruit, the phases of the moon. Don't be alarmed—just turn it off when it starts seriously leaking.

4- Then stir. WATCH OUT!! IT'S HOTTER THAN HECK! Use oven mitts. CAREFULLY lift a corner of Saran Wrap that's away from you (THE STEAM IS HOTTER THAN HECK, TOO). Stir. The jam should boil for a total of 8 minutes, so put it back in the microwave and nuke in 1- or 2-minute spurts, stopping before it boils over too much. If you want to save the spilled jam, just scrape it up and return to the Pyrex (assuming your microwave was clean and not crusted with pizza sauce when you started).

5- Now uncover, stir, and nuke a couple of minutes at a time, until you've cooked it about 5 minutes more. You are thickening the jam so it gels. Traditional jam making does this by cooking for a very long time on the stove or by using packaged pectin. There are times for tradition, but not if you have a quart of overripe berries and you have to go to work in the morning. As the jam thickens, your spoon will feel the weight more and start leaving a trail as you stir.

6- Add lemon juice to bring out the flavor and color, if you wish. Then pour into the clean jars. This is where a pour spout, like on the Pyrex, is useful.

That's it. You made jam. Try it tomorrow morning on toast. You will be very impressed with yourself. It will keep for at least a week in the fridge. Otherwise, put it in the freezer, where it keeps for 6 months. You have not preserved these preserves, so they need to stay refrigerated or frozen.

Produce

Double-Ginger Rhubarb Chutney

2 C. chopped rhubarb

½ C. dry white wine

½ C. sugar

1 tsp. minced garlic

¼ tsp. nutmeg

1 T. minced crystallized ginger

2 tsp. minced fresh ginger (a walnut-size piece)

½ tsp. crushed red pepper

¼ C. chopped (preferably toasted) walnuts

Combine all the ingredients, except the walnuts, in a saucepan. Bring to a boil, then lower the heat to a simmer. Simmer 5 minutes, add the walnuts, and simmer another few minutes or until the rhubarb breaks down and the sauce thickens.

Persimmon Chips

Fuyu (NOT Hajiya) persimmons

cinnamon-sugar mix (or try five-spice powder and sugar)

Preheat the oven to 300°. Wash the persimmons, but do not peel or core. Slice them paper thin, crosswise, cutting right through the core on a V-slicer or mandoline. This leaves a lovely starlike pattern in the middle. Place a rack over a baking pan. Spray with nonstick cooking spray. Arrange the persimmon slices in one layer on top of the rack. Sprinkle lightly with cinnamon-sugar. Bake for 30 to 45 minutes. If they seem to be cooking unevenly, rotate the pan midway through. The persimmon chips are done when they color slightly and curl a bit. (If these are stored in an airtight container, I think they last a while, but we've always eaten them the day they're made, so I'm not sure.)

Produce Stores

It seems that big chain supermarkets have increasingly replaced their produce departments with more aisles of snacks, pop, and prepared foods. They say nobody cooks anymore. (Heard about the rich family who renovates their kitchen, complete with a Wolf range, a Sub-Zero refrigerator, etc., but never even bothers to connect them?) The top two vegetables in the American diet are French fries and ketchup. Scary, ain't it? Maybe the pendulum is finally swinging. There are more farmers markets and more interest in organic agriculture these days. In its small way, even the short-lived low-carb craze helped some folks realize that living on bread, pasta, and Snackwells was the road to fatville. Nobody ever got fat eating too many fruits and veggies.

There is a wonderful world of produce out there beyond potatoes and tomatoes. It's quite a revelation to see all the different types of greens for sale in an Asian market or to be able to choose from eggplants that are white, striped, green, or pale purple. Ethnic markets are great places to broaden one's horizons. It seems to me that most of them give more square footage to produce and that it's usually fresher and cheaper

than in a chain supermarket.

The stores in this section are those that specialize in fruits and veggies, but you should also keep in mind the supermarkets in the "Multiethnic" chapter (pp. 258–264), especially:

A & G International Fresh Market (p. 258)

Marketplace on Oakton (p. 260)

Westbrook Market (p. 263)

For organic produce, don't forget:

Trader Joe's (p. 6)

Whole Foods Markets (p. 8)

Wild Oats Natural Marketplace (p. 64)

Andy's Fruit Ranch
4725 N. Kedzie Ave.
773/583-2322

This one is worth making a detour for. Andy's seems to pride itself on offering the widest range of fresh produce anywhere in the city. You can purchase groceries and canned goods, including a good selection of condiments, dried legumes, and seasonings, but it's the produce that really shines. Here is a list of the less common items available the times I visited, but chances are if it is in season or in demand, Andy's will have it: **bitter melons**, **cactus fruit** (tuna), **chayotes**, **cherimoya**, **daikon**, **green mangos**, **green papayas**, **guavas**, **Haitian mangos**, **horseradish**, **jicama**, **malanga** (yautia, amarilla), **mamey**, **ñame** (white yam), **Philippine mangos**, **plantains**, **pomelos**, **sour oranges**, **taro** (dasheen, eddo), **tomatillos**, **young coconuts**, and **yucca** (cassava). The exceptions when I was there were specifically Asian items (no durian or lychees) and Indian items (no wing beans or tindora).

Berwyn Fruit Market
3811 S. Harlem Ave.
Berwyn
708/795-6670

A combination of **Latin American, Eastern European, and Middle Eastern ingredients** in one store. When I shop here, I come home with a world tour of ingredients. You can pick up **labna, ajvar, tomatillos, Polish pickles**, and **fresh dill weed**. Produce is very cheap, and the emphasis is on Latin American items. This is one of the few places that regularly has the **spiny version of Mexican chayote**. You'll find a full-service butcher here, too.

Carrot Top
1430 Paddock Dr.
Northbrook
847/729-1450
www.carrottopmarket.com

This produce market is hard to find but worth seeking out if you live north. It's just off Willow Road south on Old Willow Road. You'll find exotic offerings: **chanterelle mushrooms, oyster mushrooms**, and **morels in season**, as well as **passion fruit, lychees, baby artichokes**, and other **baby vegetables**. Carrot Top also carries **fresh herbs, locally grown produce**, and the usual lettuces, roots, and fruits. Another Carrot Top store next door carries meat, fish, and prepared food.

Family Fruit Market
4118 N. Cicero Ave.
773/481-2500

Good prices on mostly mainstream produce are what this large, bright market offers. It's an excellent place to stock up on basics like apples, potatoes, and lettuces. Some **Latin items**, such as **yucca**, are also available. Groceries emphasize **Balkan, Eastern European, and Greek offerings**. The convenient mid–North Side location offers plenty of parking.

Jerry's Fruit and Garden Center

7901 N. Milwaukee Ave.
Niles
847/967-1440

This big, sprawling market is a North Side favorite for great prices on fruits and veggies. It's clean, well laid out, and almost always crowded. You'll find all the standard offerings plus some ethnic choices. Jerry's always has **many kinds of eggplant, jicama, yucca**, and **cactus**. Dry goods feature **Polish, Greek, and Balkan specialties (jarred pickles, jams**, and, of course, **ajvar**). Jerry's also has a decent dairy and cheese selection.

Lincolnwood Produce

7175 N. Lincoln Ave.
Lincolnwood
847/329-0600

This supermarket has some of the most neatly arranged produce I've seen. Selection is good and includes some **Asian and Mexican fruits and veggies**, such as **daikon** and **poblano peppers**. There is a full-service butcher as well as a fairly standard deli. Groceries include **Greek and Middle Eastern specialties (grape leaves, pomegranate molasses, mastic)**, some **Italian and Mexican items**, and lots of **Balkan and Eastern European products**.

Northeastern Fruit

6000 N. Lincoln Ave.
773/338-0610

Tucked into a corner at the busy Peterson-Lincoln intersection for generations, Northeastern Fruit has decent prices on mainstream fruits and veggies, as well as a good selection of **Greek products**, such as **trahana, canned grape leaves**, and **jams**.

Rogers Park Fruit Market

7401 N. Clark St.
773/262-3663
See "Africa and the Caribbean" chapter (p. 177).

Stanley's Fruits and Vegetables

1558 N. Elston Ave.
773/276-8050

Stanley's doesr'
really exotic
prices an'
ment c
recer
to

Produce

products as well as fruits and veggies. Quality is generally good, and food stylists often shop here.

Candied Kumquats

1 pint kumquats

2 C. sugar

1 C. water

Wash the kumquats and cover with water in a medium saucepan. Bring to a simmer, cook for 5 minutes, and drain. When they are cool enough to handle, cut each kumquat in half and remove the seeds and any pulp that is tough or fibrous. Combine the measured sugar and water in a saucepan. When it is simmering, add the kumquats. Cook about 10 minutes and let cool in the syrup for several hours or overnight. Remove and let dry. Stuff with a walnut or an almond, if you like, and roll in granulated sugar.

Equipment

Equipment

Next time you're tempted to give your credit card a workout at Williams-Sonoma, try a restaurant supply store instead. Most will be happy to sell to you, the home chef. They generally have a sales force that calls on restaurants, but their showrooms are usually retail stores that are open to the public and lots of fun. Many of them are only open Monday through Friday, 9 A.M. to 5 P.M. Call for hours.

For things like **sheet pans** (baking pans), **food storage containers**, and **gadgets** of all descriptions, you can't beat 'em. You'll find some real bargains. They also carry things you'd have a hard time finding in a cookware store, from **ladles in weird sizes** (really tiny or huge), to **enormous colanders**, to **ramekins**, to **catering-style chafing dishes**, to **heat-proof spatulas in any size and color**. **Cutting boards** come in a rainbow of colors and are cheap enough to stock up on.

Paper goods are a deal. You get **a year's supply of** for a buck. You can buy kind of "to-go" con- (Chinese food car- ke nifty gift boxes.) hese things would be worth the trip alone, but if you're picking up other items, why not stock up.

When it comes to **pots and pans**, you'll find good quality at reasonable prices—especially if you're in need of **large-capacity cookware**. Be wary of the very reasonably priced commercial aluminum pots and pans, however. They are perfectly okay 90 percent of the time, but they do react with some ingredients and turn cream sauces a very nasty gray color.

You'll find all sorts of delightful gadgets you never knew you needed. Better yet, simple tools like **graters** and **melon ballers** are often better made, sharper, and more efficient than the grocery-store versions. Proprietors are friendly and helpful (unless they're swamped with commercial clients), and you don't have to pretend you own a restaurant.

Small Equipment

butane torches
cutting boards, all sizes
 and colors
food storage containers,
 all sorts

garnishing tools
hand blenders
ladles
mandolines
melon ballers
nutmeg graters
oyster knives
parchment paper
pastry bags and tips
pastry brushes
pizza stones and peels
ramekins
rolling pins: French,
  marble
scales
sheet pans
silicon baking sheets
  (Silpat)
skimmers
spatulas (heatproof)
squirt bottles
steel gloves
stockpots
tamis (a sauce strainer)
thermometers
tongs
V-slicers
whisks

Large Equipment

barstools
butcher-block tables
carts
coffee brewers and urns
pot and pan racks
professional blenders,
  toasters, processors,

slicers, mixers, etc.
shelving
stainless prep tables

You can also find the real restaurant professional items, like **deep fryers** and **Viking ranges**, in some of these stores, though most such equipment is not appropriate for home use. In fact, it's illegal to have a professional range in your home, for fire safety reasons. Not only do they require a major, very expensive, make-a-hole-in-your-wall vent, they are not insulated well enough to be safe. They're quite seductive, though, since at first blush the prices are reasonable. If you want a professional stove, you'll have to pay for the professional version that's been modified for home cooks. Check the **Something's Cooking** listing (p. 54). Many upscale appliance stores, like Plass, also carry professional and European brands of stoves, refrigerators, and such. Much of the other equipment is just too expensive for home use. Th usually no need to heavy-duty versions like toasters and ble

One of my restaurant s **prep tab** stainle resta sc

in

the high-tech look, they'll fit into your kitchen. Check them out if you're remodeling— they'd make a gorgeous island. They cost $150 and up, depending on size and accoutrements. (You can even occasionally find used ones on sale.) Customize with **drawers**, **pot racks**, **shelves**, **butcher-block tops**, and so forth.

Many of these stores also sell lovely, old-fashioned **John Boos solid butcher-block tables**. You can also buy **high-tech–looking wire shelving** (Metro and other brands) that restaurants use in their store rooms.

For **ethnic gadgets**, like **sushi rollers** or **tortilla presses**, you're better off at a supermarket devoted to that cuisine. See the appropriate listings.

How to Play on Your Mandoline (or V-Slicer)
Vegetable Chips

Try weird and wild veggies— taro, plantain, beets, turnips—any starchy tuber. The humble sweet potato also makes a great chip.

Peel and slice vegetables paper thin on your slicer. Dry thoroughly. Heat 1 to 3 inches of oil to 350° in a deep pot. Fry chips in a single layer. (Always do beets last! They turn everything red.)

Remove with a skimmer when crisp and slightly colored. Salt immediately. Keep warm in a low oven.

Equipment Stores

Alliance Paper and Food Service
913 W. Randolph St.
312/666-6424

This small place in the West Loop food-service neighborhood stocks **restaurant-size containers of spices, salad dressings, and canned goods**, as well as **paper products**, including **parchment paper sheets**.

Chef's Catalog
3009 N. Clark St.
773/327-5210

151A Skokie Blvd.
Highland Park
847/831-1100

These retail outlets for a big catalog company carry a full selection of all the well-known brands of cookware and equipment, including **All-Clad, Calphalon, Cuisinart**, and **KitchenAid**. It's a good place to buy **knives—Wüsthof, Henckels**, and other brands—and **all kinds of electronics**, such as **hand blenders, deep fryers**, and **food processors**. They have frequent sales with discounted prices.

Chefwear
3111 N. Knox Ave.
800/568-2433

Located over the factory in an industrial neighborhood, this outlet has good buys on **chef's pants, coats, hats, shoes, and aprons**. Call first. Their hours are limited, and it's hard to find. The chef's pants are comfortable and indestructible and have lots of pockets.

Chiarugi Hardware
1449 W. Taylor St.
312/666-2235

This old-fashioned Italian hardware store is the place for **winemaking equipment**, like barrels, corks, and chemicals. They sell **huge wine presses, citric acid, wine yeast, malt extract**, and **mother of vinegar** (to start your own batch of vinegar). They carry **Vittorio strainers, ravioli presses, cavatelli makers**, and, of course, **pasta machines**.

Equipment

49

Cost Plus World Market

2844 N. Broadway St.
773/477-9912

1623 N. Sheffield Ave.
312/587-8037

1725 Maple Ave.
Evanston
847/424-1022

145 Skokie Blvd.
Northbrook
847/509-1800

2155 W. 22nd St.
Oak Brook
630/573-9826

105 Orland Pl.
Orland Park
708/349-6111

3555 E. Main St.
St. Charles
630/587-1011

1055 E. Golf Rd.
Schaumburg
847/413-0400

9454 Skokie Blvd.
Skokie
847/674-2241
www.costplusworldmarket.com

Cost Plus World Market is sort of like Pier One (imported products), only with a large selection of cooking equipment and supplies. They carry **canning jars**, baskets, **madeleine pans**, condiments, **spices** (Spice Hunter), **flavored vinegars**, **oils**, **teas**, **woks**, strainers, **gadgets**, **grill equipment**, **biscuit cutters**, and an eclectic bunch of **serving ware and dishes**. I've purchased cool square bamboo plates for noodles here, as well as cruets for vinegar. You'll find good prices, but the selection changes frequently, so don't go looking for something specific.

CB2

3757 N. Lincoln Ave.
773/755-3900

800 W. North Ave.
312/787-8329
www.cb2.com

The merchandise at this younger, hipper version of Crate and Barrel includes **funky kitchen gadgets**, **serving dishes**, **martini glasses**, and the like, as well as home decor. There is not as big a selection of cookware as at the mother store, however.

Crate and Barrel

646 N. Michigan Ave.
312/787-5900

850 W. North Ave.
312/573-9800

1775 Lake Cook Rd.
Northbrook
847/272-8920

35 Oakbrook Center
Oak Brook
630/572-1300

40 Old Orchard Shopping
Center
Skokie
847/674-6850

1515 Sheridan Rd.
Wilmette
847/256-2723
www.crateandbarrel.com

Crate and Barrel was one of the first retailers to carry **professional-quality cookware** marketed to the home cook. The bright, uncluttered stores have all the name brands, including **Calphalon**, **Cuisinart**, and **KitchenAid**. You'll find an amazing assortment of **kitchen gadgets**, **cutlery**, **cookware**, **baking equipment**, and **electronics**.

Crate and Barrel is also justifiably famous for reasonably priced, **well-designed dishes, glasses, and other tabletop things**. A small but up-to-date collection of condiments and cookbooks rounds out the shopping experience.

Don Outlet Store
2525 N. Elston Ave.
773/489-7739

Edward Don is one of the biggest food service suppliers in the area, and this is their retail outlet, so it's crowded with goodies. You'll find many geared toward the home cook, like **Emeril's line** of cookware and **Wilton cake-decorating equipment**.

There's **paperware**, gadgets like **fish tweezers** (no, no, no—you use them to remove bones) and **Microplane graters**, **pressure cookers**, and **lots of pots**.

GFS Marketplace
220 E. Roosevelt Rd.
Villa Park
630/832-3354

8146 S. Cicero Ave.
Burbank
708/424-4335

15606 S. Harlem Ave.
Orland Park
708/532-0794
800/968-6525
www.gfsmarketplace.com

This chain belongs to Gordon Food Service, one of the big restaurant suppliers in Chicagoland. They have only a

Equipment

small selection of equipment, but it's the place to go for **restaurant-size cans of tomato sauce or chocolate topping**. There are good buys on **paper and plastic goods**, as well as a frightening assortment of frozen prepared foods that restaurants use.

Gold Brothers
1140 W. Madison St.
312/666-1520

At this downtown spot for chef shopping, parking is impossible, and they are a bit less welcoming than some other places, because they're so busy with restaurant customers. Still, they have—or can get—anything. Don't miss the interesting showroom of **used restaurant equipment and furniture**, too.

Krasny Supply
2829 N. Clybourn Ave.
773/477-5504

A well-established wholesaler with a strong retail business as well, Krasny carries **pots and pans**, **glassware**, **gadgets**, and some electrical equipment.

Marc Bakery Equipment
1015 W. Lake St.
312/243-6556

This restaurant supply store specializes in **equipment for baking and pastry making** and is a good spot to purchase **Ateco pastry tips** (they have every one), **tart pans**, and **sheet pans**. They cater to the institutional market and carry huge pieces of equipment, as well as some **giant sizes of ordinary stuff**. Ever see a 20-inch bread knife? Some of the **rolling pins** were so heavy I could barely lift them. They do NOT carry paper goods.

Marlinn Restaurant Supply
7250 S. Cicero Ave.
708/496-1700

This very pleasant store offers lots of things for the home cook, including **Emeril's product line** and an excellent selection of **garnishing tools**, **V-slicers**, and gadgets. Expect good prices on **professional aprons**, dishes, and glasses. They carry **bar supplies**, **Wilton cake-decorating equipment**, **stockpots**, **cutting boards**, and **heatproof spatulas**, plus some exotica, like **escargot plates** and **teensy (¼-inch di-

ameter) cutters in star and other shapes.

Northwestern Cutlery
810 W. Lake St.
312/421-3666
www.cutleryandmore.com
See "Knife Sharpening" (p. 58).

Olympic Store Fixtures
4758 S. Cicero Ave.
773/585-3755
773/585-3366

This was one of the first supply places I visited, and it was quite a trip! A ton of **used equipment** culled from failed restaurants makes for one chaotic jumble of things all smooshed together in a small space. Used **deep fryers** and **popcorn machines** are displayed next to racks of **tongs** and **spatulas**, the usual selection of **commercial sauté pans**, and **thermometers**. It's fun for types who enjoy digging through sale bins. The staff is very busy and will leave you alone to look, unless you ask for help (which you must do for a lot of small items behind the counter). Prices seem to be somewhat negotiable.

Pierce Chef Mart
9685 W. 55th St.
Countryside
708/354-1265

While Pierce carries a lot of **used restaurant equipment**, they also have a front room oriented toward the home cook. You'll find **baking supplies**, **pastry bags and tips**, **pepper mills**, and the like, as well as the usual **sheet pans**, **stockpots**, and **paper products**. The back room, however, is devoted to used equipment from out-of-business restaurants, meaning they sell everything from banged-up napkin holders and silverware to huge glass-door refrigerators like the kind in 7-Eleven stores. Most of this stuff (like **Hobart mixers** big enough to climb into) isn't appropriate for home chefs, but it's fun to look at. Pierce cultivates the home cook's business with Saturday hours.

Ramar Supply
8223 S. Harlem Ave.
Burbank
708/233-0808

Here is another worthy resource for all the usual stuff, but without as big an assortment as found at many other places. There are some used things and **lots of plastic and paperware**.

Equipment

53

Schweppe Foodservice Equipment

376 W. North Ave.
Lombard
630/627-3550

A very home cook–friendly place, this big warehouse-showroom offers just about everything you could imagine—and even has the Food Network showing on television monitors.

They carry **all sizes of ladles and tongs**, a huge selection of **restaurant dishes**, **ramekins**, **pizza peels**, **knives**, **colanders**, **mandolines**, **chafing dishes**, and on and on. There are even **restaurant-size packages of condiments, soups, and spices**, as well as some **chef's clothes**. If you are in the western suburbs, don't miss it.

Something's Cooking

1131 W. Madison St.
312/455-8410

This showroom features **professional appliances for home use**, including **Viking**, **Garland**, **Gaggenau**, **Traulsen**, **Sub-Zero**, and more. Something's Cooking will give you the information you need about venting, safety, and such. The sad news is that professional equipment designed to be safe and legal for home use is quite expensive.

Sunlight Kitchen and Hardware Supplies

2334 S. Wentworth Ave.
312/225-8388

This relatively new addition to the Chinatown scene stocks restaurant-type equipment with the emphasis on the Asian. You'll find **woks**, **strainers**, **cleavers**, and **skimmers**, plus mainstream pots and pans. It's more of a general supply store and less home cook–friendly than Woks 'n' Things.

Superior Products Mfg. Company

1920 Beech St.
Broadview
708/344-6500
www.superprod.com

This is a superstore that is part of a huge national food service supplier based in Minnesota. It's located in an industrial neighborhood where they have a warehouse. Don't be intimidated, however; they are extremely nice and have a lovely showroom. And although it is not oriented toward home cooks, there is no minimum purchase required.

Equipment

Superior stocks everything a restaurant needs and has a big catalog as well. You can purchase the usual **pots, pans, ladles**, and **strainers** off the rack in the showroom. Their assortment of **food storage containers** is particularly extensive. Choose clear or frosted, round or square, in dozens of sizes.

This is also an excellent place to check out **prep tables**, since they have quite a few on display and will explain things to you, including how to order. You can also order most of their stock online.

Sur La Table

755 W. North Ave.
312/787-5111

54 E. Walton St.
312/337-0600

55 S. Main St.
Naperville
630/428-1110
www.surlatable.com

These retail stores offer an eclectic selection of equipment and serving ware. In addition to **All-Clad** cookware and **Henckels** knives, you'll find Moroccan **tagines** and **couscoussières**, as well as **Weck canning equipment**, **Kuhn Rikon pressure cookers**, and many items imported from France. They carry **Le Creuset cast-iron cookware**, **Provencal garlic pots**, **copper tarte tatin pans**, and much more. Sur La Table has one of the best collections of **bakeware**, too, including all the latest silicon. Call for a schedule of cooking classes in their demo kitchens. (Shameless self-promotional plug: I sometimes do market tours and demos for Sur La Table in the summer months.)

Williams-Sonoma

900 N. Michigan Ave.
312/787-8991

Renaissance Place
Highland Park
847/681-9615

Market Square
Lake Forest
847/295-7045

9 W. Jackson Ave.
Naperville
630/369-4167

Oakbrook Center
Oak Brook
630/571-2702

362 Orland Square
Orland Park
708/226-0672

Equipment

Woodfield Mall
Schaumburg
847/619-0940

Old Orchard Center
Skokie
847/933-9803

Wheaton Town Square
Wheaton
630/665-7250
www.williamssonoma.com

Williams-Sonoma is one of the oldest gourmet kitchen equipment stores and still one of the best. **Microplane graters, pasta machines, cappuccino machines, butane torches, mandolines, KitchenAid mixers**—they carry it all, including brand-name cookware (**All-Clad, Calphalon**) and knives (**Wüsthof, Henckels**).

There are also **cookbooks**, including a complete series of single-subject books published by Williams-Sonoma itself, and a full line of gorgeous **table linens, gourmet condiments**, and ingredients to tempt you as well.

To top it off, Williams-Sonoma offers frequent cooking classes and has an extremely knowledgeable group of sales associates. You may be able to find some things cheaper elsewhere, but you won't find more inspiration anywhere.

Wilton Homewares

Chestnut Court Shopping
Center
7511 S. Lemont Rd.
Darien
630/985-6000

All the Wilton **cake and candy equipment** is available in this outlet. For baking you'll find **cake pans** in all sizes, **pastry bags and tips, paste food colors**, decorations, **equipment for wedding cakes**, plenty of **gadgets**, and the elusive **egg white powder**. For candy making they carry umpteen **molds, flavorings**, and **decorating supplies**, alongside all the essential ingredients.

Woks 'n' Things

2234 S. Wentworth Ave.
312/842-0701

At this Asian cooking supply store in the heart of Chinatown, you'll find a huge selection of **woks, cleavers, steamers, strainers**, and **skimmers**, as well as tools for non-Asian cuisine. (You can't have too many strainers!) Check out the intricate **garnishing tools**, including the very elaborate (expensive) **vegetable cutters** that let you make carrots into butterflies or Chinese characters. They carry some books on garnishing, too.

The staff is quite knowledgeable and will help you choose a wok and explain how to cure it. Fellow shoppers are an interesting mix and often happy to chat about Asian cooking.

And don't forget:

Bed, Bath & Beyond
Multiple locations

Linens-n-Things
Multiple locations

These two "big-box" stores are warehouse-style discount chains specializing in home goods. Both carry a decent selection of the basic brands of cookware and kitchen appliances. Be somewhat cautious, however, since sometimes brands create cheaper versions of their products especially for these stores.

Marshall Field's Marketplace
Multiple locations

All the name brand cookware is here, such as **Calphalon** and **All-Clad**, as well as a good assortment of **gadgets and bakeware**.

How to Paint a Plate

It will like you went to chef school, but it's easy. In fact, I usually enlist the kids to paint the dessert plates at dinner parties.

1- Fill a plastic squirt bottle (available at any of these stores and also craft stores) with sauce, your own or store-bought, or some seedless jam thinned with liqueur.

2- Squiggle a design on the plate before you add the piece of pie or cake. Try circles, Vs, or whatever. (If you want that spider web effect, do circles and then drag a knife through at right angles.) This also works on top of things, like cheesecake.

3- For non-dessert items, use a squirt bottle of sauce to add spots or squiggles. Try colorful contrasts, like dots of basil oil on top of a marinara sauce.

Knife Sharpening

Just do it. If you're still waiting for the cart with the bell to pull up in front of your house, give up. You need to take your knives to one of these establishments. It's easy, fast, and cheap. And with the possible exception of using good fresh spices, nothing will improve your cooking quicker. Dull knives are not only dangerous, they mash things up instead of slicing. You'll be amazed at how your knife skills improve when you're using a sharp one. (Don't try to sharpen those Ginzus, though.)

Bagat Bros. Sharp Knife Service
7621 W. Roosevelt Rd.
Forest Park
708/366-2818

This tiny hole-in-the-wall just west of Harlem Avenue sharpens knives for hundreds of restaurants but is happy to oblige you, too, at very reasonable prices. They usually open at 7 A.M. and close around 2 P.M., but call first. At this writing it cost about $2 to sharpen a 10-inch chef's knife.

Maestranzi Sharp Knife Service
4715 N. Ronald St.
Harwood Heights
708/867-7323

I didn't personally visit this place, but on the phone they gave me a cost of $2 to sharpen a 10-inch chef's knife. They will do it while you wait except at lunchtime when the guys aren't there.

Northwestern Cutlery
810 W. Lake St.
312/421-3666
www.futurechef.com

This place is practically a culinary institution. It's located in the Fulton Market section of town, so while you're here, check out some of the other treasures nearby, like **Isaacson's** (p. 32) for fresh fish.

In addition to sharpening knives, Northwestern sells them. There's a big display case of many brands, including **Henckels**, **Forschner**, and the ultracool **Japanese brands**.

They also carry tons of **gadgets** and quite a lot of **cookware**, so you can shop for equipment while you're getting sharpened.

Equipment

The staff is friendly and fun, albeit a bit macho. Ask one of the sales guys how sharp a knife is, and he may just slice a hair on his arm in two to illustrate, while a coworker looks on saying, "I hate when he does that."

Sur La Table

(See p. 55.)

Sur La Table stores will sharpen your knives for 50¢ an inch. You need to drop off the knives and then pick them up 48 hours later.

(Japanese vegetable knife)

Equipment

Top 10 Equipment Picks

1. V-slicers/mandolines* (p. 48)
2. instant-read thermometers
3. squirt bottles* (p. 57)
4. scales
5. tongs
6. chef's pants
7. heatproof spatulas
8. handheld blenders
9. silicone sheets/parchment paper
10. restaurant sheet pans

Runners-up

food storage containers
Microplane graters
butane torches
strainers in assorted sizes

*tip or recipe included

Health Food
and Nuts

(rice cakes, sprouts, and dried apples)

Health Food Ingredients

Although they are primarily vitamin stores, some of the bigger health food stores also stock hard-to-find food items. They make a good source for **oddball grains, oils, vinegars**, and **anything to do with soy**.

alfalfa seeds
amaranth
avocado oil
barley
blue cornmeal
carob chips
egg whites, powdered
flaxseed
fructose
grits
groats
honey: unfiltered, tupelo, other varietals
kamut
kasha
lactose
millet
molasses, blackstrap
nut butters: macadamia, soy, almond, cashew
oat bran
quinoa
rice: wehani, japonica, brown basmati
rye
sea vegetables
soy cheeses
soy milk and powder
soy nuts
spelt
sprouting seeds and equipment
stevia
tahini
teff
tempeh, flavored
tofu, baked and flavored
TVP (texturized vegetable protein)
vinegars: cider, brown rice, umeboshi
wheat germ
whole wheat

Health Food Stores

Bonne Santé

1512 E. 53rd St.
773/667-5700

This Hyde Park market has an organic juice bar, **bulk nuts and grains**, **organic dairy products**, **oils**, and **vinegars**. There is a small selection of fresh foods, frozen foods, and, of course, lots of vitamins and herbal remedies.

Fruitful Yield

4334 E. Fox Valley Center Dr.
Aurora
630/585-9200

7003 Cermak Rd.
Berwyn
708/788-9103

154 S. Bloomingdale Rd.
Bloomingdale
630/894-2553

2159 W. 75th St.
Downers Grove
630/969-7614

214 N. York Rd.
Elmhurst
630/530-1445

149 Skokie Valley Rd.
Highland Park
847/831-0460

229 W. Roosevelt Rd.
Lombard
630/629-9242

130 W. Golf Rd.
Schaumburg
847/882-2999

This chain of health food stores is long on vitamins and short on edibles. They do carry a limited selection of **organic produce** and also stock **grains**, **vinegars**, **oils**, and frozen foods.

People's Market

1111 Chicago Ave.
Evanston
847/475-9492

The name of this place and even the logo (a guy with his fist raised, clutching an apple) make me feel like I'm back in my hippie days reading the *Peking Review*. People's Market is not communistic, though, but rather is part of the Wild Oats chain. This store is smaller than the Wild Oats in Hinsdale but has **organic produce**, a salad bar, and **meat and fish counters**, as well as vitamin supplements.

Sherwyn's Health Food Shop

645 W. Diversey Ave.
773/477-1934
www.sherwyns.com

This huge store has what is probably the city's widest selection of **grains, nuts, fruits, soy products**, and frozen convenience health foods. They stock **every kind of flour—buckwheat, rye, oat, amaranth, chestnut, tapioca,** and then some—as well as **whole wheat couscous,** many varieties of **dried beans,** and an assortment of **lentils** that includes **French, beluga, Spanish, green, and red**.

The respectable Asian goods section features **organic tamari and soy sauce,** plus **ume** (red plum) **vinegar** that is flavored with **shiso** and becoming a hot chef's ingredient. There's also a small selection of fresh produce plus a good choice of equipment, including **dehydrators** and **juicers**.

Southtown Health Foods

2100 W. 95th St.
773/233-1856

This South Side institution offers a small selection of **organic fruits and vegetables,** as well as **grains, whole wheat flour, spices,** and the requisite vitamins, minerals, and **soy products**.

Whole Foods

Multiple locations
www.wholefoodsmarket.com

In addition to an extensive array of **organic produce,** Whole Foods stocks **Asian specialties, whole grains in bulk,** and a full line of **soy products**.

Wild Oats Natural Marketplace

500 E. Ogden
Hinsdale
630/986-8500
www.wildoats.com

This big, beautiful supermarket is quite similar to **Whole Foods.** You'll find lots of **organic produce, meats that are naturally raised,** and an entire section devoted to herbal and homeopathic remedies and vitamin products. The freezer case is loaded with vegetarian entrées, and they even stock **Uncle Eddie's Vegan Cookies**.

There is a schedule chock-full of in-store events, too, from cooking classes to massage therapy.

Nuts

Nuts on Clark

3830 N. Clark St.
773/549-6622
www.nutsonclark.com

This purveyor of **bulk nuts and candies of all kinds** is famous for its **caramel corn**.

Ricci & Company

162–164 W. Superior St.
312/787-7660

A wholesale nut merchant that is open to the public, Ricci carries just about **any nut you could want, any way you could want it**. Almonds come blanched or not, sliced, slivered, or whole, for instance. Prices are good and quality is top-notch. Ricci also has **dried fruit**, **candy**, **soy nuts**, and **chocolate-covered coffee beans**. They have limited weekday hours, so call first.

Superior Nut & Candy Company

4038 N. Nashville Ave.
773/282-3930

This retail thrift store for a wholesale distributor is located just off Irving Park Road in an office building complex. The product emphasis is on candy, but they also sell **nuts in bulk** at good prices. It's a fun place to stop for your **Halloween candies** as they stock quite an assortment of **old-fashioned goodies** and lots of **gummy candies**, in the shape of spiders and other scary creatures.

Kosher Food

(Kosher mac & cheese, gelatin, snacks, and matzo)

Kosher Food

The market for kosher foods is huge and growing. It's hard to accurately estimate the dollar value, since many mainstream products, like Oreo cookies, are certified kosher—and the folks buying Oreos mostly don't care. What does seem to be the case, though, is that many folks look for kosher products for reasons other than Jewish dietary laws. Just as halal/zabiha meat is considered almost kosher, so are many kosher products considered acceptable to a growing Muslim population. Many who are allergic or sensitive to milk products trust kosher labels and rely on them. This is because keeping dairy separate from meat is part of eating kosher. While all labels must list ingredients by law, many non-kosher foods will have milk products listed in a form that is not easily recognizable. Kosher labels make it clear whether or not dairy in any form was used to make the product. The same goes for strict vegetarians who are often looking for items like gelatin that are not derived from animal products. There is also a group who believe kosher products are prepared under more careful and cleaner conditions and choose them for that reason.

There are some arguments for choosing kosher meat and poultry that have nothing to do with religion, too. Like halal meat, kosher meat must be slaughtered not by a machine but by a human, who says a prayer while he slits the animal's throat with a very sharp knife. Some say this is a more humane method. (There are also many who claim it is crueler.) Meat must also be koshered within three days and may not be frozen, so you can be pretty sure that kosher meat hasn't been in storage for weeks.

Kosher poultry has one huge plus, in my mind, and that's how it's plucked. According to USDA standards, poultry must have its feathers removed. Conventional methods do that by dipping slaughtered birds in a steaming hot vat of water, which is used over and over. Some say this water quickly becomes a bacterial soup, which can contaminate poultry. Kosher chickens, on the other hand, have their feathers loosened under cold running water. This is according to Trudy Garfunkel in her excellent book *Kosher for Everybody*.

Whatever your reasons for seeking out kosher food, here are some markets that specialize in it. And here's something to remember if you're not Jewish: All these places are closed Saturdays and are crowded late Friday afternoons.

Chaim's Kosher Bakery and Deli

4956 Dempster St.
Skokie
847/675-1005

This busy spot offers a little bit of everything kosher. There is a deli with the usual **lox** and **kishke**, as well as an extensive bakery counter offering sweets, **hallah**, and **bagels** and a freezer full of **Empire kosher chicken and turkey products**. Shelves are stocked with a modest assortment of kosher goods arranged somewhat haphazardly. Chaim's also does quite a good business in carryout food of all sorts, from full meals to soups and blintzes to a salad bar.

Ebner Kosher Meat Market

2649 W. Devon Ave.
773/764-1446

This small butcher shop on the western edge of the Devon shopping district carries **fresh meat and poultry**.

Good Morgan Kosher Fish Market

2948 W. Devon Ave.
773/764-8115

This kosher fish market is at the western, Russian-Jewish end of the Devon shopping area. It's the place to go to get **ready-ground fish for homemade gefilte fish**, among other things.

Hungarian Kosher Foods

4020 Oakton St.
Skokie
847/674-8008

According to their grocery bags, Hungarian Kosher offers "complete supermarket convenience all under kosher supervision." This is definitely the place to visit if you're in need of **nova** or **gefilte fish**. The grocery aisles are packed with **matzo in many flavors** and from many brands. There are kosher **gelatins**, "Kosherific" **fish sticks**, and many **Israeli imports**. (They claim the largest Midwest assortment of products from Israel.) Also available are giant (40-ounce) bottles of **Asian duck sauce**, for some reason. The deli features **three kinds of pastrami** (veal, shoulder, and chuck), as well as

Kosher Food

69

prepared **kugel** and **chopped liver**. There is a butcher shop and a small fish market. The **kosher wine** selection is extensive and is claimed to be the largest in the Midwest. Oh, yes, and the gefilte fish—you'll find three aisles of it!

Kol Touhy Kosher Foods

2923 W. Touhy Ave.
773/764-1800

This small market is on Touhy Avenue near the North Shore Bakery. It calls itself "The Heimishe Store," which translates to a warm, homey, friendly store. Aisles are packed with kosher **canned goods**, **matzos**, **kasha**, and some **Israeli imports**. There is a modest assortment of refrigerated goods, including **kosher cheeses**. They also have a small freezer case, but no deli.

Kol Tuv Kosher Foods

2838 W. Devon Ave.
773/764-1800

A bustling grocery store at the Jewish end of Devon (where it's called Golda Meir Boulevard), Kol Tuv has aisles crammed with the usual packaged goods, such as **Tam Tam crackers**, **kosher gelatins**, **matzos**, etc.

What's So Kosher About Kosher Salt?

If you're a serious cook, you're probably using kosher salt already. It has a cleaner flavor than regular table salt, which has additives (iodine and anticaking ingredients). That's not why it's called kosher, though. Because of the larger surface area of the flakes, the salt is better for koshering meat, which involves drawing out the blood. (Blood ain't kosher.) The salt clings better to the surface of meat, and that's part of what makes it a favorite with chefs. The texture makes it easier to pick up with your fingers, too. Kosher salt is about half as salty as regular table salt by volume, however, so adjust accordingly. Be careful, though, because not all brands of kosher salts have the same size crystals. It's always best to undersalt, taste, and adjust.

There is no full-service deli, but some prepared goods are available. Refrigerated cases offer a good selection of **spreads**, **cheeses**, and such, including the amusingly named **kosher cheeses from Mitzva Farms**. You can purchase Yetta Chedda, Muenster Mench, Mazel-Rella, and more. Oh, yes, this is also the place that carried **kosher low-carb kugel**, though by the time you read this, low-carb will be so over. . . .

Roberts Fish

2916 W. Devon Ave.
773/761-3424

A large stuffed swordfish hangs on the wall of this clean **kosher fish** market just down the street from **Ebner's**.

Romanian Kosher Sausage Company

7200 N. Clark St.
773/761-4141

This kosher butcher shop has been around for more than 30 years. The first time I drove by, I thought the place was permanently closed, since there were empty boxes stacked haphazardly near the windows. Turns out they were just closed for a few days. It does look sort of unoccupied from afar, though, so don't be discouraged. The interior is spacious and filled with a huge butcher and deli counter, where you can order **sausages made on the premises** as well as some prepared items, like salads

and **grilled beef liver** and **smoked turkey**. Refrigerator and freezer cases display **chicken**, **duck**, all the permitted **kosher cuts of beef**, and some ready-to-cook specialties, such as **chicken breasts stuffed with kishke**. Prices are high, but that's a given for kosher meats. They have a convenient parking lot, which is a blessing in this neighborhood.

New York Kosher

2900 W. Devon Ave.
773/338-3354

Another store in the Devon kosher enclave, New York Kosher (sometimes listed in the phone book as Moshe's New York Kosher) has a small deli. And while it's not as big a market as **Kol Tuv**, there is a decent selection of packaged goods, including **Israeli imports**, such as **crushed Israeli tomatoes** in convenient jar-type aseptic packs instead of cans.

And don't forget:

Many Chicago-area mainstream supermarkets carry kosher brands, like **Natural Ovens**, **King David bakery goods**, **Empire frozen poultry products**, and **kosher packaged goods**. In many neighborhoods, Jewel or Dominick's has a specific section devoted to kosher products.

Lee's Borscht
(Serves 8 to 10)

1-½ to 2 lb. flanken (beef from the chuck end of the short ribs)

1 large onion

1-½ quarts vegetable broth or 1-½ quarts cold water plus 1 T. bouillon powder

1-½ C. thinly sliced potato

1 C. thinly sliced FRESH beets

1 stalk celery, chopped

1 medium carrot, sliced

1 small head cabbage, shredded (use less cabbage if you prefer your borscht soupier)

freshly ground black pepper

1 scant tsp. caraway seed

1 tsp. salt (to be adjusted later)

1 tsp. dill

1 to 2 T. cider vinegar

1 to 2 T. brown sugar

1 C. tomato puree

Place the meat and onion in the broth. Simmer until the meat is tender. Remove the onion, cut the meat off the bones into small pieces, and return it to the pot. If humanly possible, refrigerate the meat until fat solidifies on top and then remove. (Or else, as so many cookbooks so blithely put it, "skim fat from top." Hah! I've never been able to make that one work!)

Meanwhile, prepare the vegetables: Cook the sliced potatoes and beets in water to cover—RESERVE THE WATER. Cook the celery, carrot, and cabbage in 2 cups of the reserved beet-potato cooking water, until tender.

Combine all the vegetables and their cooking water, plus all remaining ingredients, including any leftover beet-potato water, in a large soup pot. Add the cooked meat, with its broth and juices, to the soup pot, too. Simmer at least 15 more minutes. Taste and adjust the seasonings. Refrigerate overnight. Skim the fat and reheat.

Cooking Schools, Groups, and Books

(chef's hat and pants)

Cooking Schools

Cooking classes can be recreational, professional, hands-on, or demonstration only. Many individuals or chefs (including me!) teach an occasional class or series, and these offerings change constantly. The schools listed here are those with a regular location and a more or less year-round schedule; they are intended for home cooks, not professionals. Be aware that most community colleges offer cooking classes, too, as do many gourmet stores, wine shops, and supermarkets. The Chicago Botanic Gardens hosts a free summer Great Chef Series every weekend in their vegetable garden.

For a more comprehensive listing (more than 80, last time I looked), check the *Chicago Tribune* or *Chicago Sun-Times* in late August. They each publish an updated annual guide to cooking schools. The *Tribune* listing can also be accessed at www.tribune.com.

Calphalon Culinary Center

1000 W. Washington St.
312/529-0100
www.calphalonculinary
center.com

This 8,000-square-foot facility has three different teaching areas, including a hands-on classroom with cooktops and video monitors for each student, as well as a library, wine cellar, and private dining room.

Chez Madelaine

425 Woodside Ave.
Hinsdale
630/655-0355
www.chezm.com

Classes are offered on a variety of subjects, such as healthy eating, French technique, and vegetarian cuisine.

The Chopping Block

4747 N. Lincoln Ave.
773/472-6700

Merchandise Mart Plaza #107
312/644-6360
www.thechoppingblock.net

The Chopping Block holds daily hands-on and demo classes at all three locations. Topics include knife skills, ethnic cooking, menus for entertaining, kids' cooking classes and much more. Equipment and ingredients are for sale at the school, too. You'll also find **truffle oil**, **sherry** vinegar, **copper cookware**, **Microplane graters**, and gorgeous but pricey **Japanese knives**. They even have the very odd Asian **Kewpie Mayo**. This product comes in a squeeze bottle and has a grotesquely cute Kewpie on the front. It's used in sushi maki rolls.

Coachouse Gourmet

735 Glenview Rd.
Glenview
847/724-1521
www.coachousegourmet.com

Julie Kearney offers hands-on classes on such topics as hors d'oeuvres, entertaining, and quick gourmet meals.

Corner Cooks

507 Chestnut St.
Winnetka
847/441-0134
www.cornercooks.com

Demonstrations and hands-on classes are scheduled evenings and weekends. You can also arrange to plan and cook (with professional help) a private dinner party or set up a personalized cooking party. Prepared foods are available for takeout.

Flavour Cooking School

7401 W. Madison St.
Forest Park
708/488-0808
www.flavourcookingschool.com

Demo and hands-on classes are offered, including a hands-on sushi party once a month.

Kendall College

900 N. North Branch St.
312/752-2000
www.kendall.edu

Kendall moved to brand-new quarters in Chicago (from Evanston) in 2004. While Kendall is for professionals, they do offer a series of adult education evening cooking classes. There is also a dining room open to the public.

Northshore Cookery

Port Clinton Square
600 Central Ave.
Highland Park
847/432-COOK
www.northshorecookery.com

This school offers a wide selection of hands-on and demo classes taught by 19 different chefs. Courses range from the basics to ethnic cuisines to cooking for couples, kids, and even teens. They also carry

cookware, ingredients, and **cookbooks**.

Wilton School of Cake Decorating and Confectionery Art

2240 W. 75th St.
Woodridge
630/810-2211
www.wilton.com

More than 90 courses and workshops are offered at Wilton, from cake decorating, pulled sugar confections, cake assembly, and advanced fondant art to starting a business and displaying your cakes on the Internet. Individual classes and a course of instruction are both available.

The Wooden Spoon

5047 N. Clark St.
773/293-3190
www.woodenspoonchicago.com

Classes run the gamut from hands-on to demo, from ethnic specialties to healthy weeknight cooking. The Wooden Spoon also operates a retail shop with a full line of **cookware**, **gadgets**, and accessories (including **wooden spoons**).

World Kitchen

66 E. Randolph St.
312/742-8497
www.worldkitchenchicago.org

These affordable classes are sponsored by the city and held in professional teaching kitchens in Gallery 37's basement across from the Cultural Center. Some hands-on and some demo, the classes focus on techniques for all levels and on a variety of subjects, from Latin flavors to Lithuanian Christmas (I taught that one) to caviar. World Kitchen classes almost always sell out very quickly, so don't dawdle if you see something that interests you.

Clubs and Organizations

American Institute of Wine and Food
www.aiwf.org

This national organization devoted to the exploration and celebration of food and wine was started decades ago by Julia Child and Robert Mondavi. The Chicago chapter is currently inactive.

Chicago Cooks
www.chicagocooks.com

Chef Dana Benigno offers a Web-based resource for Chicago-area cooks. The site posts foodie events, news, farmers market locations, and other useful information and also offers menus and recipes for entertaining.

ChicaGourmets
Don Newcomb, president
708/383-7543
www.chicagourmets.org

This gourmet club's members plan events that let them experience new restaurants, cuisines, and the chefs who create them. Don Newcomb is well plugged into the Chicago culinary scene and has helped arrange many

food-oriented lectures by visiting chefs and authors, so his is a good mailing list to be on. You'll find ChicaGourmets events listed at www.culinary-historians.org. (Don is vice president of that organization.)

Cooking with the Best Chefs
630/980-6800
www.bestchefs.com

Founded in 1996 this organization offers a year-round schedule of chef-taught cooking classes in various suburban and Chicago locations. Restaurant tours, wine dinners, mushroom foraging, food-themed travel and children's classes are also offered.

Culinary Historians of Chicago
contact:
Susan Ridgeway
815/439-3960
www.culinaryhistorians.org

Meetings are usually held monthly at the Chicago Historical Society; lectures and events relate to food history, ethnic cuisines, and the food business. Memberships and events are very reasonably priced and often feature tastings, too.

Savoring Chicago
2735 N. Clark St.
Box 173
866/820-2787
www.savoringchicago.com

Lydia Marchuk publishes this knowledgeable quarterly newsletter about Chicago food shops, markets, and producers. Past issues have covered Devon Avenue, chocolate shops, and wine stores, among other things.

Slow Food
www.slowfoodchicago.org
www.slowfoodusa.org

This international organization began in Italy in 1986 and is now active in 50 countries, with more than 80,000 members. Slow Food USA supports sustainable agriculture and believes we should slow down and take honest pleasure in the foods we eat. They sponsor local and national events on food education and tastings. The local chapter helps make heritage turkeys available for purchase at Thanksgiving time. They have also authored *The Slow Food Guide to Chicago Restaurants, Markets, Bars.*

Cookbooks

Certainly, buying recent cookbooks at any bookstore is easy enough. (The online discount source Jessica's Biscuit [www.ecookbooks.com] has some bargains.) There is a growing interest in old cookbooks that have been out of print for years. They have become collectibles and are often found in antique stores.

The Frugal Muse
Chestnut Court Shopping Center
7511 S. Lemont Rd.
Darien
630/427-1140

This bookstore, which is pretty far out in the burbs, offers one of the best selections of used cookbooks I've seen anywhere. The prices are incredibly low. They also discount **new books, music, and videos. Wilton Homewares** (p. 56) is in the same mall.

Kay's Treasured Books
847/256-4459
kaysbooks@aol.com

This is not a retail store but a knowledgeable local source with more than 3,000 out-of-print cookbooks in stock. If you're looking for a particular volume, give Kay Sullivan a call. She says she has a 95 percent success rate with searches, and she has a real passion for her business.

Little Treasures
7502 W. Madison St.
Forest Park
708/366-9198

A large collection of old cookbooks (amidst the antique jewelry and bric-a-brac) makes this an enjoyable destination for cookbook lovers. You'll find classic sets, like the Time-Life Foods of the World series, and early editions of Julia Child titles and The Joy of Cooking, as well as lots of interesting but unknown volumes. The staff will help you find something specific or just let you browse. Remember to bring your checkbook or cash as they do not accept credit cards.

Latin America

(guajes, tomatillos, peppers, and tortillas)

Latin American Ingredients

Chicago is a rich treasure trove of foods from Mexico, Central America, and South America. If you're used to the Mexican section at Jewel, a visit to a real Mexican (or other Latino) grocery may surprise you with its foreign feel and wealth of unidentifiable ingredients. It's a lot more fun, and you can expect better quality, selection, and prices than you get in a gringo store. So if you're looking for **fresh tortillas**, **dried chiles**, or just excellent **quality herbs and meat**, it's worth seeking out a nearby Latin American grocery, even if you never cook anything authentic at all.

Meat is almost uniformly top quality in even small groceries. For one thing, they usually carry **choice grade**, which is a huge improvement over the select grade available in regular supermarkets. For another, there is a real live person standing behind the counter to assist you. Language can sometimes be a barrier, but there's always pointing and acting things out. I have found myself explaining the cut I wanted by using my own rump or shoulder as an example. I was understood completely. There's usually not a huge selection of seafood (at least compared with an Asian store), but you will almost always find **raw, head-on shrimp**, plus **sea bass**, **cod**, or **snapper**, and usually **mussels** or **clams**, too.

Meat and Fish

bacalao (dried cod)
beef tongue
carnitas, ready-made
chicharrónes (pork rinds)
chicken feet
chorizo sausage
cow feet
lamb hearts, liver
pig, every part but the oink: ears, heads, tails, spine, trotters
shrimp, head-on
skirt steak
tripe

Produce

These shops are very good places for veggies in general, as well as specialty items. There is an abundance of things you'd expect, like **peppers** and **avocados**, as well as excellent **lettuces** and **herbs**. At any one time you won't find all the items listed, but you can expect to find those that are in season.

(Fresh **chiles** and **herbs** are included here; dried ones are in the Spices and Seasonings list.)

boniato
calabaza
chamomile
chayote
cherimoya
chiles: Anaheim, arbol, habanero, jalapeño, peron, poblano, serrano
cilantro
epazote
garbanzos, fresh
green coconuts
guajes
guavas
huazontle
jamaica (dried hibiscus)
jicama
lita squash (a kind of zucchini)
malanga (yautia)
mangos
mint
ñame (white yam)
nopales (cactus paddles), whole, cleaned, and chopped
papayas
plantains
prickly pear fruit (tuna)
tamarillo
tamarind
tomatillos
verdolaga (purslane)
yucca (cassava)

Love That Lita

I'm not sure whether lita squash (sometimes called calabacita) is strictly a Mexican import, but it's wonderful. You'll find it in most Latino groceries as well as Middle Eastern ones. It's shorter and fatter than a zucchini, with an earthier, nuttier flavor and less bitterness. The flesh is crisp and dense and the seeds unnoticeable. Use it wherever you would regular zucchini. It even tastes good raw.

Spices and Seasonings

achiote paste
achiote seeds
adobo seasoning
bouillon cubes: flavored with tomato, annatto, coriander
canela (Mexican cinnamon)
chamomile
chile con limón (fruit seasoning)
chiles (dried): ancho, arbol, chipotle (red are moritas or colorados, brown are mecos), guajillo, pasilla

Yucca with Marilyn's Mojo

(Serves 4 to 6)

1 lb. yucca (2 or 3 tubers)

Peel the yucca. Do NOT attempt this with a potato peeler. Instead, cut into 2-inch sections. Then cut a slit through the barklike skin and the purple underlayer. Insert a paring knife and peel both layers off. Cut into hunks and rinse off. Immediately place in water to prevent discoloring. Salt the water and bring to a boil. Cook until the yucca becomes translucent and can be pierced with a fork. Watch carefully as different pieces may be done at different times. It will take about 20 minutes. Drain the yucca and keep hot. There is a hard, central stringy core, rather like a candlewick, which should be removed either before or after cooking.

Marilyn's Mojo

3 T. olive oil

1 T. butter

1 red onion, peeled, halved, and sliced into thin half-moons

1 red pepper, julienned

1 peron pepper or a serrano or habanero

2 cloves garlic, minced

juice of 3 limes

½ C. orange juice

1 bunch cilantro, chopped

salt and pepper to taste

Heat the oil and butter in a sauté pan. Cook the onion and the sweet and hot peppers until wilted. Add the garlic and cook until fragrant. Add the lime and orange juice. Season to taste. Add the cilantro and serve atop the hot yucca.

chipotles in adobo
hot sauces, all kinds
Mexican oregano
mole paste, various kinds
salsas, lots of unusual ones
tamarind paste

Carbs

The land of corn. You will find many versions, from huge dried kernels (often called **"mote"**) to prepared **masa** for making your own tortillas and tamales. (Buy yourself a tortilla press. I was very humbled by trying to do it bare-handed. In fact, I am still humbled by trying to make them—even with a press.) **Canned hominy** is very versatile and can be used in soups and stews; it also tastes great sautéed with greens.

hominy, dried and canned
masa, fresh (see p. 97)
masa, prepared for tortillas or tamales
masa harina (flour to make corn dough)
mote blanco (white dried field corn)
tortillas, all kinds

Rice and beans are also very important carbohydrate sources in these cuisines, and most stores offer good prices on these staples. Since the turnover is huge,

freshness is almost guaranteed. You'll discover many new kinds and colors of beans (including pink!), both canned and dry.

beans, dry or canned: black, canary, coba, pink, pinto, white, kidney
habas (fava beans, broad beans)
pigeon peas (gandules), dry or canned
refried beans, canned
rice: medium grain, long grain, Valencia (pearl, short grain)

Groceries

chufa (tiger nut, earth chestnut)
corn husks
empanada wraps
guava paste/puree
huitlacoche (corn smut), canned
lard (the hydrogenated kind—yuck—or lard that is rendered on the premises and is often available in plastic containers near the butcher section)
mango paste/puree
panela (loaf-shaped brown sugar)
passion fruit paste/puree

pigeon peas
piloncillo (cone-shaped brown sugar)
plantain flour

Dairy

cajeta (caramel sauce made from goat's milk)
crema (Mexican sour cream)
dulce de leche (caramel sauce made from milk)

Mexican cheeses (quesos) go by many different names and brands. The list here is far from definitive. In general, **queso fresco** is mild, fresh, soft cheese; **queso añejo** is aged and harder. Queso fresco is good crumbled on top of things, but it won't melt. It's a nice addition to any kind of salad. Queso añejo is more like Parmesan and is often grated onto things.

queso añejo (an aged version of queso fresco)
queso asadero (a melting cheese)
queso blanco (creamy white cow's milk cheese)
queso Chihuahua
queso cotija (hard, sharp grating cheese)
queso criollo (yellow cheese similar to Muenster)

queso enchilado (queso añejo with a spicy red coating)
queso fresco (crumbly white mild cheese)
queso Oaxaca (a melting cheese, "Mexican mozzarella")
queso ranchero (same as queso fresco)

Miscellaneous

chicharrónes (pork rinds)
fava beans, spicy
Mexican chocolate (YUM!)
peanuts, spicy
pumpkin seeds and nuts, flavored with chiles, lime, etc.
tropical juices: guava, mango, etc.
tropical sodas: Jarritos and other brands

Equipment

comales (griddles)
lime squeezers
molcajetes (lava mortars)
molinillos (chocolate frothers)
tortilla presses

Hibiscus Drink (aka Jamaica)

(Makes 2 quarts)

Hibiscus flowers can be purchased at any Latino grocery. They're sold dried, in plastic bags (usually labeled "Jamaica"), often hanging on pegs with the spices and chiles. They are very pretty and look like something you should add to a potpourri, but they're even more gorgeous when brewed into a drink, since the color is a deep pinkish red (which stains like crazy). The flavor is flowery and sour and refreshing.

8 C. water

2 C. hibiscus flowers

1 C. sugar (or to taste)

grated fresh ginger (optional)

Bring the water to a boil and add the hibiscus. Squash it to submerge and let brew for 20 to 30 minutes. Strain and add sugar and ginger, if you're using it. Serve over ice.

Simple Mango Salsa

(Serves 4 to 6)

2 mangos, cut into bite-size chunks

2 jalapeños or other hot chiles of your choice, minced

½ medium onion, chopped fine

3 cloves garlic, minced

juice of 2 limes

1 bunch cilantro, chopped

salt to taste

Mix it all together, adjust the seasoning, and allow flavors to mingle for at least 30 minutes.

Taste and adjust the seasoning again. Serve with grilled or roasted meats.

Also good as a dip.

Latin American Stores

Armando's Finer Foods

2639 S. Kedzie Ave.
773/927-6688

This large, clean grocery is near the Little Village archway entrance. The packaged goods, meats, and produce are fairly standard, but the store seems relatively serene, perhaps because it's not on the main drag. Shelves are well tended, and produce looks fresh. There's even a parking lot.

Armitage Produce

3334 W. Armitage Ave.
773/486-8133

In the heart of Humboldt Park, this nice grocery caters to the needs of its Puerto Rican and Central American neighbors and has the biggest, best selection of **tropical tubers** I've seen— **malanga lila**, **malanga blanca**, **yucca**, and more. They're also worth the trip for the **breadfruit**, a good **spice selection**, the **full-service butcher**, and those big, flaky, crunchy island-style crackers simply called **galletas**.

Belmont Produce

3239 W. Belmont Ave.
773/267-5800

Nothing too exciting, but this market is close to the freeway (you can see the sign from the Kennedy as you zoom by the Belmont exit) and carries everything in the way of Mexican foods. Products are carefully arranged, and the store is clean. Produce includes all the **Mexican specialties** and is very well priced. A full-service butcher shop offers good prices on **choice beef**, and there are carryout **carnitas** and **barbacoa**.

Carnitas and Barbacoa

Most stores with a full-service butcher shop prepare traditional meat dishes to take home from the deli. Carnitas is pork, slow-cooked until it's falling off the bone. Barbacoa is barbecue beef, but Mexican style. Each is utterly delicious and usually available only on weekends. They make great fillings for tamales or enchiladas, too.

Brazil Legal

2153 N. Western Ave.
773/772-6650

This teensy store specializes in **things Brazilian**. There is a small refrigerated section with **cheeses** and two aisles of packaged goods, including **mixes for pao de quijo**, the tasty cheese bread made from tapioca, as well as many brands of **guaraná soft drinks**. Guaraná is a tropical berry that provides a lift similar to a caffeine jolt. You'll also find **manioc (cassava) flour**, **guava paste**, and Brazilian soccer jerseys.

Carniceria Guanajuato

1436 N. Ashland Ave.
773/772-5266

3140 N. California Ave.
773/267-7739

6040 W. Diversey Ave.
773/836-2816

The Ashland store (Guanajuato #1) just might win the prize for having the cleanest, most beautiful meat case in town. Everything, even the **cow feet**, looks delicious. You'll see butchers who really look like they know what they're doing carving up **primal cuts**. Of course, they offer **carnitas**, **chorizo**, and **barbacoa**.

The produce selection is fine, and the packaged goods, **beans, peppers**, and **seasonings** offer everything you'd need for a Latin meal. There is the usual abundance of **dried chiles** as well as powdered versions of **ancho**, **guajilla**, and others. Try some of them in your next batch of chili!

Carniceria Jimenez

3850 W. Fullerton Ave.
773/278-6769

4204 W. North Ave.
773/486-5805

2140 N. Western Ave.
773/235-0999

37 S. York Rd.
Bensenville
630/766-0353

This well-established chain of stores is listed as a resource in Rick Bayless's book, *The Mexican Kitchen*. I've visited only the one on Fullerton, which is big, well stocked, and clean and has a parking lot. You will find most anything you need, particularly good produce, **lots of meat (all choice grade)**, a huge selection of **seasonings** and **chile peppers (both fresh and dried)**, **frozen empanada dough**, **frozen tropical fruit pulps** (mango, guava, etc.), and some equipment. There is also a small restaurant attached.

Chicago Produce

3500 W. Lawrence Ave.
773/478-4325

Similar in size to **Lindo Michoacán** (p. 94), this store, as its name suggests, offers plentiful produce, including **herbs**, **tamarind**, **plantains**, **calabaza**, **jamaica**, and **yucca**. The butcher shop carries some unusual items, like **lamb hearts**, **pig tails**, **lamb liver**, and **lard**. To keep things interesting, there's even a small selection of **Polish specialties**.

Delray Farms

3311 W. 26th St.
773/762-2598

5205 N. Broadway St.
773/334-2500

2330 W. Cermak Rd.
773/523-7100

6500 W. Fullerton Ave.
773/745-9600

This chain of produce and grocery stores used to be everywhere, but there seem to be fewer of them lately. Perhaps because of the competition from the bigger, newer supermarkets, such as Pete's. I've listed only the city stores I'm aware of, but there are suburban locations as well. Delray carries **chiles**, **tomatillos**, corn **husks**, and all the other basics, and it has a butcher shop. The prices are good, but the quality varies, so shop with care.

Edgewater Produce

5509 N. Clark St.
773/275-3800

Edgewater Produce is smaller than many other markets in this category, but it made the cut because it is clean, is well laid out, and has excellent prices. You'll find a small meat counter and deli, as well as a good selection of produce, including all the **Mexican specialties**.

El Guero Supermarket

1701 W. 47th St.
773/523-2350

4023 S. Archer Ave.
773/847-1600

1900 S. Blue Island Ave.
312/733-6820

2101 W. Cermak Rd.
773/247-0622

9029 S. Commercial Ave.
773/978-4981

El Guero has excellent prices on **all things Mexican**. The Pilsen store (on Blue Island) is the one I visited. It looks pretty shabby from the outside, but inside it's just fine. (Pretend you're in NYC, where a rough exterior often hides glamour inside.)

El Mercado Food Mart

3767 N. Southport Ave.
773/477-5020

This small but extremely well-organized market specializes in **South and Central American foods**. Shelves are organized by region. The section for Brazil holds **pao de quijo mix** (cheese bread), **manioc and tapioca flour**, and an **assortment of sweets—sweet pumpkin and coconut jam** looked intriguing. **Argentinian goods** include **dulce de leche, yerba maté, guava, quince**, and **sweet potato paste**. There are several brands of **canned hearts of palm**. From Peru there are **yellow chile (aji amarillo) pastes** and some **exotic corn products—purple corn flour, ground toasted corn**, and **Peruvian popping corn** (maiz para tostada or cancha)—and also **Inca-brand peeled wheat** and **fava flour**. A small refrigerated case holds some **sausages** and **cheese**, and there is a freezer with meat products, including **tripe, tongue**, and **matambre** (a type of flank steak). A few

prepared products, including **empanadas**, are stowed by the checkout.

Fiesta Market

3925 W. Lawrence Ave.
773/478-2882

The very nice produce in this supermarket features all the **tubers** (including **boniato, yucca**, and **malanga**), plus herbs like **epazote** and **huazontle**. They also carry **masa** from **La Guadalupana**, as well as a full selection of the usual **cheeses, canned goods**, and **meats**.

Joe's Food and Liquor

3626 W. Lawrence Ave.
773/478-1078

This smallish grocery offers a huge selection of **dried beans and corn**, a small selection of produce and meat, and many **Central American specialty items**. They will also prepare **roast pigs** for your fiesta!

La Casa Del Pueblo

1810 S. Blue Island Ave.
312/421-4640

A big, well-established market in the Pilsen neighborhood, La Casa is clean and friendly and carries all the basics (though they didn't have prepared masa when I visited). The store is now part of the Certi-Saver chain, which may be the reason it seems more American to me than the other Latino markets in Little Village or on the Northwest Side. That probably makes it a very good place to pick up your Cheerios and Tide at the same time as your **epazote**. They have a big deli, a **good produce** section (lots of **chiles, fresh and dried**), and a nice **meat selection**. Street parking, I suspect, may be a problem during busy times. La Casa operates a taqueria next door, and the famous Mexican bakery El Nopal is two doors down.

La Chiquita

3555 W. 26th St.
773/522-0950

2637 S. Pulaski Rd.
773/542-0950

4926 W. Cermak Rd.
Cicero
708/780-7157

9655 Franklin Ave.
Franklin Park
847/455.2724
www.laschiquitas.com

This chain of stores began with the Little Village (the 26th Street) store in 1972. La Chiquita is a real super-

market with fine, well-priced produce (**guajes, fresh chiles, epazote**), a butcher shop, and all the standard **mole pastes, salsas, cheeses**, and **beans**. Each store also has a restaurant, as do many Latino markets.

La Guadalupana

"La Casa de la Masa"
3215 W. 26th St.
773/847-3191

4637 S. Archer Ave.
773/843-1722
773/TAMALES

Tamale heaven! La Guadalupana is justifiably famous for **prepared tamales** and **masa of all kinds**. When you visit, proceed beyond the grocery section to the rear for masa and tamales. You can choose **masa for tortillas** or **masa for tamales (either plain or sweet)**. Here you can purchase masa by the pound, but La Guadalupana also distributes its products to most Mexican stores in the city. In fact, some have just appeared in my Oak Park Jewel! And don't leave without taking home some of their tamales. Fantastic! There are always four or five varieties, and they are totally delicious.

Julie's Ancho Pepper Dip

(Makes about ¾ cup)

6 ancho chiles

1 T. minced garlic

2 T. chopped cilantro

½ C. sour cream

1 tsp. lime juice

salt and pepper

Reconstitute the anchos by covering with boiling water. Let stand at least 30 minutes. Drain. Remove the seeds and stems. Puree in a food processor with the garlic and cilantro. Combine the ancho puree, sour cream, and lime juice. (Start with 2 teaspoons of puree and add more for a deeper flavor.) Season. Serve with crackers or veggies.

La Justicia

3644 W. 26th St.
773/277-8120

I suspect La Justicia is losing business to bigger, newer markets, like Tony's and Pete's. There used to be two stores in Little Village, but they're down to one. The market offers **canned goods**, **cheese**, **produce**, **chiles**, **salsas**, and so on. There is also a butcher shop with **pig heads** and **every kind of pork product**, as well as **cow feet**. Of course, huge slabs of **chicharrónes** (pork rinds) are for sale on top of the meat counter, where blocks of **guava paste** are also displayed. (Be advised that this guava paste has seeds. It's one time when canned is better.)

La Unica Foodmart

1515 W. Devon Ave.
773/274-7788

La Unica is unique. This fascinating store specializes in **Central American and Cuban ingredients**. When you first walk in, you'll see **racks of chips**—not potato, but **plantain, taro, and yucca**. They have several varieties of **fruit paste, like guava and quince**, as well as **syrups flavored with passion fruit, tamarind, and guava**, to name a few. One section is filled with **dozens of different tins of fish: sardines**, of course, in various sauces, but also **octopus**, **squid in its own ink**, **mussels**, **cockerel**, **scallops**, and more. The **canned fruit** is just as exotic. (Try **canned guava shells**.) There are **flours and mixes to make breads and fritters**, including **manioc flour, barley flour, bean flour**, and **pea flour**. **Canned olives** come stuffed with such things as tuna and hot peppers. **Yerba maté** (a South

93

American drink) is here, as well as a big collection of **medicinal teas and herbs**.

There are many frozen pre-pared foods to choose from, too. The **arepas** (Colombian corn cakes) that I tried had an English muffin shape and a fresh corny flavor. Stocking **tamarillo, morro, guanabana,** and **mamey,** La Unica also has one of the widest varieties of **frozen tropical fruit purees** I've seen.

Finally, there's a small selection of equipment, plus a choice of **beers and booze from El Salvador, Peru, Honduras, and the Caribbean**.

The restaurant attached to the store offers Cuban specialties at good prices, as well as tropical smoothies made from passion fruit, mango, and guava.

As you check out, check out the pomades, exotic soaps, and little tins of medicinal herbal salves across from the register.

Lindo Michoacán

3142 W. Lawrence Ave.
773/279-8834

Located in one of my favorite neighborhoods for food shop-ping—the area around Kedzie and Lawrence in Albany Park—this complete store has **beauti-ful produce**, including a big selection of **Mexican items**

and herbs. Besides the usual **epazote**, you'll find (in season) **huazontle, guajes, pepicha**, and my favorite, **verdolaga** (purslane). The **complete meat department** is next to a deli that offers **carnitas** and other specialties prepared on the prem-ises. Oh, yeah, there's a big park-ing lot, too.

Maxwell Street Market

1500 S. Canal St.
Sundays, year-round
7 A.M. to 3 P.M. (go early)

This is the new Maxwell Street open-air market, set up to replace the much-lamented old Maxwell Street. It's big, crowded (especially on nice days), and loaded with junk. As my mom used to say, if you like that sort of thing, it's just the sort of thing you'll like.

On my last visit, Maxwell Street was somewhat short on produce and long on used tools and vac-uum cleaners, but it is still great fun. You will find a good selection of **dried and fresh chiles** at a produce stand on the south end of the market, along with **jicama, tomatillos, guajes,** and **fresh garbanzos**.

The real reason to go, however, is the food stands. Don't miss the **papusas** at the north end of the market. These Salvadoran masa

Chile Table of Correspondence

DRIED	FRESH
ancho	poblano
chipotle (moritas, mecos)	jalapeño
pasilla	chilaca
guajillo	mirasol

In general, larger, rounder thick-walled chiles are milder than smaller, pointy thin-walled ones. Individual variations exist: Some jalapeños are mild, and others fairly hot.

pancakes are filled with a choice of cheese, beans, chicharrónes, etc. Each one is handmade, and the woman who does it makes it look so easy! Tables are happily shared, and if you show an interest, somebody will help you order or offer recommendations. **Salsas** and **pickled vegetables** are in big jars or pitchers on the table. Try something different. How wrong can you go when steak tacos cost a buck?

For the definitive guide to Maxwell Street, you need to consult David Hammond, a writer and the self-styled Gorilla Gourmet. He has created a film and an invaluable PDF of the must-visit Maxwell food tents, complete with photos and maps. To download the guide, visit www.dchammond.com/gorilla/ HammondMaxwell.pdf. You can order a copy of the film at the same site. David's is a more adventurous palate than mine (which is going some), and he reports on delicacies like **eyeball tacos**. This is good information to have even if you just want to AVOID eyeball tacos. He also writes of an herb called **papalo**, used as a taco add-in. I have not seen it in regular markets but will be on the lookout for it next visit to Maxwell.

Pete's Fresh Market
4700 S. Kedzie Ave.
773/523-4600

5724 S. Kedzie Ave.
773/925-6200

4343 S. Pulaski Ave.
773/927-4300

These are big supermarkets specializing in Latin American goods, but with an international feel. You'll spot the store from afar since there is a large drawing of a guy (Pete, I presume) awkwardly holding a basket of produce. They carry nice, inexpensive produce featuring **Mexican specialties**, such as **epazote**, **xoconostle** (a kind of sour cactus fruit), **verdolaga**, **chiles**, etc.

A huge deli offers **tamales**, **chicharrónes**, and **carnitas**, along with the usual slice-to-order meats. There is an eat-in area as well, so you can take a rest and sample the store's **tacos**, **churros**, and such. Everything about Pete's is large—a large butcher shop, a large dairy case with **dozens of brands of crema and Mexican cheeses**, and large, wide aisles, too. Some **Polish goods**, especially baked goods, and a smattering of other ethnic specialties are here, too. Pete's is definitely worth a visit (unless you live in Evanston!).

Santa Maria Lacteos
3424 W. 26th St.
773/277-1760

This small shop specializes in **dairy products imported from Mexico**. They have all the **quesos**, including **Oaxaca**, **cotija**, and **asadero**, as well as **yogurt**, **cajeta**, and **crema**.

(Super) Tony's Finer Foods
2099 N. Mannheim Rd.
Melrose Park
708/345-4700
See "Multiethnic" chapter (p. 261).

Tony's Finer Foods
4608 W. Belmont Ave.
773/202-1760

2500 N. Central Ave.
773/804-1556

4137 N. Elston Ave.
773/866-0010

3607 W. Fullerton Ave.
773/278-8355

Tony's almost didn't make the cut for this book. It's part of the Certified chain so is a little too corporate to be really cool. Nevertheless, my Tony's on Central is a good shopping experience and has excellent **pico de gallo** as well as decent **carnitas**. (These are the somewhat skewed standards on which I judge.)

Tony's is a big American-style supermarket and is easy to love. All the normal Jewel or Dominick's stuff is here, but there is also a complete selection of **Latin American produce**, including **fresh epazote**, **guajes**, **nopales** (cactus paddles), and more. There's a big butcher shop, some **fresh fish**, and tons of frozen goodies, including Latin specialties, such as **empanada wrappers** and **tostones** (fried plantains).

Fresh Masa: What It Is and Where to Get It

Those of you who pay attention to our local foodie hero, Rick Bayless, know that one of the advantages of living in Chicago is the availability of fresh masa from tortilla factories. I must say, I first thought buying fresh masa sounded too scary. Where were these factories? Would I have to speak Spanish?

Masa just means "dough." Fresh masa is the dough used to make corn tortillas—dried corn cooked with lime water and then ground. (No, you can't grind up sweet corn and lime juice in your food processor to get masa. If you really want to make your own masa from scratch, you are a big-time overachiever, but you can find the instructions in Diana Kennedy's *From My Mexican Kitchen*.) Fresh masa is insanely perishable. You must use it the day you buy it, and it doesn't freeze well. That's why there are prepared refrigerated masas (with preservatives) and masa harina (corn flour for tortillas) in grocery stores.

Don't be scared to buy fresh masa—just go to a tortilla factory early in the day. The ones listed here are open to the public. There will just be a counter and a clerk. Don't be shy—step up and order a pound or more of masa for tortillas or tamales. The grind on the corn is coarser for tamales. Most places will also sell you the best fresh, hot tortillas for low, low prices and offer other goodies, like nopales salad. They may also have masa that's prepared for tamales. That means it has the fat added (sometimes salt, flavorings, as for sweet tamales, and preservatives, too). You will get a plastic bag of something that is the consistency of Play-Doh. It smells wonderful and is very inexpensive. Freshly ground masa is easy to work with, and if you make your own tortillas, I'd say it's a necessity. I tried to make tortillas

Cheater's Tamales

Here's a sneaky modern way to enjoy tamales more often. Also a great use for leftover roast chicken or pork.

1 tub of La Guadalupana Masa para Tamales

dried corn husks, soaked in hot water for at least an hour to soften

prepared salsa, homemade or store-bought

fillings: cheese, corn, chicken, pork, or beef, in small chunks or shreds

Set out all the ingredients, and find a big pot with a steamer insert (or one that will hold a vegetable steamer) and that has a cover.

Lay a drained husk on a flat surface, and spoon a heaping tablespoon of the masa on it. Use your fingers or the back of a spoon to smear it into a square layer in the middle of the husk, leaving the pointy ends naked. In the middle of the masa, arrange a bit of cheese and/or meat. Top with a spoon of salsa.

Wrap up the tamale by lifting the two long ends and folding them over so the masa encloses the filling. Don't get too concerned if a bit of filling leaks out or the job is not perfect. Then fold over the pointy ends of the husk to make a package, and tie it shut with cotton twine or a strip of corn husk. Set aside and go on to the next one. You will get better at adjusting the amount of filling and wrapping.

To cook, stand the tamales upright in the steamer. It is okay if they touch, but they must be in a single layer. Put several inches of water in the bottom of the pan. Bring the water to a simmer, and steam the tamales gently for an hour, adding water to the pan if needed. Tamales are done when the husk pulls away from the masa without sticking.

Tamales freeze well and reheat beautifully, so make lots!

with dough mixed from masa harina (impossible) and used the La Guadalupana–prepared masa (almost impossible). Then I tried fresh-from-the-factory masa (possible, though not easy).

Both Pilsen and Little Village have tortilla factories. To decide which one to patronize, pick the one whose tortillas you like best. I've heard that Bayless likes El Popo masa. Me, I'm an El Milagro fan. For instructions on tortilla making, consult Bayless's excellent book *The Mexican Kitchen*.

El Milagro

1923 S. Blue Island Ave.
312/433-7620

26th and Albany
(no phone listed)

El Popocatepetl

1854 W. 21st St.
312/421-6143

Sabinas Food Products, Inc.

1503–09 W. 18th St.
312/738-2412

Breads, Sweets, and Other Delights

Bombon Bakery

1508 W. 18th St.
312/733-7788

The **tres leches cake** at Bombon is light, elegant, and perfect. Pastries are made by owners Luis and Laura, who are trained in classical techniques and use them to create **traditional Mexican desserts**, as well as some wonderful variations of their own. From joyous **children's birthday cakes** to **molded sugar skulls** for the Day of the Dead, Bombon's delights are not to be missed.

Dulcelandia

3300 W. 26th St.
773/522-3816

3855 W. Fullerton Ave.
773/235-7825

6123 S. Kedzie Ave.
773/737-6585

This Mexican sweet shop stocks all sorts of goodies not available anywhere else. Piñatas hang from the ceiling, and usually an employee walks around with free samples. You can buy **mango-flavored marshmallows**, **tamarind candy**, and dozens of **by-the-pound sweets**.

Top 10 Latin American Ingredients

1. ancho, chipotle, and other dried peppers* (p. 95)
2. jalapeño, serrano, habanero, and other fresh peppers (pp. 84 & 87)
3. lita squash* (p. 83)
4. masa* (pp. 97 & 98)
5. Mexican chocolate
6. carnitas and barbacoa* (p. 88)
7. tropical fruit purees
8. mango* (p. 87)
9. hominy
10. verdolaga (purslane)

tip or recipe included

Tips on Tropical Tubers

A visit to the produce department of any Latin American, Caribbean, African, or Asian store will present you with a number of lumpy, bumpy potato-like vegetables that may be new to you. Yucca, malanga, taro, and their tuberous relations are the ugly ducklings of the vegetable bin, but looks aren't everything.

These starchy, filling, pleasantly bland ingredients are the backbone of some African and Caribbean cuisines. Worldwide they are used more than the potato, and they generally can be used in similar ways, so tubers are definitely worth getting to know, though that's not always easy.

Part of the problem is that each of them has many different names, depending on the ethnicity of the person labeling them. To add to the confusion, they are often mislabeled or unlabeled, and most of them come in more than one variety.

Probably the most important shopping tip I can offer is this: Make sure that the tubers you take home are fresh. Purchase them in a market that has a lot of product displayed. Usually one or two samples will be cut open to reveal the interior and showcase its freshness. Please do squeeze—a fresh tuber is firm without soft spots.

Tubers can be used in many ways, so consult an ethnic cookbook or Web site for ideas. I can provide you with one foolproof recipe, however. They all make great deep-fried veggie chips! (See recipe, p. 48)

Yucca (also spelled yuca, often called cassava or manioc)

It can be boiled, baked, deep-fried, stewed, and used in dessert. Yucca is an important food every place it grows. Most Americans only know it in the form of tapioca. There are many kinds, and the bitter kind is poisonous if not cooked, so cook it! Yucca is a good side dish, simply boiled or steamed first and then sautéed in olive oil with heaps of garlic. (See recipe on p. 84.)

Malanga (also called yautia or cocoyam)

The many varieties are often labeled by the color inside (lila for lilac, blanca for white, etc.). The outside is shaggy and ringed and looks a lot like taro, with which it is often confused. Malanga makes tasty and pretty home-fried chips, especially the lilac version, which has specks of color.

Taro (also called dasheen or eddo)

This tuber is also shaggy and ringed. The commonest kind here seems to be the small turnip-shaped taro. It is used to make Hawaiian poi, among other things. The flavor is mild and nutty. (See recipe on p. 204.)

Boniato (sometimes labeled batata or Cuban sweet potato)

This sweet potato has a texture that is fluffier and a flavor that is more like a baked potato than our sweet potato. The shape is bumpier and the skin is paler and patchier, but boniatos may be cooked in all the same ways as regular sweet potatoes—and they're delicious.

For more information, consult *Vegetables from Amaranth to Zucchini*, by Elizabeth Schneider (see the bibliography, p. 277). She explains things clearly, offers recipes, and provides photos.

All photos life-size.

taro, dasheen, eddo

malanga, yautia, cocoyam

103

boniato, batata, Cuban sweet potat

malanga lila, yautia

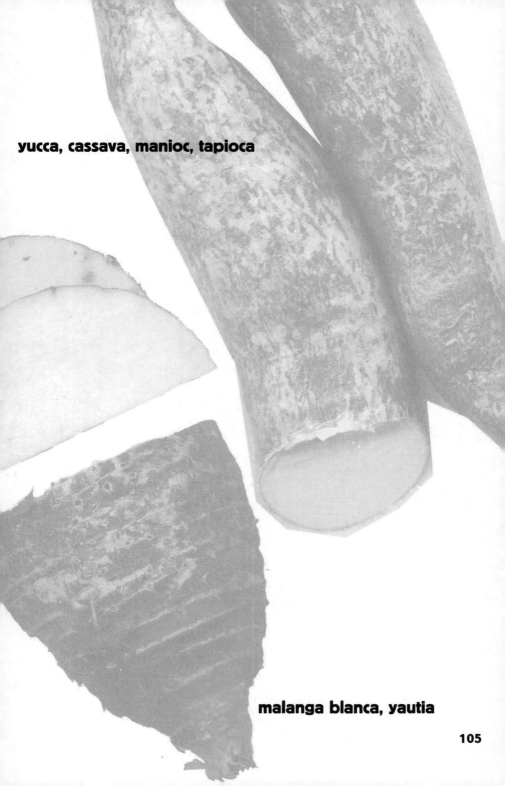

yucca, cassava, manioc, tapioca

malanga blanca, yautia

105

Eastern Europe

(savoy cabbage)

Eastern European Ingredients

Chicago has a population of Poles rivaling that of major Polish cities, not to mention a huge number of Lithuanians, Czechs, Estonians, and Russians. This provides a wonderful resource for cooks, even if they're not particularly interested in the cuisines of Eastern Europe. In a good Polish store, you'll find cuts of **meat**, **mushrooms**, **honey**, **syrups**, **cheeses**, **grains**, and **spices** you can't get elsewhere. And prices are generally quite low, too.

Meat and Fish

Eastern European butcher shops are excellent and cheap. Even small stores have **extensive delis** with an assortment of very good **bacon**, **lunch meats**, and, of course, **sausages** galore.

calf liver
chicken, whole, smoked
chicken gizzards
deli meats, including
    headcheese, **pork loin**,
    liver sausage
fish, smoked: trout,
    salmon, **whitefish**
ham, fresh
herring, every kind
lard

pâté
pork of any kind, including **trotters** and **pork belly**, **smoked items**
sausage, dozens of kinds
smoked butt
sweetbreads
tongue
tripe
veal bones for stock

Spices and Seasonings

Eastern European cuisine isn't known for its spices, but you will find an assortment of **seasoning packets** for making Polish-style fried chicken, borscht, etc., as well as a seasoning mix called **Vegeta**, which is a popular blend of vegetables and MSG.

citric acid
dill, fresh
horseradish, fresh or
    jarred, with or without
    beets
paprika, Hungarian
poppy seeds
sorrel, fresh
Vegeta

Carbs

Bakeries are usually quite good, especially for **rye breads**. Do try **Lithuanian sourdough rye** from the Baltic Bakery, a brand that's widely distributed.

barley, all kinds
kasha (buckwheat), toasted
   or not
oats/oat bran
rye bread, pumpernickel
spelt
whole wheat, wheat
   berries

Groceries

The **jams** of Eastern Europe are delightful and come in exotic flavors, like **rose hip**, **aronia**, and **gooseberry**. I used to think to get those you had to make them yourself. **Honey** is also taken seriously, as are **pickles and pickled things**.

exotic jams: aronia, gooseberry, rose hip
honey: acacia, buckwheat,
   others
mushrooms, **pickled**,
   including porcini and
   chanterelle mushrooms
peppers, **pickled**
pierogis
porcini mushrooms, dried
   (aka cèpes or boletus)
sauerkraut

Lithuanian Potato Gratin

(Serves 6)

5 or 6 potatoes

1 jar (5 oz.) horseradish

2 T. chopped fresh sage

salt and pepper

1 C. heavy cream

bread crumbs

1 T. cold butter in pieces

Preheat the oven to 350°. Slice the potatoes paper thin. Put a layer in a shallow, buttered casserole. Smear with some horseradish and seasonings. Repeat until potatoes are used up. Pour on the cream, making holes with a knife so it penetrates all the layers. Top with crumbs, dot with butter, cover, and bake for about an hour. Uncover for last 15 minutes to brown.

Dairy

Eastern European shops are the home of one of my favorite ingredients—**fresh farmer's cheese**. It is light, delicate, and fresh tasting. It comes in tubs like cottage cheese but tastes more like ricotta. I add it to eggs, stuff it in crêpes, and eat it straight. Dairy products in general are excellent, and a Polish store is a good place to purchase **butter**, since they stock the **high-fat European varieties**. Some imported **Polish butter** ranks right up there with the French and Irish brands.

butter (European-style)
cultured milk (similar to kefir)
farmer's cheese, soft or pressed
kefir
Polish cheeses
Scandinavian cheeses

Miscellaneous

I won't go into detail on the huge selection of **European candies and cookies** available, but these places have everything from my favorite **chocolate-covered cherries in booze** to awesome **kolackys** and dozens of kinds of **hard candy** with hilarious names ("lobster tails," "Eddy"). For the cook, there is an array of syrups—not the kind you put on pancakes (although you could), but **fruit syrups** that can be used for jazzing up seltzer water, making a meat glaze or sauce, or flavoring cheesecake.

European candies, **cookies**, and **chocolate**
fruit syrups: morello cherry, currant, rose hip, more
pierogis, **frozen** and **prepared**

Drinks

These stores are great for **juice drinks** and **teas**, including **medicinals**. My daughter's Polish nanny used to give her chamomile tea as a baby to cure her colic. Sometimes it worked.

fruit and vegetable drinks, boxed: cherry, carrot, currant, etc.
kvas (a fermented drink made from rye bread)
teas: chamomile and more

Cham-Polski

A pretty drink and a nice change from ordinary white wine.

Pour a little fruit syrup (morello cherry or black currant is good) in a wine glass. Fill with champagne, white wine, or sparkling water.

Eastern European Stores

A-J Meats
3541 W. 99th St.
Evergreen Park
708/422-4130

This tiny, friendly deli and meat market is tucked away on a side street on the South Side near St. Laurence High School. The neighborhood is Lithuanian, and so are many of the products. The Pleinis family, who are the owners, specialize in homemade **Lithuanian, Polish, and Italian sausage** and offer **prime meat cut to order**. You can also pick up **kugelis** and **bacon buns** (better than my grandma's), and at Christmastime you can get the dumplings used to make **shlisikai**, or poppy seed milk soup.

A & T International
2858 W. Devon Ave.
773/973-2642

This little shop is primarily a Ukrainian bakery. Once the wonderful odors hit you, I defy you to leave without a loaf of bread. In addition to an assortment of **authentic rye, sourdough, and other breads and pastries**, they carry **deli meats**, **honey** of all sorts, **jams**, and other grocery imports.

Andy's Deli & Bakery and Mikolajczyk Sausage Shop
1737 W. Division
773/394-3376

5421 N. Milwaukee Ave.
773/631-7304

Chicago is a town that runs on sausage, and Andy's has been around fueling us since 1918. The original store is the one on Division. The new Andy's is the one on Milwaukee. In addition to the **legendary sausage and deli products**, they also offer a large grocery selection, including **bread and sweets from various bakeries** and all the **Polish specialties** you'd expect. There is also a café, and prepared foods are available for takeout as well.

Bobak's Sausage Company
5275 S. Archer Ave.
773/735-5334

100 Burr Ridge Pkwy.
Burr Ridge
630/655-2100

955 W. 75th St.
Naperville
630/961-9200

Bobak's Plaza
159th and Wolf Rd.
Orland Park

A South Side favorite, the original Bobak's in the city is a good-size grocery with a restaurant attached. While the grocery selection is not quite as broad as it is at **Wally's**, you can find most of the same things, like lots of **sausage**, prepared foods, and an **extensive meat section** that carries **geese** and **ducks**. The suburban locations are newer and grander than the original. As of this writing, the Orland Park store (which will have a whole mall named after it!) had not as yet opened.

Burbank Deli
7903 S. Nagle Ave.
Burbank
708/233-0557

This small but full-service Polish grocer, deli, and meat market is on the corner of Nagle and 79th Street, right next door to John's Bakery. The deli counter offers **sausages**, a huge selection of salads, prepared foods, and **homemade pierogis** by the pound—every variety is available, including **blueberry**. Shelves are well stocked with **Polish jams**, **grains**, **pickled mushrooms**, and more.

Dunajec Bakery and Deli
8339 S. Harlem Ave.
Bridgeview
708/598-9451

Dunajec is another **sausage** lovers hot spot. On Saturdays the line for the deli stretches from one end of the store to the other. While you're waiting you can check out the shelves of **jams**, **grains**, and **pickled things**. There is also a very small offering of produce. Plenty of prepared foods are available, too, such as **borscht**, **beet salads**, and **pierogis**.

E & J Sausage
6556 W. 79th St.
Burbank
708/598-1121

This tiny butcher shop and deli is located just across 79th from **Burbank Deli**. The **meat** is the thing here. On Saturdays the narrow aisles are filled with folks waiting in line to purchase **homemade sausage** and also a full range of **poultry**, **pork**, and **beef** from the butcher's counter. There is also a small selection of dry goods and a

Helen Szajkovics's Famous Kolackys

Helen was from Bratislava, Czechoslovakia, and her daughter, Pam, often treats lucky friends to these rich, traditional cookies.

3 C. flour

3 egg yolks (separate and hold whites on side)

½ lb. butter

½ cake yeast or 1 packet of active dry yeast, dissolved in ¼ C. lukewarm milk

¼ pint sour cream

1 T. sugar

Fruit filling:

purchase at any Polish store—your choice of apricot, prune (povidla), raspberry, pineapple

Preheat the oven to 350°.

Mix all ingredients except the fruit filling. Let the dough rest, covered with a towel, for an hour.

Roll out thin on a floured board. Cut in squares and fill with a small spoon of fruit filling. Cross opposite corners; dab with water to hold together. Place on a cookie sheet. Brush with egg white. (Just whip with a fork, not a blender.)

Bake for 15 to 20 minutes, or until golden brown.

freezer case with **pierogis** and the like. I didn't try the sausages (how much sausage can one girl eat?!), but based on the crowd, lovers of encased meats might do well to stop off here if they're in the neighborhood.

Eurostyle Deli, Inc.
4861 Oakton St.
Skokie
847/329-1430

Russian sausages made on the premises and **smoked fish** fill the deli case in this suburban store, which is practically next door to **Marketplace on Oakton** (p. 260). Eurostyle also offers imported packaged goods, including **Lithuanian products, frozen pelmeni**, and **blintzes**. There is a staggering array of **booze**, two examples being **Georgian blackcurrant vodka** and **Armenian pomegranate wine**. The dairy case holds **farmer's cheeses** as well as **Ryazenka**, a fermented yogurt drink kind of like kefir only more so. They even have funky-looking Russian colognes and beauty products.

Family Euro Deli
800 E. Roosevelt Rd.
Lombard
630/495-3185

Hidden behind what used to be a Frank's gardening store on the north side of Roosevelt Road, Family Euro Deli is worth seeking out if you live or shop in the western burbs. The grocery section offers all the Polish necessities, such as **pickled things, Vegeta, medicinal teas**, and **canned fish**. The selection of

different **imported juices in boxes** is huge. Besides the usual **black currant** and **sour cherry**, they have **pithaya** (dragon fruit) and **passion fruit blends**. There is a big deli with many prepared foods and even a few tables and chairs, if you wish to eat on the premises.

Gene's Sausage Shop and Deli
5330 W. Belmont Ave.
773/777-6322

Though Gene's is a little off the beaten (Polish) path, don't miss this large grocery, deli, and butcher. Customers line up at the counter for **pork belly, trotters**, and plenty of **house-prepared sausages**.

Gene's stocks an assortment of all kinds of **sweets, grains**, and **seasonings** (**Vegeta** being one, of course), with notable selections of **European candies, fruit syrups, tort wafers**, and **jams** in flavors like **wild blackberry** and **aronia-apple**. The dairy case is small but has the basics, including the usual brands of **farmer's cheese**. Almost an entire aisle is devoted to **tinned fish**. In addition to **sardines in every imaginable oil and spice**, they stock **sprats, herring**, and others.

Finally, they have a strong

Aunt Emily's Gruzdis

(Makes about 3 dozen gruzdis)

I raided my aunt Emily's recipe box for this one. She is an amazing cook, though she has slowed down a little since she passed 90. These fried dough treats are called crullers in Polish bakeries and sometimes also "bow ties." The name gruzdis is, as far as I know, not translatable. I suspect it was something we made up.

3 egg yolks	**¼ tsp. vanilla**
3 T. sugar	**¼ tsp. almond extract**
5 T. sour cream	**¼ tsp. salt**
1 T. rum or brandy	**2-¼ C. flour, sifted**

Beat the yolks until light. (I use a stand mixer.) Add the sugar gradually and continue beating. Add the sour cream, rum, vanilla, almond extract, and salt; mix well. Add the flour a little at a time until a ball of dough forms. (You may not need all of the flour.) Knead by machine or on a floured board until the dough is no longer sticky when cut. Divide the dough into two or three balls, wrap in plastic, and let rest at least 10 minutes.

Heat oil for deep frying to 375°. Roll out the dough paper thin on a floured board. (Aunt Emily never did this, but the easiest way to get paper-thin dough is to run the pieces of dough through a pasta machine just as you would pasta dough. Start with a setting of 1 and end with 5.) Cut into 3-inch by 1-inch strips. Cut a slit in the middle of each strip and bring one end through the slit. Deep-fry a few at a time for about 3 minutes on each side. Drain on paper towels. Sprinkle with powdered sugar before serving.

liquor and wine depart-ment, featuring unusual items like **chocolate vodka**, **peach liqueur** from France, and plenty of **Polish beer and vodka**.

Gilmart

5050 S. Archer Ave.
773/585-5514

Gilmart is east of Midway Airport, between Pulaski and Cicero. They are known for having great **Polish sausage**, but a complete deli and meat counter also offers **herring, house-cured bacon**, salads, and **many cuts of pork**. There is the expected variety of **syrups**, **pickles**, and **jams** in jars, as well as **pickles** (cucumber) and **pickled fish** in barrels. Prices are good, and the place is usually bustling. A small restaurant is tucked into a corner.

Grandpa's Bakery & Deli

7312 W. Irving Park Rd.
Norridge
773/589-0300

This combo grocery, bakery, and restaurant is just west of Harlem in the Polish neighborhood that stretches along West Belmont for many miles and encompasses much of Harwood

Heights and Norridge. Grandpa's offers shelves of **Polish jams**, **pickles**, and such. A large bakery shop proffers **house-baked breads, pastries**, and those retro pastries called **apple slices** that I remember fondly from my youth. The deli is crammed with prepared foods but doesn't have the huge selection of sausages you'll find in **Wally's** or **Rich's**. The freezer case offers **pierogis**, of course, but also boasts **frozen vegetables and dumplings imported from Poland**.

Joe & Frank's Homemade Sausage

7147 W. Archer Ave.
773/586-0026

3334 N. Milwaukee Ave.
773/283-0310

8720 S. Ridgeland Ave.
Oak Lawn
708/599-3800

Though the biggest store is the one on Archer, each location has an **excellent butcher shop**, lots of **homemade sausages**, and the usual Polish specialties—**farmer's cheese**, **syrups, pickles**, etc. This is also where I found **mushroom powder**, a tasty addition to homemade pasta, among other things. The Mil-

Eastern Europe

waukee Avenue store is no longer owned by the original Joe & Frank's but still carries their products.

Kurowski Sausage Shop/Rich's Bakery

2976 N. Milwaukee Ave.
773/645-1692

Kurowski is a good-size market with an especially comprehensive assortment of **sausages**, **teas**, and **spices**. Teas include the Indian and Chinese varieties, as well as every sort of herbal, fruit tea and many unrecognizable combinations. They also have dieter's tea and other medicinal types. **Spice products** include several variations on the all-purpose, ubiquitous **Vegeta**.

Mulica's Deli

3118 N. Milwaukee Ave.
773/777-7945

Beyond the usual **spices** and stuff, there is lots to drink at Mulica's. A large assortment of **herbal teas** is displayed, and **beer from Eastern Europe** is available by the single bottle, so this is a good place to try out some of the dozens of different brands. Let me make a special pitch for **Utenos beer**, a Lithuanian brand that is excellent.

Rich's Deli

857 N. Western Ave.
773/235-5263

Rich's is a Ukrainian Village neighborhood institution. They have a **meat counter**, a **deli**, and a **liquor** section. In grains, I found the usual **buckwheat**, as well as **spelt** and **barley**. They also carry **saltpeter**, **pork fat**, and lots of different **breads**.

Rich's Foods and Liquors

4747 N. Harlem Ave.
Harwood Heights
708/867-6663

This large market is located in a mall just off Harlem. Rich's offers an excellent assortment of **all things Eastern European**. The deli is packed with **sausages**, **meats**, and prepared foods. It's usually packed with customers, too, so take a number and keep a watchful eye on the progress, since they call out numbers in Polish. There are refrigerated cases filled with prepared foods, including several varieties of **borscht**, **hunter's stew** (bigos), and various salads.

Rich's may even have **Wally's** beat when it comes to **dairy products**. There are at least a dozen varieties of **European-style butter**, plus tons of brands of **farmer's cheese**, **kefir** (including **chocolate kefir**!), **yogurt**, **flavored cheese spreads**, and more. Dry goods shelves are stocked with **honeys**, **jams**, **pickled things**, **barley**, **kasha**, and **powdered mixes** to make Polish soups and other dishes. There is a small fresh produce section, a very representative assortment of **breads and sweets from most Polish bakeries**, and big **barrels of sauerkraut and pickles**. The small liquor section offers **Polish and Lithuanian beers**, myriad brands and flavors of **vodka** (Polish, Russian, and Scandinavian), and **Polish honey liqueur**. To the best of my knowledge, this Rich's is unrelated to the one in the Ukrainian Village.

Three Sisters Delicatessen
2854 W. Devon Ave.
773/465-6695

In this busy, crowded establishment, you'll hear mainly Russian spoken. Of course, **smoked fish** of all sorts, sold whole or by the pound, is a big seller, but Three Sisters is a complete deli and also stocks many kinds of **sausages**, **pickles**, **breads** from various bakeries that specialize in Eastern European styles, and a good assortment of **jarred fish**, **mushrooms**, **relishes**, and **jams**.

Several kinds of **caviar** are available by the ounce.

Ukrainian Village Grocery
2204 W. Chicago Ave.
773/486-6619

This small grocery stocks **Russian and Polish goods**. You'll find **pickled mushrooms**, **borscht**, **jams**, **honey**, and the absolute **best selection of imported vodkas** I've seen anywhere.

Wally's International Market
6601 W. Irving Park Rd.
773/427-1616

3256 N. Milwaukee Ave.
773/736-1212

The original store on Milwaukee in Little Poland is a bit smaller and shabbier than the Wally's on Irving Park, east of Oak Park Avenue. Both are real supermarkets. You will be delighted with the assortment. The prices are very good, too. Check out the **smoked fish**, the jars of **pickled things**, and the **jams**. The deli has more kinds of **sausages** than you probably knew existed, as well as a large assortment of

house-smoked meats. They also prepare many of their own **cold cuts**, which are excellent and reasonably priced.

Wally's bakery is awesome. Try the **"Starapolski" (old Polish–style) bread**—a huge crusty loaf that smells wonderful and tastes even better. Don't leave without some **bread**, jam, and **farmer's cheese** at least. A minor warning: You need to put a quarter into a slot in order to get a shopping cart at the Irving Park Wally's. You can also offer a shopper who's finished a quarter for her cart. You get the money back when you return the cart or "sell" it to someone else. (This can be confusing when you don't speak the language and folks start offering quarters.)

The Best Scrambled Eggs in the World

fresh, organic eggs

fresh farmer's cheese (the kind in a tub)

salt, pepper, and chives

a few T. of cream or milk

butter for frying

Add 1 tablespoon of cheese for every egg you're using. Whisk it into the eggs along with seasonings and cream or milk. Fry in butter. The cheese makes the eggs fluffy and delicious even if over-cooked.

Breads, Sweets, and Other Delights

Baltic Bakery
773/523-1510

You must have the **Lithuanian Medium Rye Bread**, unsliced. Don't try to go to the bakery—it's not a retail outlet. You can pick up the bread at pretty much any market in the city, Polish or not. Slice your loaf thinly; wrap and freeze the portions you're not going to eat in the next several days. (Generally, this bread keeps quite well and freezes even better. I often send a loaf to underprivileged Lithuanian friends elsewhere.) Eat your slice with a thick smear of European-style butter. If you want to bow to healthy eating, top the butter with sliced radishes and a sprinkle of sea salt.

Oak Mill Bakery
8012 N. Milwaukee Ave.
Niles
847/318-6400

5635 W. Belmont Ave.
773/237-5799

5747 S. Harlem
773/788-9800

3256 N. Milwaukee Ave.
773/736-1212

For **fancy coffee cakes**, **tortes**, and **pastries**, you can choose one of the four locations of the Oak Mill Bakery. This is THE place to go for **paczki** on Fat Tuesday, too.

Racine Bakery
6216 S. Archer Ave.
773/581-8500

For **Polish and Lithuanian specialties**, especially **kolackys** and **crullers**, head to Archer Avenue. Racine Bakery also has a deli that sells **smoked fish**, **prepared kugelis**, and other specialties.

Lietuvele
5741 S. Harlem Ave.
847/845-3972

My South Side Lithuanian heritage prompts me to include this small store that is neither a grocery nor a bakery. Lietuvele stocks Lithuanian books, music, souvenirs, and imported foodstuffs. You'll find **honey**, **jams**, **mixes for blinis and zeppelinis**, and assorted **cookies and candies**. It's also the place to buy T-shirts touting Lithuanian basketball, as well as the latest CDs from what we used to call the old country.

Lithuanian-Style Beet Salad

(Makes about 12 servings)

6 medium beets

1 C. hazelnuts

6 T. sour cream (NOT low fat)

6 tsp. prepared horseradish

salt and pepper

Preheat the oven to 375°. Trim and scrub the beets. Wrap in foil and bake on a baking sheet for about an hour, or until they yield slightly to pressure when squeezed. Meanwhile, toast the hazelnuts for 4 to 6 minutes, until they smell nutty. Chop coarsely and reserve.

After the beets cool, peel and cut them into ½-inch dice. You should have about 6 cups of diced beets. Combine the beets, hazelnuts, sour cream, and horseradish. Taste and add salt, pepper, and more horseradish, if you like. Serve cold.

Eastern Europe

Casmira's Pennycakes

(Makes about 12 six-inch pennycakes; can be doubled)

My Lithuanian grandma called these thick crêpes pennycakes.

1 C. flour (preferably Wondra)

1 C. milk

3 eggs, preferably organic

4 T. melted butter, divided

generous pinch of salt

pinch of freshly grated nutmeg (optional)

farmer's cheese and smoked salmon for filling

Measure the flour into a bowl and add the milk gradually, whisking out as many lumps as you can. Minimizing lumps is the reason for Wondra Flour. (You'll find it in a tall canister in the flour section of most groceries.)

Whisk in the eggs one at a time, then stir in 2 tablespoons of the melted butter, the salt, and the nutmeg. You should have a pourable batter, thicker than heavy cream.

Heat a 5- or 6-inch nonstick frying pan over medium heat. Brush the surface with a little of the remaining butter. Pour a puddle of batter into the center of the pan. Tilt the pan to spread the batter over the bottom. When the center begins to get dull (less than a minute), shake the pan to loosen the pennycake. And this is the fun part—flip it! Yes, you can do it. Toss the pennycake by jerking the pan up and away and back toward you in one motion. Keep your eye on it so you can position the pan under it on the way down. You'll probably miss a few times, but have a utensil handy and unfold the messed-up pennycake, or pick it off the ceiling, or let the dog have it. Let it cook for another 5 seconds and it's done. Cool on a rack. (Can be frozen.)

Put a small slice of smoked salmon and a tablespoon of fresh farmer's cheese in the middle of each pennycake, fold over the sides, and roll into a package. Bake at 350° until the cheese melts.

Stella's Stuffed Cabbage

(Serves 4)

1 head cabbage, washed, leaves separated

1 C. rice

1 T. butter or oil

1 onion, chopped

1 lb. ground pork

½ lb. ground beef

2 eggs

1 carrot, shredded

1 tsp. Vegeta

salt and pepper to taste

prepared mushroom or tomato sauce

Preheat the oven to 350°. Pull off the cabbage leaves and cut out the hard center core section at the bottom of each one. Bring a big pot of water to boil. Meanwhile, cook the rice in 2 cups of water until done. Put the cabbage leaves in the water and cook until wilted (5 minutes). Reserve the cooking water.

Heat the butter or oil in a sauté pan and cook the onion until limp, but not brown. Combine the meat, cooked rice, egg, carrot, and seasoning. Lay down each cabbage leaf and spoon on some filling. Fold over the sides and roll up into a package. Place in a baking dish seam side down. When all the cabbage rolls are assembled, add 1-½ cups of the cabbage cooking water. Bake at 350° for about 45 minutes, or until the meat is cooked through.

Serve with mushroom and/or tomato sauce.

Top **10** Eastern European Ingredients

1. farmer's cheese* (pp. 119 & 122)
2. fruit syrups* (p. 110)
3. house-cured bacon and sausage
4. jams and fruit fillings* (p. 113)
5. pork, especially fresh ham, butt
6. smoked fish* (p. 122)
7. horseradish* (pp. 109 & 121)
8. honey
9. bread and pierogis (not really ingredients . . .)
10. European-style (high-fat) butter

tip or recipe included

Germany, Ireland, and Scandinavia

(flatbreads, potatoes, cod roe, and spaetzel maker)

Germany, Ireland, and Scandinavia

I apologize for lumping together three such different cuisines. (Although they are all big on potatoes!) There weren't quite enough stores in any category to warrant an entire chapter.

Folks of German, Irish, or Scandinavian descent and the grocers catering to them have pretty much disappeared into the mainstream. Lincoln Square, once filled with German businesses, now features yoga parlors, Mexican restaurants, and antique shops. Andersonville has also both gentrified and diversified from its Scandinavian roots. As for the Irish, they are such an integral part of the city's political life (da mayor) and social life (da bars) that finding an Irish neighborhood in Chicago only requires walking out your door. In Chicago it's a lot easier to find nopales or Sriracha sauce than lefse or quark. Here are a few of the remaining grocers that offer goods from the old country in the new.

German

Meyer's Delicatessen
4750 N. Lincoln Ave.
773/561-3377
www.delicatessenmeyer.com

This is a real (wonderful) throwback to a time when sausage was made at the butcher shop and Lincoln Square was a heavily German neighborhood. The **brats** and **wurst** you find here are not anything like the grocery store version. They're plump and still attached to each other. You can choose from **knackwurst**, **veal and Sheboygan-style brats**, **blood sausage**, and **wieners** (Meyer's, not Oscar Mayer's). It's also the place to go for **liverwurst**, **veal bologna**, **Black Forest ham**, and **Westphalian ham**. The salesgirls speak German and wear little white lacy caps. The patrons frequently speak German, too.

The deli is gorgeous and holds **herring** and **cheeses**, including **quark** (a mild, fresh cheese, also known as **glumse**) and **Limburger** (not so mild). There are some prepared foods, and you can pick up a **spaetzle maker** or **springerle pin**. There is a good selection of **German and Alsatian wine**, **imported beer**, and liquor. Don't miss all the **chocolate**, **European candies**, and imported **jams** either.

Irish

Winston's Market

4701 W. 63rd St.
773/767-4353

7961 W. 159th St.
Tinley Park
630/663-7500

Winston's is a South Side favorite famous for **corned beef** and **Irish soda bread**. Actually all of their meat is quite popular. They make **"bangers"** (Irish/English sausages), **black and white "puddings"** (breakfast sausages), **pickled pork**, and **smoked pork butt**. All these items are seasoned but uncooked. There is also an assortment of imported goods, including **marmite, HP Sauce, YR Sauce, Irish oats, canned marrofat peas, salad cream, candies**, and **jams**. The Chicago store is tiny, and the prep kitchen is in the back. The Tinley Park market is much larger, has a restaurant, and sells Irish dishware and even jewelry.

Scandinavian

Andersonville, the traditional Scandinavian neighborhood around Clark and Foster, is the place to go for **lingonberries** and **lutefisk**. (A newer, Middle Eastern presence has brought diversity, with stores like **Pars Persian Store**, p. 165.) While you're in the area, stop by **Ann Sather's** restaurant (Swedish, 5207 N. Clark), especially for breakfast, or **Reza's** restaurant (Persian, 5255 N. Clark), for lunch or dinner. And don't forget dessert at the **Swedish Bakery** (5348 N. Clark).

Erickson's Delicatessen

5250 N. Clark St.
773/561-5634

This is the smaller of the two Scandinavian delis in Andersonville. They carry an excellent assortment of **cheeses** (including **gouda** and **havarti**), **flatbreads, lingonberries, cod and herring paste, lefse**, and **lutefisk**.

Wikstrom's Gourmet Food

5247 N. Clark St.
773/275-6100
www.wikstromsgourmet.com

This deli's small café draws a huge lunch business with its excellent sandwiches. Wikstrom's Scandinavian specialties include **lutefisk, lefse, Swedish brown beans**, **lingonberries (jarred or frozen), herring paste, cod paste**, and imported **flatbreads**. Check their Web site for a more complete listing of products. Wikstrom's will be happy to put together a gift basket featuring Swedish, Norwegian, Danish, or Finnish products.

Germany, Ireland, and Scandinavia

Italy

(radicchio and pizzelle)

Italian Ingredients

Italian is usually the first cuisine we think of as Mediterranean. Certainly Italian cooking has been mainstream for a long time, especially here in Chicago, land of pizza and Italian beef. Many ingredients, like **fresh basil**, **instant polenta**, **pine nuts**, and **risotto rice**, are available at almost every Jewel and Dominick's. Therefore, the markets included have something special to offer—either more exotic ingredients or a better selection or both. I'm aware that there are dozens of local Italian delis that escaped my notice and/or selection criteria, so apologies if your favorite was left out.

Fish

anchovies, in salt, in tins, or by the pound
baccalà (salt cod)
clams
mussels
octopus
sardines, fresh
squid

Meat

rabbit, often frozen
veal breast
veal cutlets
veal shanks (osso bucco)

Meat and Fish

A big Italian market will usually carry a slightly skewed choice—the steak and chicken you'd find in a regular market, but also more **deli meats**, **veal**, and **lamb**. Same with seafood, though these stores are generally great places for **sardines** and **squid**.

Cured Meat

bresaola (cured raw beef)
pancetta: regular (round) or smoked (strips)
prosciutto: crudo and prosciutto di Parma (cured, but uncooked)
prosciutto cotto (cooked)
sausages, homemade: all kinds, depending on the region of the maker

Frico (Cheese Crisps)

A frico is a wonderful thing. This recipe was inspired by Lidia Bastianich's recipe for Montasio Cheese Crisps in her book *Lidia's Italian Table*. They are so tasty that she opened an entire restaurant based on serving them. Unsurprisingly it's called Frico.

Frico are wonderful as hors d'oeuvres, are addictive as potato chips, and make a dandy platform for a salad. According to Bastianich, Montasio cheese is the preferred kind. I've always made them with Reggiano. Even preshredded Asiago works in a pinch.

They're easy to make, once you get the hang of it, like crêpes. The trick is to have faith. They need to cook for longer than you probably think.

Heat a heavy nonstick pan or griddle. Test the temperature by tossing on a shred of cheese. It should melt quickly, but not sizzle. Arrange a thin layer of cheese in a circle of whatever size you want on the hot pan—small for hors d'oeuvres, larger if you're making a "basket" or other shape. Watch the cheese melt. The oil will come out around the edges. The frico should loosen a bit from the pan when it's ready to be moved. This usually takes about 3 minutes. Flip it with a spatula or tongs, or slide it onto a plate and turn it upside down back onto the pan to cook the other side. Frico can also be created by baking circles of shredded cheese on a nonstick surface (parchment or, better yet, Silpat) in a medium-hot oven. It's probably easier, but not as much fun.

While still warm, frico can be shaped by draping them over a bowl. When they cool a bit, you have a very chichi (and delicious) salad container.

Italy

Produce

We'll skip the obvious eggplants and peppers, but know that all these relatively ordinary items are cheap and good.

artichokes, **baby**
arugula
broccoli raab (rapini)
cardoons (cardi)
chicory
dandelion
escarole
fava beans
fennel (finocchio)
figs, fresh
olives, uncured
radicchio

Spices and Seasonings

balsamic vinegars: red, white, aged
basil, fresh
caper berries
capers, in brine or salt-packed
Italian parsley, fresh
oregano, fresh
rosemary, fresh
sage, fresh
syrups: Torani and other brands; almond, hazelnut, other flavors
wine vinegars

Carbs

farro (spelt)
flours: 00 (hard flour, like semolina), chestnut, chickpea (ceci), semolina (pasta flour)
pasta: squid ink, orecchiette, many wild shapes and imported brands
pizza crusts, ready to top
pizza dough (for pizza, focaccia, or calzones)
polenta, instant or regular
rice: Arborio, Carnaroli, Vialone Nano (all for risotto)

Groceries

artichoke paste
beans: borlotti, cannellini, lupini
cannoli shells
chestnuts
olive paste, green or black
peppers, roasted
pesto, green or red
porcini mushrooms, dried
tomatoes, San Marzano canned
tomatoes, sun-dried

Dairy

Cheeses:
Asiago
Bel Paese
caciocavallo
Fontina
Gorgonzola
grana Padano
mascarpone
montasio
mozzarella: fresh cow's
    milk, buffalo milk (moz-
    zarella di bufala), smoked
Pecorino Romano
Reggiano Parmesan
ricotta
ricotta salata
scamorza
Stracchino
Taleggio

Is Real Reggiano Worth It?

Yes! You can be sure you're buying the real thing by checking the rind to see the word Reggiano stamped there in pinpricks. Enjoy this luscious treat on its own, paired with fruit and wine, or grate it over your pasta. Grana Padano is similar, cheaper, and fine for most cooking, but not as tasty.

pizzelle (crisp waffle-type
    cookies in many flavors)
tarelli (hard, pretzel-shaped
    cookies)

Miscellaneous

Biscotti, **grissini**, and
amaretti are available in
even the most modest Italian
delis, alongside a great assortment of bread from our
local Italian bakeries.

amaretti (almond cookies)
biscotti, many flavors
crostini (crackers in many
    shapes and flavors)
grissini (very thin, crisp
    bread sticks)

Drinks

**espresso beans and other
    coffee products**
Italian fruit syrups
Italian liqueurs: amaretto,
    Campari, limoncello,
    maraschino, sambuca,
    Strega, etc.
Italian sodas: Aranchiata,
    Chino, Crodino,
    Limonata, Orangina, etc.
mineral water

Italy

Caprese Salad

This classic combination of fresh mozzarella, tomato, and basil is so perfect it doesn't really need a recipe. In tomato season, I can (and have) eaten Caprese for breakfast, lunch, and dinner. I consider myself an expert. Here's what I've learned:

1. The quality of mozzarella varies wildly. The best is usually made where it's sold. It should be soft, not mushy, and should exude cream when you cut into it. Caputo Cheese Market (p. 137) makes a good one.

2. Fresh mozzarella is sold covered by a water-whey liquid. When you store mozzarella in your refrigerator at home, you should keep it in a container filled with water. Change the water daily if you don't eat up all the mozzarella immediately.

3. Don't even bother making Caprese unless you have really fresh flavorful tomatoes. Ditto basil.

4. The very best dressing is simply salt, pepper, and a drizzle of aged balsamic vinegar (the pricey kind). Balsamic vinaigrette is also good and has the advantage of letting you pass the dressing at the table so everyone can use what they want. Leftovers keep better undressed.

5. Making your own mozzarella is sort of fun, but it takes a gallon of milk to make a lousy ¾ of a pound! One experiment convinced me that store-bought is not only better, it's worth every penny.

6. You can create a stunning salad with combinations of different color tomatoes interspersed with different kinds of basil. Or try cherry tomatoes, whole basil leaves, and bocconcini (little balls) skewered shish kebab style for a stylish handheld salad.

Genna's Spinach Risotto

(Serves 4 to 6)

5 C. chicken broth (low sodium preferred)

2 T. olive oil

1 medium onion, chopped small

2 tsp. minced garlic

1 C. raw Arborio rice

1 tsp. dried basil

1 bunch fresh spinach, washed and chopped (or 1 box frozen)

salt and pepper to taste

½ C. fresh grated Reggiano Parmesan

⅛ tsp. fresh ground nutmeg

Heat all the broth and keep it just below a simmer for the duration. Heat the oil in another, wider pan. Add the onion and cook until softened, then add the garlic. In 30 seconds, put in the raw rice and stir it around for a minute.

Now comes the fun part. Put a ladle full of hot broth into the rice and stir. When the rice absorbs it, add more. The rice mixture should stay at a low simmer. Don't worry. This is really hard to screw up, as long as you don't let the rice dry out and burn. Add the basil when you feel like it. (You can use fresh basil, but don't add that till the end of the cooking.)

Taste and season after 15 minutes. When the rice is soft on the outside but still hard in the middle, stir in the spinach.

Keep adding broth and checking the doneness of the rice. It's difficult to be precise about amounts and timing since it depends on the rice, the size of the pan, and the vibes of the person stirring. The whole process takes between 20 and 40 minutes. You may not use all the broth or you may run out. If it's the latter, add some water or white wine.

The risotto is done when just cooked through. Turn off the heat, add the Parmesan and nutmeg, and adjust the seasoning.

Italy

135

Italy

Broccoli Raab and Polenta

(Serves 4)

quick-cooking polenta (enough for 4 or more)

½ C. grated Parmesan or Asiago cheese

2 T. butter

salt and pepper to taste

1 large bunch of broccoli raab (or substitute chard, spinach, or mustard

greens)

3 cloves garlic, minced

3 T. olive oil

2 tsp. balsamic vinegar

2 tsp. soy sauce

¼ C. pine nuts, preferably toasted

salt and pepper to taste

I am somewhat embarrassed to admit to using instant polenta, but for a weeknight supper it's a lifesaver. If you have the time, do it the long way.

Wash the broccoli raab and chop it into bite-size pieces. Heat a big sauté pan, add the oil, then the garlic. After 30 seconds put in the thicker stem sections of broccoli raab (or other greens), stir to coat with oil and garlic, then cover for 5 minutes to help the greens cook. Uncover and add the leafy parts. Stir again and cook until the desired degree of tenderness is reached. Season with balsamic vinegar, soy sauce, salt, and pepper.

Meanwhile, make the polenta. Bring the salted water to a boil, and add the polenta in a steady stream while stirring. When the polenta is thick enough, turn off the heat, add the butter and grated cheese, season, and cover to keep warm.

Top a big scoop of polenta with the broccoli raab, and sprinkle pine nuts on top. Easy and delicious! Leftover polenta can be packed into a loaf pan and refrigerated, then cut into slices and fried in butter or oil the next day.

Italian Stores

Italy

Bari Foods

1120 W. Grand Ave.
312/666-0730

Bari has been around forever and with good reason. It's a small store jam-packed with imported Italian goods. They make **their own sauces and deli items**, which are excellent. Stop by **D'Amato's Bakery** next door (1124 W. Grand) for some real old-fashioned Italian bread while you're at it.

Caputo Cheese Market

1931 N. 15th Ave.
Melrose Park
708/450-0074

Although it's down an industrial side street off North Avenue and just west of First Avenue, Caputo's is worth seeking out for good prices on **all kinds of cheeses**, from Manchego and cheddar to a huge choice of Italian ones. They make their own **fresh mozzarella and ricotta**. Caputo's is also an Italian grocery, selling **prosciutto**, **deli meats**, prepared food, **spices**, and the usual canned and dried Italian items. They recently expanded and now offer an even

bigger selection of imported goods, including some wonderful **Italian mineral waters** that are cheaper than most U.S. brands (better, too). The owners are only vaguely related to the other Caputo's (cousins, if I remember correctly).

Caputo's

2560 N. Harlem Ave.
Elmwood Park
708/453-0155

510 W. Lake St.
Addison
630/543-0151

1250 Lake St.
Hanover Park
630/372-2800

166 E. Lake St.
Bloomingdale
630/924-0900

Caputo's is an institution—a must for anyone who cooks. They have a huge and well-priced selection of produce, an awesome Italian deli, plus **fish and meat**. The sign outside used to proclaim, "If we don't have it you don't need it." Produce is their forte, and you'll find not only hard-to-locate

137

Italian items, like **baby artichokes** and **escarole**, but also Latin American and Asian produce, like **persimmons** and **malanga**. You can buy by the case, too: **strawberries**, **figs**, **uncured olives**—whatever's in season.

Caputo's grocery aisles offer a lot of **Polish items** (including **farmer's cheese**!) and a fair selection of **Middle Eastern and Latin American foods**. The **Bella Romana brand** is Caputo's own and provides real bargains on **canned Italian goods** and **pasta**.

The deli (be sure to take a number and remember your assertiveness training) displays wonderful **homemade sausages**, **imported prosciutto**, and all kinds of **olives** and **prepared salads**, as well as the classics. The bakery shelves hold just about **every local brand of Italian bread**, so it's a good place to try the different kinds.

The original store (on Harlem) recently remodeled to double its size, and it's just as jammed as ever. Negotiating a shopping cart is a trick, and finding parking in the lot can be a challenge. It's fun if you're in the mood, since the clientele is a diverse mix, but if you can help it, don't go on a Saturday or Sunday afternoon.

The Addison store lacks the atmosphere, but it has wide aisles and more of everything. Parking is easy, and you don't have to deal with the crazed motorists on Harlem. It's still always jammed, though!

Conte di Savoia

1438 W. Taylor St.
312/666-3471

A lovely store in the old Italian Taylor Street neighborhood, Conte di Savoia is not huge but is nice. They have an upscale deli with a good selection of **cheese**. You'll also find **truffle oil**, **aged balsamic vinegar**, **canned chestnuts**, and **exotic pastas**, like **salmon tagliatelle**. The liquor section has Italian specialties, such as **limoncello** and **Cynar**. There's also a small café space where you can enjoy your cappuccino.

Convito Italiano

1515 Sheridan Rd.
Wilmette
847/251-3654
www.convitoitaliano.com

Convito is a restaurant, deli, and Italian gourmet shop. For starters, there's a wide selection of oils and vinegars: **aged balsamics**, **olive oils pressed with lemon** and other citrus fruits, **truffle oils**, and **nut**

and grapeseed oils. They also stock three kinds of **risotto rice**—**Arborio**, **Carnaroli**, and **Vialone Nano**—in addition to **high-end pastas**, **canned San Marzano tomatoes**, and gourmet sauces and condiments of all kinds. The deli displays a small selection of mainly **Italian cheese**, **sausages**, and a large choice of prepared foods.

D'Andrea Italian Market

7055 W. Cermak Rd.
Berwyn
708/484-8121

Tucked away at the eastern end of a mall (the one with the sculpture that consists of cars on a huge skewer), D'Andrea has been around serving the near western suburbs for decades. The narrow aisles are packed with **pastas**, **risotto rices** (**Arborio** and **Carnaroli**), and other canned imported Italian goods. **Fresh mozzarella, ricotta, Reggiano Parmesan, prosciutto, homemade sausages**, and **antipasti** are highlights of the big full-service deli. Prepared sauces, **frozen ravioli, pizzas**, and **pizza dough** are also on hand.

Gino's Italian Imports

3420–22 N. Harlem Ave.
773/745-8310

In the Piazza Italia on Harlem, this small Italian grocery and deli also carries some **equipment**. When I visited they had **imported pasta-serving dishes**, as well as huge $300 **grinders**. (I'm not sure for what.) There were a couple of odd choices on the shelves, like **maté**, the South American tealike drink. Next door is a fresh pasta shop, where you can purchase homemade **pumpkin ravioli, rottoli**, and more.

Joseph's Food Market

8235 W. Irving Park Rd.
773/625-0118

Joseph's, a large deli and grocery at the far western end of Irving Park Road, offers all the staples (**anchovies, porcini, balsamic, semolina**, etc.). While the meat and fish department is small, they carry **rabbit** and **octopus**. The produce section is also modest, but they have **fig trees** and **basil plants** for sale in the summer. The variety of **equipment**, however, goes way beyond the usual. You'll find **pasta machines**, of course, but also **cavatelli makers, espresso machines,**

Vittorio strainers, huge expensive wine presses, and a "torchietto spremi," which is, according to the directions posted, "a food squeezer to flatten for preservation or extract oil and liquids."

L'Appetito

30 E. Huron St.
312/787-9881

875 N. Michigan Ave.
312/337-0691

This small deli-grocery downtown does a booming business in sandwiches at lunchtime. They also carry a modest assortment of Italian necessities, like **Arborio rice**, **Reggiano**, and more.

Mercato del Pesce

2623 N. Harlem Ave.
773/622-7503
See "Fish and Seafood" chapter (p. 32).

Minelli Brothers Italian Specialties

7780 N. Milwaukee Ave.
Niles
847/965-1315

Milwaukee Avenue is a real UN of food stores, and this is the Italian delegate. Minelli offers sausages, pasta, prepared items, a small meat counter, and **imported canned goods**.

Nottoli & Son Sausage Shop

7652 W. Belmont Ave.
773/589-1010

The Nottoli family has been in business since 1947. In addition to the **sausages** they are famous for, Nottoli & Son offers their own **gardiniera**, **marinara**, and **meat sauce**. They also do a booming lunchtime business in sub sandwiches. There is another deli named Nottoli at 5025 N. Harlem, but one of the employees at the original Nottoli informed me most emphatically that there is no connection whatsoever.

The Pasta Shoppe, Inc.

3418 N. Harlem Ave.
Elmwood Park
773/745-5888

This small store on the Italian strip on Harlem specializes in **homemade pasta**. You can watch the pasta makers at work through a window. The Pasta Shoppe also carries a selection of specialty goods.

Riviera Market

3220 N. Harlem
773/637-4252

This small shop is a *salumeria*, selling **sausages**, **cold cuts**, and **pork products**, but no produce or other meat. They do stock imported **olive oils**, **pasta**, some canned goods, and Italian soccer jerseys.

You Don't Have to Baby Baby Artichokes

If you love the flavor of artichoke but hate the time-intensive task of trimming and dechoking, try the baby version available in the spring. No bigger than a real baby's fist (but a lot pointier), they're very easy to handle because they haven't yet developed a fuzzy choke or all those tough outer leaves. Just whack off the top and stem and cut them in half or quarters, and they're good to go. They are an excellent addition to pasta with pesto.

Breads, Sweets, and Other Delights

D'Amato's Bakery #1
1124 W. Grand Ave.
312/733-5456

D'Amato's Bakery #2
1332 W. Grand Ave.
312/733-6219

Why are there two D'Amato's only blocks apart? Beats me, but they do make one of the best Italian breads in the city. (I wouldn't dare suggest which Italian bakery is the absolute best, for fear of reprisal from readers who disagree.) I'm especially partial to the whole wheat loaf D'Amato's sells on Fridays.

"Original" Ferrara, Inc.
2210 W. Taylor St.
312/666-2200

Established in 1908, this pastry shop is at the western end of Little Italy and separated from the main drag by miscellaneous unattractive urban developments. Seek it out for the famous **cannolis** (**chocolate**, too), **cookies**, and other delicacies, but mainly because it is a Chicago landmark. You can read the newspaper clipping blown up and displayed on the wall about a huge wedding cake Ferrara created in the '40s in the form of an archway big enough for the happy couple to stand under. There's table space and a limited selection of soups, pastas, and sandwiches served on the premises. Or take home some frozen lasagna or stuffed shells to enjoy with your cannolis later.

Top 10 Italian Ingredients

1. Arborio rice* (p. 135)
2. Reggiano Parmesan* (pp. 133 & 135)
3. basil* (p. 134)
4. fresh mozzarella* (p. 134)
5. baby artichokes* (p. 142)
6. prosciutto de Parma
7. balsamic vinegar* (pp. 134 & 136)
8. broccoli raab (rapini)* (p. 136)
9. ready-to-use pizza dough
10. polenta* (p. 136)

tip or recipe included

Greece, Turkey, and the Balkans

(grape leaves and gigandes beans)

Greek, Turkish, and Balkan Ingredients

The lands of southeastern Europe between the Adriatic, Ionian, Aegean, and Black Seas are the Balkans—a land of political upheaval and countries with names and borders that morph and mutate. Many Chicago immigrants hail from these places, and markets accommodate them with imported products from Bosnia and Herzegovina, Serbia, Albania, Romania, Croatia, Macedonia, and Slovenia. Although Greece and Turkey are also Balkan, they have a more entrenched and familiar ethnic presence in Chicago. All these cuisines have many overlapping flavors and ingredients. They also use many of the same ingredients as used in the Middle East, so check out that chapter as well.

where or settle for frozen at Athens Grocery. You will find a sampling of **sausages** and other **preserved meat** and **fish** in even the smaller stores. Supermarkets generally offer some **fresh (or defrosted) seafood**, as well as **lamb, including ground lamb**, which is often hard to find in mainstream stores.

basturma (cured beef)
cod roe, smoked
Hungarian sausages
lamb, ground
salt cod
soujouk (spicy beef sausage)
taramasalata (the pink cod-roe spread served in Greek restaurants)

Meat and Fish

Balkan diets are generally grain and dairy based, rather than meat based. Greek lamb is legendary, of course. Unfortunately the Greek butcher shop that used to be on Halsted Street is gone now, so you'll have to get your lamb else-

Produce

The larger markets offer all the mainstream produce you'd expect, with an emphasis on **peppers**, **eggplants**, and **root vegetables**. Smaller places stick to items with a long shelf life.

apricots, dried
dates

figs
nuts: pine nuts, walnuts, almonds (fresh), hazelnuts, pistachios, more
olives, all kinds

Spices and Seasonings

caper berries
capers
cardamom
citric acid
fenugreek
lemons, dried
limes, dried
mastic
molukhia (Jew's mallow)
orange blossom water
paprika, hot or regular
pomegranate concentrate (pomegranate molasses)
rose water
sesame seeds
sumac
syrups: almond, tamarind, mulberry
tahini (sesame paste)
tamarind paste

Carbs

basmati rice
bulgur wheat: coarse, medium, fine
chickpea flour
couscous

hulled wheat
Israeli couscous (the big kind)
lentils: brown, red, yellow
trahana, sour or sweet (a pebble-shaped Greek pasta)

Groceries

ajvar (pepper-eggplant dip)
almonds, raw
ammonium carbonate (baker's ammonia)
beans: brown, fava
carob molasses
cashews, raw
gigandes (giant lima beans)
grape leaves
grape molasses/syrup (pekmez)
halvah

Ajvar and Friends

Balkan countries all produce one or more spreads based on a combination of tomato, peppers, eggplant, and other vegetables. Ajvar (pronounced EYE-var) is the most common. It's a handy condiment—great served on toasts, as a vegetable dip, or as a quick sauce for just about anything from pasta to broccoli.

honeys: date, sage, more
ikra (eggplant dip)
ljutenitza (tomato-pepper dip)
pepper puree
peppers, stuffed (usually with cabbage)
phyllo, in sheets and in shreds (kataifa)
preserves: rose, plum, bitter orange, fig, walnut, bergamot, quince, kumquat

Dairy

cheese, **Balkan**: halloumi (Cyprus), kashkaval
cheese, **Greek**: kasseri, kefalotiri, myzithra (grating), manouri
kajmak (thickened heavy cream)
kefir
labna (yogurt cream cheese)
yogurt

Miscellaneous

baklava
Jordan (candy-coated) almonds
lavosh
pita bread, white or wheat, many sizes
Turkish delight (rahat loukoum)

"Phun" with Phyllo

Phyllo (or filo) is paper-thin pastry. You buy sheets of it rolled up in a box from the refrigerated or freezer section of any Middle Eastern or Greek store. There are two tricks to working with phyllo:

1. It dries out in a heartbeat, so keep it covered with a damp cloth as you work.

2. Don't get upset when it rips; just cover it up with another sheet.

Phyllo is versatile. Roll a buttered layer around apples and sugar for strudel. Cut into circles or squares and stuff into muffin tins, one buttered layer at a time, to make puff pastry cups that can be filled with almost anything sweet or savory. One traditional recipe is on p. 153.

Greek, Turkish, and Balkan Stores

Andy's Fruit Ranch
4725 N. Kedzie Ave.
773/583-2322
See "Produce" chapter (p. 41).

Arax Foods
9017 N. Milwaukee Ave.
Niles
847/966-1808
See "The Middle East" chapter (p. 162).

Athens Grocery
324 S. Halsted St.
312/332-6737

This has been a Greektown landmark since the '60s. After having lunch or dinner on Halsted, stop here to pick up **feta**, **Greek oregano**, **olive oil**, **canned goods**, and groceries. **Frozen lamb** is also available.

Berwyn Fruit Market
3811 S. Harlem Ave.
Berwyn
708/795-6670
See "Produce" chapter (p. 42).

Best Turkish Food
2816 W. Devon Ave.
773/764-5093
www.bestturkishfood.com

This pretty little shop is tucked into the Indian-Pakistani majority on Devon Avenue. A small deli features **Turkish cheeses** (like **kasseri**) and meat specialties (like **soujouk** and **basturma**). The jam-packed shelves hold **Turkish coffees**, **teas**, interesting **jams and preserves**, and packaged mixes for bulgur pilaf and such.

This is the best place to buy your **Turkish delight**, as they stock several kinds. Ask one of the friendly clerks for a recommendation or simply go for the expensive one. (Cheap Turkish delight is nasty, gluey stuff.)

Brillakis
9061 N. Courtland Ave.
Niles
847/966-1250

The emphasis here is on Greek specialties, including **liquors and liqueurs** (featuring a great selection of **ouzo**). They also carry many brands of

Gigandes with Giant Flavor

(4 to 6 servings)

½ lb. gigandes dried beans

4 strips bacon

1 medium onion, chopped

2 cloves garlic, minced

1 can (14-½ oz.) diced tomatoes

2 T. grape molasses

2 tsp. oregano

3 to 4 tsp. salt

freshly ground black pepper

Make sure to purchase your beans from a store with a lot of turnover. The dried beans should be cream colored, not yellow, broken, or shriveled. Soak the beans, covered by twice the water, for 4 to 6 hours or overnight. They will soften and swell to double the size. (They don't call 'em gigandes for nothing!)

Simmer the beans in fresh water to cover until almost tender. This will take from 40 minutes to 1-½ hours, depending on the age of the beans. Add 1 teaspoon of salt toward the end and another when they are done. Drain the beans and refrigerate (for a day or two, if you like) until ready to finish cooking).

Sauté the bacon until crisp; remove, drain, and reserve. There should be about 2 tablespoons of fat in the pan. If there is a lot more, pour some of it out. Preheat the oven to 350°. Sauté the onion until soft; add the garlic and cook for a minute. Add the tomatoes, oregano, grape molasses, and a bit more salt (1 teaspoon) and pepper. Simmer 5 to 10 minutes. Mix the beans with the cooked tomato mixture in a casserole dish. Add ½ cup water (more if you want the beans to be soupy). Bake 45 minutes, until bubbly. Adjust seasonings and stir in crumbled bacon.

Greece, Turkey, and the Balkans

phyllo, **giant limas**, and **cracked wheat**.

City Fresh Market
3201 W. Devon Ave.
773/681-8600

This clean, fair-sized market is located on Devon and Kedzie, at the edge of the main Devon Avenue shopping strip. The offerings are multicultural, with the emphasis on **Balkan, Middle Eastern, and Russian**. You'll find a good selection of produce, including some **Asian greens**, **bitter melon**, **yucca**, **fava beans**, and a good assortment of **peppers** and **eggplants**. **Exotic jams, like rose petal and fig**, line well-organized shelves that also hold **rose water**, **honey**, **ajvar**, and many kinds of **grains**, both Middle Eastern (**couscous**, **bulgur wheat**) and Eastern European (**barley**, **buckwheat**).

The meat counter is huge and well stocked with the normal and the slightly strange (**pork spines**). There is a small fish counter, displaying **whole fish on ice** and many sizes of **head-on shrimp**. The freezer case holds more kinds of **pelmeni** (Russian dumplings) than I've seen anywhere, including **Siberian pelmeni**. You'll find a wacky array of multiethnic offerings—**frozen fried plantains**, **coconut**, and more. Most **pita breads**

and **Eastern European loaves** are also represented.

Devon Market
1440 W. Devon Ave.
773/338-2572

This place looks like a perfectly ordinary supermarket outside, but inside it's a bustling combination **Balkan and Latin American** grocery. Expect to find several kinds of **ajvar**, a red-pepper-based vegetable spread, plus **peppers stuffed with cabbage, smoked beef, Hungarian pickles**, and an assortment of **syrups** and **fruit and vegetable drinks** in boxes, including some not seen elsewhere, such as blueberry. Grains, like **buckwheat**, **millet**, and **barley**, are fresh, as is the produce, with the requisite peppers, tubers, and fruits. The fairly big butcher shop makes their own **sausage** and **smoked salmon**, and the seafood selection includes **head-on shrimp** and a tank of **live tilapia**.

Lalich Delicatessen
4208 W. Lawrence Ave.
773/545-3642

8133 N. Milwaukee Ave.
Niles
847/581-1120

This small, charming deli has

Opah!

If you've eaten in Greektown, you've probably had saganaki. This fried cheese appetizer is easy to make with halloumi or kasseri. Just dredge a 1/2-inch-thick slice in flour and panfry in butter. If you want to go the whole way, flame the cheese with brandy and douse the fire with lemon wedges. (Do so at your own risk!) These cheeses are excellent on the grill as well.

been serving the Yugoslavian (Serbian) community in Chicago for 20 years, according to owner Vera Lalich. Their main business is in **smoked meats, homemade sausage**, and **barbecued lamb and pigs**. I'm fond of the slightly spicy **sremska ljuta sausage**. Shelves are stocked with **teas, coffees, pickled peppers, stuffed peppers, whole wheat (wheat berries)**, and several kinds of **ajvar**, of course.

Lincolnwood Produce

7175 N. Lincoln Ave.
Lincolnwood
847/329-0600
See "Produce" chapter (p. 43).

Marketplace on Oakton

4817 W. Oakton Ave.
Skokie
847/677-9330
See "Multiethnic" chapter (p. 260).

Produce World

8325 W. Lawrence Ave.
Harwood Heights
708/452-7400
See "Multiethnic" chapter (p. 261).

Ted's Fruit Market

2840 W. Devon Ave.
773/743-6739

This large store on multicultural Devon sells a good selection of **produce** and a huge **assortment of breads**, including **Ukrainian ryes**, as well as many **Middle Eastern flat breads and pitas**. **Greek specialties** are well represented in the grocery section. There are **pastas** (including **trahana**), **Greek jams, honeys** of all kinds, and much more. You'll also find a selection of **Middle Eastern yogurt, labna**, and **kefir**.

Spinach-Cheese Phyllo Triangles

(Makes 6 to 10 appetizer servings)

1 box frozen chopped spinach, thawed and squeezed dry

1 T. olive oil

½ onion, chopped

1 egg

½ C. crumbled feta

½ C. farmer's cheese or ricotta

salt and pepper to taste

2 tsp. dill weed

½ box of phyllo sheets

½ stick butter, melted

Make the filling first. Sauté the onion in oil for a few minutes. Add the squeezed spinach and cook another minute or two. Mix the cheeses in a bowl with the seasoning and egg, then add the cooled spinach mixture. The mixture can be refrigerated for a few days in a covered container.

Preheat the oven to 350°. Clear a large work surface, place the melted butter in a dish with a pastry brush, get the baking sheet out, and dampen a clean dish towel to cover the phyllo. Unroll the dough and cut it the long way into strips about 3 inches wide (a pizza cutter works well). Remove one single strip from the stack. Immediately cover the rest. Brush gently with the butter. Place a teaspoon of filling near one short end about an inch from the edge. Fold the corner over to cover the filling and make a triangle. Keep folding and making triangles, like folding a flag, until you've used up the strip. Trim off any extra and place on the baking sheet with the loose end down. Continue until you fill the baking sheet and use up the filling and phyllo. Bake for 15 to 20 minutes, until puffed and golden.

Greece, Turkey, and the Balkans

153

Breads, Sweets, and Other Delights

Greek Islands

200 S. Halsted St.
312/782-9855

Sure, you know the restaurant, but did you know that they also sell some of the products they import, including an outstanding **Greek olive oil**? They'll even make up a gift basket of Greek products, if you so request.

Pan-Hellenic Pastry Shop

322 S. Halsted St.
312/454-1886

Baklava and **custard wrapped in phyllo** are just a few of the Greek goodies available. Greek butter cookies (**kouambeithes**) are dangerous—so light and flaky you can't help but eat five or six. **Diples** are honey-soaked after being deep-fried. Greek pastries are delicious and indulgent. A little goes a long way.

Rahat Loukoum

Turkish delight, as it is called in English, is a legendary sweet that everyone should try at least once. Kind of a clear, gummy candy coated in sugar, it comes in wonderful flavors, like rose, pistachio, and mastic.

There is an entire song about it in "Kismet," where it features in a seduction. It is also a magical, addictive candy offered to children by the bad witch in C.S. Lewis's Narnia series. Nothing can live up to all this, of course, but it is tasty—sort of a cross between gummy bears and Jell-O. And it's extremely pretty. Go for the more expensive brands; the cheap stuff is nasty in the extreme.

Top **10** Greek, Turkish, and Balkan Ingredients

1. phyllo dough* (pp. 148 & 153)
2. Greek yogurt
3. ajvar* (p. 147)
4. giant lima beans (gigandes)* (p. 150)
5. tahini
6. grape leaves
7. Greek olive oil
8. halloumi, kasseri, and kashkaval cheeses* (p. 152)
9. Turkish delight* (p. 154)
10. feta cheese* (p. 153)

tip or recipe included

The Middle East

(figs, pistachios, chickpeas, and rosewater)

Middle Eastern Ingredients

Whether the store is owned by a Jordanian, a Lebanese, or a Syrian, a Middle Eastern grocery is a wonderful place for the home cook. The **pita bread** and **feta** alone are worth the trip. **Nuts**, **dried fruits**, and **olives** are fresh and cheap. There are wonderful **spice blends**, **rose water**, **phyllo sheets**, and plenty more.

dates, many varieties
figs
olives, all kinds

Meat

Quite a few of these stores do offer meat, and the lamb is most often raised in the United States and is of good quality. Even smaller places often have deli items, such as **soujouk** (sausage) and **basturma** (dried beef). In addition to the Middle Eastern stores, you can also obtain **lamb** or **goat** at any of the **halal butcher shops** on Devon (p. 190).

Produce

Most Middle Eastern groceries don't offer much in this category. I think they just don't have the turnover or the space to handle perishables in quantity. They do have a few unusual things in season, however, often stocked at the front of the store.

A Little Lamb

Is the smallest lamb always the best? According to the USDA, to be called lamb, the animal must be less than a year old. Baby lamb (6 to 8 weeks old) and spring lamb (3 to 5 months old) must be milk fed. Much of our supermarket lamb is imported from Australia and New Zealand, and these cuts—leg, chops, whatever—are generally smaller than American-raised lamb. It's not because they're slaughtered younger, but because they're a different breed of animal. American lamb is usually considerably milder than the kind from down under since it is grain finished. Most Middle Eastern shops carry American lamb, which I personally prefer.

Spices and Seasonings

Here's where these shops become a gold mine for cooks, as they have many spices and seasonings you just won't find in other places. Sometimes items are not marked in English. Then there are the **spice blends** spelled in many mysterious ways, often with unidentifiable ingredients, and house blends, which can vary greatly from place to place. The famous **ras el hanout** includes at least 20 spices and means "head of the shop" because each version was put together according to the owner's unique recipe. Many herbs are sold for medicinal purposes rather than for cooking, so if you don't recognize something but want to try it, ask. (Herbs can be strong medicine.)

angelica
baharat (blend of nutmeg, peppercorns, coriander, cumin, clove, and paprika)
cardamom
citric acid
fenugreek
harissa (Tunisian chili sauce with red chiles, cumin, coriander, mint, caraway, and more)
hibiscus
lemons, dried
limes, dried
mahleb, mahlab
mango powder (amchoor)
mastic
molukhia (Jew's mallow)
orange blossom water
pomegranate concentrate (pomegranate molasses)
rose water
sesame
sumac
syrups: almond, tamarind, mulberry
tabil (blend of coriander, caraway, garlic, and chile)
tahini (sesame paste)
tamarind paste
vanilla powder
verjus (sour grape juice or grape vinegar)
zaatar (blend of sumac, thyme, and sesame)

Carbs

basmati rice
bulgur wheat: coarse, medium, fine
chickpea flour
couscous
freekah (green cracked wheat)
lentils: brown, red, yellow
maftoul (aka Jordan or Israeli couscous, the big kind)
rishta (pasta)
semolina
whole wheat

The Middle East

Groceries

amardine (dried apricot in sheets)
beans, dried: brown, fava
carob molasses
cashews, raw
chickpeas
date molasses
falafel mix
fava beans
foule mudammas (Egyptian fava beans)
grape leaves
halvah
honeys: date, sage, more
melon seeds, many kinds
phyllo, in sheets and in shreds (kataifa)
pistachios, raw or roasted
pomegranate juice
preserves: rose, pistachio, bitter orange, fig

Dairy

cheese: feta (many kinds), kasseri, touloumi, white cheese
kefir
labna (yogurt cream cheese)
yogurt

Miscellaneous

Jordan (candy-coated) almonds and chickpeas
halvah
lavash
nut mixes for snacking
pita bread, white or wheat, many sizes
sesame candies
Turkish delight (rahat loukoum)

Bagels and Labna

You'll find cartons of labna, the cream cheese of the Middle East, in the refrigerated dairy case. It tastes like cream cheese with an attitude (a sour attitude). Try it anywhere you would normally use cream cheese. Or smear some on toasted bread, crackers, or pita; drizzle on olive oil; and top with coarse salt and fresh cracked pepper for a delicious new take on cheese and crackers.

Tomato–Red Lentil Soup

(Serves 4 to 6)

This recipe is my attempt to create a soup similar to one served at Reza's restaurant. The secret ingredient is sumac. Sumac is a sour spice used almost like salt in some parts of the Middle East. It's also an ingredient of zaatar, a table seasoning frequently sprinkled on flat breads.

2 T. olive or vegetable oil	**4 C. chicken stock or broth**
1 medium onion, chopped	**½ C. red lentils**
1 large stalk celery, chopped	**2 T. dried parsley (or one bunch fresh, chopped)**
1 medium carrot, chopped	**1 to 2 tsp. sumac (to taste)**
2 cloves garlic, minced	**salt and pepper to taste**
1 large can (28 oz.) chopped tomatoes	**juice of 1 small lemon (optional)**

Heat the oil in a soup pot over medium heat. Add the onion, celery, and carrot, and cook until softened (a few minutes). Add the garlic, then in a minute add the tomatoes and chicken stock.

Simmer for about 20 minutes, season, and let cool. Puree the soup, then strain it back into the pot. This removes tomato skins and most seeds. Add the lentils and return to a low simmer.

Taste a lentil in about 15 minutes to see if it's tender. If not, continue cooking, but don't let them get mushy. Add the parsley and sumac. Taste for seasoning and add lemon juice, if you like. Serve with a dollop of yogurt.

Middle Eastern Stores

Al-Bayan Grocery

3136 N. Narragansett Ave.
773/622-6593

I spotted this relatively new shop only because it's on my daily commute—it's not really near any other Middle Eastern stores that I'm aware of. Al-Bayan has all the essentials, and while it's not quite as comprehensive as Al-Khyam, it's a lot closer to my place! There are the usual canned goods (**favas**, **chickpeas**, etc.), a refrigerated case with **cheeses** and **yogurt**, and a decent-size butcher counter offering **halal/zabiha** cuts.

Al-Khyam Bakery and Grocery

4738 N. Kedzie Ave.
773/583-3077

Al-Khyam makes the **best whole wheat pita bread**. In fact, it's carried in many other stores, but as long as you're here, buy it at the source. It's often still warm from the oven. This well-stocked grocery has expanded to fill three storefronts and carries pretty much everything Middle Eastern. There are the basics, including **bulgur wheat**, **pomegranate concentrate**, **grape**

leaves, and much more. A butcher counter offers fresh meat of all kinds, such as **lamb tripe**, **intestines**, and **kidneys**, as well as **soujouk**, **makaneh**, and **merquez sausages**. Canned goods feature the largest selection of **canned favas** in the world. There are also **pickled wild cucumbers**, **sumac**, **date molasses**, **zaatar**, **jahlab syrup**, and dozens of brands of **jam**, **Turkish delight**, and **tobacco for your hookah**. (If you're not already hookahed, you can purchase one.) Bulk bins are filled with **nuts**, **spices**, and **grains**, even a **dark bulgur wheat**, which I've not seen elsewhere. The cheese case holds the usual **labnas** and **yogurts** as well as some **Balkan cheeses**. In front there are bins filled with nuts, and they are addictive—especially the **kri-kri peanuts**, which are coated with sesame, spices, and other yummy stuff.

Arax Foods

9017 N. Milwaukee Ave.
Niles
847/966-1808

This clean, brightly lit store prides itself on stocking ingredi-

Pomegranate Chicken

(Serves 4)

2 whole boneless, skinless chicken breasts

1-½ C. walnuts

¼ C. flour

2 eggs, beaten lightly

salt and pepper

2 to 4 T. olive oil

1-½ C. chicken stock

¼ C. pomegranate concentrate

Rinse and separate the chicken into four pieces. Flatten by removing the tenderloin (that little skinny part underneath) and then covering with plastic wrap and pounding until thickness is fairly even, about ½ inch. Chop the walnuts coarsely with the flour in a food processor. Put the eggs and the walnut mix into separate shallow dishes. Salt and pepper each chicken piece, then dip into the beaten eggs, followed by the walnut coating. Press the coating onto both sides so it sticks.

Heat the oil in a sauté pan. Add the chicken and brown both sides. Cook through, about 10 to 15 minutes total. Don't crowd the pan and don't worry about some walnut mixture falling off (it thickens the sauce). Remove the chicken and keep warm.

Add the chicken stock and pomegranate concentrate to the pan. Cook, scraping up the brown bits, for about 5 minutes, until the sauce thickens slightly. Taste and adjust seasoning. Pour over the chicken and serve.

ents for all the Middle Eastern cuisines—**Persian, Jordanian, Armenian, Egyptian, Turkish, Palestinian**—as well as **Greek** cooking. You will find the best selection of **spice mixes** here alongside single-note **herbs and spices** of all kinds. There are **bins of snacks and nuts**, a well-stocked freezer case, **jams**, a deli for **cheese**, and a good selection of **bakery goods**, along with the usual items.

City Noor Meat Market

4718 N. Kedzie Ave.
773/267-9166
See "Meat, Poultry, and Game" chapter (p. 21).

Farm Meat Market

4810 N. Kedzie Ave.
773/588-1266
See "Meat, Poultry, and Game" chapter (p. 22).

Holy Land Bakery and Grocery

4806 N. Kedzie Ave.
773/588-3306

This delightful store has been around for years, and it's easy to see why. It's well stocked and the staff is helpful. They carry a good range of **grains**, **nuts**, **jams**, and **sweets**, as well as the usual bins of **bulgur**. There's an excellent deli loaded with **olives** and **cheeses**, not to mention a good choice of **yogurts**, **labnas**, **spices**, and **condiments**, including the all-important **pomegranate concentrate**. They also stock a mysterious-looking cone-shaped ingredient called **lektc**. It is made of yogurt and goat's milk and is grated and used in stews, according to the clerk.

One of the best parts is you can stop at Holy Land and then visit **Clark Market** across the street for Korean food (p. 253) and the big Latin American market **Lindo Michoacán** on Lawrence (p. 94). All without moving your car! (See "Delicious Day Trips" chapter [p. 272].)

Mediterranean Plus

612 E. Roosevelt Rd.
Lombard
630/424-1397

This store is an interesting addition to one of the many strip malls dotting the Route 38 shopping district. Mediterranean Plus makes a nice change from all the big-box behemoth chain stores. Their business card advertises them as carrying **Arabian, Iranian, Indian, Pakistani, and Greek foods** and also as specializing in **stuffed lamb and poultry**.

There is a complete selection of all things Middle Eastern, including vacuum-packed **grape leaves**, the usual **canned favas** and **tahini**, and bins of **bulgur** in different sizes. They also carry **tea leaves** in bins. (I thought these were some exotic dried greens until I asked.) **Pita bread**, in white or whole wheat, is fresh from several different South Side bakeries. The

Chickpea Nibbles

Preheat the oven to 400°. Drain a can of chickpeas and rinse them well in a colander, shaking to remove as much moisture as possible. Combine the chickpeas with olive oil, salt, and pepper in a large bowl. Spread them on a baking sheet in a single layer and bake 15 minutes, shaking the pan occasionally, until they begin to brown. Shake on some chili powder and some cayenne. Bake an additional 5 minutes. (You can alter the seasoning to suit your own taste buds.)

butcher cuts **custom pieces of halal meats**. The deli is very cool, and you are welcome to sample things. The **pickled turnips** are totally gorgeous—a Day-Glo hot pink—but kind of boring tasting. One aisle is devoted to **hookahs** and **exotic flavored tobacco** to fill them.

Middle Eastern Bakery and Grocery

1512 W. Foster Ave.
773/561-2224

In addition to **fresh pita** and a selection of pastry, this store offers all the staples. You'll find **couscous**, **lentils**, **dried fruits and nuts**, **bulgur**, **labna**, and a large assortment of **spices packaged in-house**, including **sumac** and **zaatar**. The Andersonville location makes for good shopping and eating nearby, but lousy parking.

Nineveh Grocery and Meat Market

2850 W. Devon Ave.
773/338-0690

Did you ever wonder what Iraqi food is like? This small store will give you a taste of **Assyrian cuisine**. Assyrians are one of Iraq's Christian minorities and represent one of the oldest civilizations on earth. Ask for a taste of the nicely **sour yogurt** they make, or take home some **frozen kibbeh**, Assyrian style.

Pars Persian Store

5260 N. Clark St.
773/769-6635

This store has been smack dab in the middle of Scandinavian Andersonville for a long time and is a good place to stop off before or after dining at **Reza's** (Persian) or **Ann Sather** (Swedish).

The Pars inventory includes many **herbs and spices**,

Meatball Pocket Sandwich

(Makes about 30 small meatballs)

(Inspired by the kofta recipes in A Book of Middle Eastern Food, *by Claudia Roden)*

1-¼ lb. ground turkey	**½ tsp. ground coriander**
1 small onion, chopped	**½ tsp. ground cumin**
2 cloves garlic	**¾ tsp. salt**
1 egg	**freshlt ground black pepper**
1 tsp. cinnamon	**1 T. raw rice**

The secret to meatballs (kofta), according to Roden, is the smooth texture of the meat. It was traditionally achieved by multiple grindings and hand pounding; however, you can get the effect in a food processor. Using turkey instead of beef or lamb is a healthy, modern twist.

Put the onion into the processor and chop until very fine. Add the garlic and pulse to chop. Then add the meat, egg, and spices. Process in pulses, scraping down the bowl frequently, until the meat mixture has a pasty, baby food texture. Mix in the raw rice. Form into walnut-size balls. (Wet your hands from time to time to prevent the meat from sticking to them.)

Place the meatballs (don't worry if they're not perfectly round) in a broad nonstick frying pan (or two) in a single layer. Add about ¼ cup water to the pan(s). Bring to a simmer, cover, and cook over low heat for 20 minutes. Add a bit more water to prevent sticking, if necessary.

Drain the meatballs and let cool a bit. Clean the pan(s), add a film of olive oil, and brown the meatballs on all sides. Serve with pita and yogurt raita.

couscous, tamarind, pomegranate concentrate, and other staples. They also have jarred harissa and a wider-than-average collection of flavoring "waters." Besides the traditional rose and orange blossom waters, Pars offers cumin, sweetbrier, and peppermint waters.

There are fresh barrels of nuts and seeds up front. At the time of my visit, they had a fruit called seyjid, which looked like a pale date, was said to be good for cleansing the digestive tract, and is a traditional food for Persian New Year's feasts.

In addition to food, they stock books, dishes, medicinal herbs, and even hookahs!

World Fresh Market

2434 W. Devon Ave.
773/508-0700

This place seems to change names and ethnic leanings periodically. It used to be World Fruit Market, offering Pakistani and some African ingredients. Now it seems more Middle Eastern. You'll still find a smattering of everything, and now some Latin American foods have been added. The produce department is extensive and stocks daikon, dandelion, methi, dill, and all the greens and tubers you could

want. The butcher shop is also large and runs the gamut from baby lamb leg to cow's feet (about the same size actually). Grocery aisles stock dried apricots, carob molasses, and everything Middle Eastern. You'll also find some Polish items as well as Indian and Pakistani staples.

Yogurt Raita

1 medium cucumber, chopped (seed and peel first if it's waxed or watery)

1 medium tomato, chopped

½ sweet red pepper, chopped

1 T. chopped fresh mint

1 T. chopped fresh parsley

juice of ½ lemon

salt and freshly ground black pepper to taste

1-½ C. yogurt

Combine all the ingredients. Taste and correct the seasoning.

The Middle East

167

Mahamorrah (Walnut-Pomegranate Dip)

2 cloves garlic

1-½ C. walnuts

1 jar roasted red peppers
(10 to 16 oz.), drained

3 T. pomegranate
molasses

½ tsp. cumin

salt and pepper to taste

about ¼ C. olive oil

Put the garlic in a food processor and pulse to chop. Add the walnuts and pulse to roughly chop. Add the red peppers, pomegranate molasses, cumin, salt, and pepper. Pulse to form a coarse puree, adding enough olive oil to smooth out the dip. Taste and adjust seasoning. Serve with whole wheat pita chips.

Whole Wheat Pita Chips

These are easy, healthy, and addictive. Preheat the oven to 350°. Split the pita, eliminating the pocket, into two circles of a single layer. Place the crust side down on a baking sheet and bake 15 to 20 minutes, until browned and crisp. You may have to cook some pieces longer than others and turn some over partway through to get the toasting even. Cool the rounds and break into chip-size pieces. These will keep in an airtight container for at least a week.

Top **10** Middle Eastern Ingredients

1. couscous
2. olives
3. pomegranate concentrate (pomegranate molasses)* (pp. 163 & 168)
4. labna* (p. 160)
5. sumac* (p. 161)
6. pita bread* (pp. 166 & 168)
7. chickpeas* (p. 165)
8. bulgur wheat
9. lamb* (p. 158)
10. dates

tip or recipe included

Africa and the Caribbean

(sugar cane, guava, and egusi seeds)

African and Caribbean Ingredients

This is a big category and a slippery one. It comprises everything from Jamaican jerk to Haitian curry and Nigerian egusi soup. Many ingredients overlap with those listed under Latin America because many items (yucca and guava, for instance) are used by several cultures. You will find stores listed in the "Latin America" chapter that specialize in Cuban (**La Unica**, p. 93) and Puerto Rican (**Armitage Produce**, p. 88), although you'll also find many of those ingredients here.

Meat and Fish

Go to African and Caribbean shops for **offal**, **cow feet**, **goat feet**, **pig tails**, and many **smoked versions** of these things. Although fresh seafood is part of these cuisines, the choices are limited compared with Asian stores. There is, however, a large variety of **smoked and dried fish**.

chicharrónes (pork rinds)
conch, frozen
cow feet
fish, smoked

goat, fresh or smoked
pig tails and snouts
salt fish, dried
salt pork
shrimp, dried

Produce

Tropical fruits and vegetables abound, and there is almost always a good selection of **greens**, **peppers**, and **tropical tubers**. (See "Tips on Tropical Tubers" [p. 102].) **Yams** in various sizes and colors are a primary carbohydrate source in most of these cuisines. (The various flours made from them are listed under "Carbs.")

boniato (batata, Cuban sweet potato)
breadfruit
chayote (christophene, mirliton)
chiles: habanero, Scotch bonnet
dasheen (taro)
guava
June plum (Jamaica plum)
mamey
okra
peanuts, green

plantains: green, black
quenepas (Spanish limes,
    mamoncillo, mamones)
sour orange
sugar cane
tomatillos
yams: white, yellow, Ghana
yautia (malanga, cocoyam)
yucca (cassava)

Spices and Seasonings

achiote
allspice (called pimento or
    Jamaican pepper)
annatto
canela (soft-stick
    cinnamon)
cassareep (flavored, con-
    centrated cassava juice)
criolla seasoning
curry powder, West Indian
egusi seed (squash seed)
filé (sassafras powder)
hot sauces, dozens of dif-
    ferent kinds
**jerk seasonings and
    pastes**
kuchela (green mango
    chutney)
piloncillo (brown sugar
    cones)
sofrito (a tomato-based
    seasoning sauce)
solomon gundy (herring
    paste)
tamarind
turbinado sugar

Carbs

Gari is cassava (yucca) flour and comes in sour or sweet versions. It is the basis for Jamaican bama bread and for egba, a classic Nigerian starch dish. You will also see something labeled "**farinha**." It's not Cream of Wheat, but another term for the same dried cassava flour. Toasted and flavored with palm oil, it is called **farofa**, a crunchy sprinkle used

Fu Fu and Coo Coo

Fu fu is the African name for a mush, usually made from pounded yam or plantain.

Coo coo is its Caribbean relation, a cornmeal mush, often including okra, but, like fu fu, open to interpretation based on available ingredients. Both dishes are bland, starchy foils for highly flavored meat or vegetable dishes.

Hominy grits are the southern U.S. form of cornmeal mush. And of course, polenta is nothing more than cornmeal mush with an Italian accent.

173

on top of many Brazilian dishes.
cane syrup/juice
cassava meal
corn flour
cornmeal: white, yellow,
    coarse, fine, hominy grits
couscous de manioc
    (attieké, cassava couscous)
fu fu (foo foo) flour (dried
    pounded flour from yams,
    plantains, corn, or rice)
gari, sour or sweet
kenkey (fermented corn-
    meal cakes, found in the
    freezer)
millet

tropical jams: guava,
    coconut, passion fruit
zomi (spiced palm oil)

Groceries

ackee, canned (a creamy
    white tropical fruit used
    in Jamaican Salt Fish and
    Ackee)
banana leaves, frozen
callaloo (soup made from
    taro greens)
cassava leaves, frozen
dende (palm oil)
gandules (pigeon peas,
    Congo peas)
jute leaves, frozen
pickled hot peppers
rice flour
semolina
tropical fruit purees:
    mango, passion fruit,
    guava

Guava Guidelines

Guava is my favorite fruit flavor, tropical and mysterious, without that overripe, decadent taste you sometimes get in mangos or papayas. The flavor and scent are tangy sweet with flowery overtones.

Fresh guava is often available in ethnic stores. While there are many varieties and the flesh can vary in color from almost white to hot pink, the kind usually sold in Chicago is small (2- to 3-inch diameter) and green on the outside with a lovely pink inside. You can recognize it by sniffing. I've always been disappointed with the taste of the fresh fruit (they tend to be VERY seedy and rather bland), but they sure make the kitchen smell good.

Guava puree is in the freezer case in Caribbean or Latin American stores. It makes an excellent smoothie or sauce.

Guava jam is a good glaze or ice cream topping.

Guava juice is available most everywhere. It is delicious but usually has a beige color instead of the gaudy pink of the familiar variety of the fruit.

Guava paste comes in a round can or a cello-wrapped brick shape in Latin American stores. It tastes wonderful paired with cheddar cheese (sounds strange, but it's a perfect match).

African and Caribbean Stores

Abyssinia Market & Coffee

5842 N. Broadway St.
773/271-7133

This tiny little shop offers a handful of Ethiopian groceries but also has **freshly made injera**, the spongy, sourdough flatbread made from a grain called tef and served in Ethiopian restaurants. It's kind of addictive.

Homeland Food Market

6046 N. Broadway St.
773/271-7133

Homeland stocks ingredients for just about every African cuisine: **Ethiopian, Nigerian, South and West African**. Shelves are jam-packed with exotic (to me anyway!) **spices**. They also have two brands of the **Jamaican hot sauce** I love, which combines papaya and pepper. There are assorted **dried fish, frozen kenkey, fu fu flour**, and, if you ask at the counter, **kola nuts**. You suck on them to get a caffeine kick that helps you get through the day. (Are you old enough to remember the commercial about "kola and unkola" nuts?)

La Fruitería

8909 S. Commercial Ave.
773/768-4969

This well-stocked grocery with a friendly, helpful staff specializes in African and Caribbean ingredients (particularly **Jamaican and Haitian**). Produce is fresh and plentiful and includes all the tropical tubers (**yucca, yautia**, and **yellow, white, and Ghana yams**). They carry fresh **guava, breadfruit, sour orange, mamey, "June plum,"** and **quenepas** (also called mamones) in season.

Spices are available in amazing variety, from some I didn't recognize (**ukazi, obgono, suya pepper, pitter**) to dozens of **mixed spices for jerk, Haitian curry**, and the complete line of the **Walker's Woods brand of Jamaican pastes and spices**, as well as the **Ocho Rios** brand from Miami. There is a small frozen section with **tropical fruit pulps** and a butcher shop that offers **cow feet, smoked goat feet**, and **pig tails** alongside more pedestrian items. They sell **smoked fish** ("boney fish"), **dried fish**, and **shrimp**, but they direct customers to a shop across the street for fresh fish.

Old World Market
5129 N. Broadway St.
773/777-7945

This is a Caribbean-African market in yet another strip mall, only a few steps away from the Southeast Asian Broadway-Argyle corridor. They carry African, Jamaican, and Caribbean foods, **spices**, and **condiments**. It's not a huge store, but it is packed with exotic stuff and lots of fun.

The odor of **dried fish** hits you when you walk in, so take a minute to get over it. Then go slowly down the aisles and check out **dende** (palm oil), **zomi** (spiced palm oil), **oil beans**, **tiger nuts**, **gari** (cassava flour), many kinds of **fu fu flour**, frozen **palm hearts** and **jute leaves**, and **teensy pickled peppers** that would look great in a martini.

Pick up **cassareep** (concentrated cassava juice used in stews), **dried bitterleaf** (used in stews and African palaver sauce), **Jamaican jerk spices**, and the whole, very good line of **Walker's Wood Jamaican products**, too.

If you are interested in African or Caribbean cooking in the slightest, don't miss this place.

Rogers Park Fruit Market
7401 N. Clark St.
773/262-3663

It was a tough call as to whether this multiethnic place should be listed here or in the "Produce" chapter. It's a microcosm of the melting pot nature of Rogers Park. There is a huge selection of fruits and vegetables, including the exotic, like **mamey** and **bitter orange**. There are **green coconuts**, **yautia**, and **yucca**, plus four different kinds of **yams**. **Plantains** are available at every stage of ripeness, and there is a good choice of Latin American vegetables, including **purslane**, **tomatillos**, **epazote**, and **nopales**.

A complete butcher shop offers **pig tails and snouts** in addition to the usual cuts of beef. There is a small selection of fish, too.

Last but not least, one of the best assortments of Jamaican ingredients is here: all the **jerk sauces** and **criolla sauces**, as well as jarred **escabèche sauce** and an array of **hot sauces**, including some I didn't see elsewhere, like **papaya-habanero**.

Breads, Sweets, and Other Delights

Caribbean American Bakery

1539 W. Howard St.
773/761-0700

Stop by this Jamaican bakery and fast-food joint for their **famous patties**—like empanadas with a reggae accent. Patties come in beef (the best seller), chicken (jerk or curry), and veggie. They are quite delish! You can also pick up **spiced buns**, **hardo bread** (Jamaican-style white bread), **totoes** (coconut cakes), and a bottle of the wonderful **Jamaican grapefruit soda**, Ting. It's the perfect antidote to a gray Chicago winter day.

In Praise of Plantains

Sometimes called the cooking banana or plátano, this relative of the regular sweet banana is versatile and delicious. Usually available in various stages of ripeness, plantains are cooked in stews or boiled like potatoes when green. When ripe the skin turns black, but the fruit inside retains a firm texture. The flavor is somewhere between banana, squash, and potato. Green ones will ripen gradually, so you can enjoy them at many stages. What an obliging fruit!

Breakfast Plantains

Peel a black-ripe plantain, cut into 3-inch lengths, and then slice vertically. Sauté in a nonstick pan with melted butter until both sides are browned. Season with salt, pepper, lime juice, and, if you're feeling frisky, some cayenne.

Dessert Plantains

Cut a black-ripe plantain (unpeeled) in half vertically. Spread a little butter on both sides. Dot with brown sugar and cinnamon or nutmeg. Cover with plastic wrap and microwave on full power for 2 to 3 minutes, until the butter melts and the sugar caramelizes. Serve with ice cream and/or rum sauce.

Top 10 African and Caribbean Ingredients

1. guava* (p. 175)
2. plantain* (p. 178)
3. jerk seasoning
4. boniato
5. sour orange
6. papaya-habanero hot sauce
7. yucca (cassava)
8. coconut
9. cornmeal or grits* (p. 173)
10. dende (palm oil)

tip or recipe included

India and Pakistan

(pappadams, mace, cardamom, and cinnamon)

Indian and Pakistani Ingredients

My first experience of Indian cuisine left me enraptured. These were tastes and also fragrances I'd never experienced before. It seemed to me I was eating perfume. No one handles spices with more subtlety and panache than an Indian or Pakistani cook. And there's no place better to buy your **saffron**, **cardamom**, or **cinnamon** than in what some Chicagoans call Little India—Devon Avenue between 2200 and 2800 west. Devon has been designated Ghandi Marg for the Indian stretch of the street. The eastern blocks are Mohammed Ali Jinnah Way, named for the Pakistani hero, and at the western end of the shopping strip, the honorary name changes again to Golda Meir Boulevard. It's my absolute favorite ethnic shopping destination.

Wandering east and west of Western Avenue on Devon and stopping at the dozens of groceries and produce markets, you'll find that these cuisines believe in **spices**, **fresh produce**, **more kinds of grains and flours** than you dreamed of, and **impeccably fresh meat**. Don't forget to stop for lunch while you're at it. Many new sweet shops have sprung up, and they offer lots of snack- and sandwich-type fare in addition to exotic desserts. (Try **Sukhadia Sweets** [p. 196].)

Devon is a good place to stock up on **cashews**, **peanuts**, and the like, as well as spices and **lentils**. This is definitely a destination for cooks, even if they never cook Indian. There are wonderful Indian convenience foods available, too. After all, if you live in Bombay, your hectic life doesn't leave you time to make everything from scratch either. Try some of the **curry pastes** or mixes. You'll also find tons of very interesting frozen vegetables and breads that only need to be heated. Even some of the prepared foods make a welcome change from another weeknight of Lean Cuisine.

The street is also lined with electronics shops that carry **rice cookers** and **pressure cookers** of all kinds and sizes. Much of this merchandise is being sold for folks to send back home to India, so if you're buying, watch the voltage. (You need to bargain, too.)

Allow enough time to explore the area. You can also get your eyebrows "threaded," buy a sari, have your hands decorated with intricate henna painting (mehndi), or purchase a 22-karat gold necklace. People are generally friendly and will answer questions if they speak enough English, which most of them do. Many shops are closed on Tuesdays.

Meat and Fish

There are dozens of butcher shops along Devon, and most advertise themselves as "**halal/zabiha**." This is the Muslim version of kosher meat (see p. 68). The halal part of the equation means it is a type of meat allowed (i.e., not pork). The zabiha designates the way it is slaughtered to meet Muslim requirements. It's interesting that they are extremely close to kosher regulations. In fact, I've been told that a kosher kitchen would accept zabiha meat if kosher were unavailable, rather than use the ordinary supermarket kind. The quality is usually very good, especially the lamb. They will butcher to order.

fish: pomfret, shrimp, prawns, hilsa, ruhu, surmai, more, all frozen

goat and kid
lamb, all kinds and cuts

Produce

Millions of Indians are vegetarians, so the produce at their groceries is varied and good. While there is some overlap with Asian cuisines, there are also unique vegetables and herbs.

amaranth
banana blossoms
bottle gourds
chickpeas, fresh
curry leaves
karela (bitter melon)
lemongrass
long beans (yard long beans, snake beans)
lotus root
mangos, green mangos
methi (fenugreek leaves)
mooli (daikon)
paan leaves (betel leaf)
parval (a gourd)
plantains
pomegranates
quinces
ratalu (purple yam)
sinqua (luffa, silk squash)
star fruit (carambola)
tamarillo
taro
tindora (like a mini cucumber or zucchini)

turmeric, fresh white (zedoary)
turmeric, fresh yellow
tuvar beans (Indian green beans)
valor beans
young coconuts (white, with conical tops)
winter melons

Spices and Seasonings

These are the best reason to visit Devon Avenue. The stores' selections are vast, their turnover is fast so things are fresh, and the prices are hard to beat.

Whole Spices:
allspice
anise seed (saunf)
caraway
cardamom: green, black
celery seed
chiles
cinnamon
cloves
coriander
cumin
dill seed
fennel seed
mace
mustard seed
nutmeg
peppercorns
poppy seed, white
saffron
sesame seed
star anise

Indian Spices:
ajowan
amchoor (mango powder)
anardana (pomegranate seed)
asafoetida (hing)
black salt (actually pink in color)
cassia leaf
fenugreek
kala jeera (black cumin, royal cumin)
kokum
nigella (kalonji, black onion seed, charnuska)
salam leaf (Indonesian bay leaf)
tamarind, paste or block
turmeric (haldi)

The idea of curry is British, not Indian. The root word means a sauce to serve with rice. There are hundreds of kinds of spice mixtures in Indian and Pakistani cuisines, from the incendiary to the delicate. All-purpose curry powder is a fine English invention made to bring Indian flavors to non-Indian cooks. It is not truly representative of Indian food.

You'll find many premixed spices as well as ready-made sauces on store shelves. One of my favorite convenience products is garlic-ginger paste. A jar in the fridge is incredibly handy. After all, who always has fresh garlic and ginger on hand and also has enough time to chop or grate it?

In general, the word **masala** indicates a mix of spices.

chaat masala (salty, spicy, sour; the name means "finger licking")

garam masala (slightly sweet with coriander, cinnamon, cumin, and cardamom)

panch phoron (a Bengali five-spice blend)

tandoori masala (hot and sour with cumin and coriander)

tikka masala, **vindaloo masala**, and many, many more

There are also cooking pastes and sauces for everything from **balti** to **vindaloo**. Mostly good. Directions in English are usually included.

Carbs

It's easy to be overwhelmed—happily overwhelmed—by the selection of **lentils**, **flours**, **rice**, and **bread**. Legumes are king here, and you'll find beautiful, cheap lentils in every color and configuration.

Dal is the word used to describe all **dried peas, beans, and pulses**. Things are complicated by the different names, not to mention spellings. Sometimes toor dal is toover dal or achar, for instance. Many can be bought either whole or split, skinned or not. Some dals are called gram, to make it even weirder. The good news is, other than having different cooking times, they are more or less interchangeable. Herewith, a superficial lesson:

channa dal (made from chickpeas)

masoor dal (red lentils)

moong dal (mung beans, sold split or whole)

toor dal (yellow lentils, also called pigeon peas)

urad dal (black lentils)

Bread is often sold frozen as well as fresh, and it's the next best thing to making your own. Many kinds also come in more than one variety or with different flavorings (cumin, saffron, etc.), but these are four of the basics:

chapatti (basic griddle flat bread)

khakhara (thin, crisp crackers, flavored with spices)

naan (leavened flat bread

made in a tandoor)

pappadam (lentil cracker bread)

paratha (griddle flat bread with flaky layers)

puri (puffy, deep fried bread)

I won't pretend to understand all the flours of the region. Suffice it to say that Indians make flour out of just about everything, including wheat. Here are some of those you'll find:

atta flour (basic wheat)
besan flour (gram flour, made from a kind of chickpea)
corn flour
dokra flour (a mix of besan and rice flour)
raggi and bajri flours (made from millet)
rice flour
semolina (hard wheat)

Indian **basmati rice** is world-famous, and you'll find a zillion brands in any of the listed stores. The two main types are **Patna** and **Dehraduni**, the latter being the more expensive and higher quality. They are named after the region where they're grown.

All rice is a good buy; the only catch is you usually have to purchase a sack of at least 10 pounds. Go with a friend and share. You can sometimes find **brown basmati** as well, in smaller quantities than the white. It's delicious but takes longer to cook. You'll also find **puffed rice** for snacking and **flattened rice**, called poha, to deep-fry or use in desserts.

Dairy

ghee (Indian version of clarified butter; usli ghee is

Ghee Whiz!

It took me a while to try Indian ghee in a jar. Somehow it seemed wrong to buy butter that wasn't refrigerated. Ghee is simply clarified butter—handy for cooking at high heat, since it doesn't brown or burn like regular butter. (The burning is caused by the milk solids, which clarifying removes.) It isn't difficult to clarify butter, but now that I've found ghee, I'll never bother again. Just look for a ghee that is pure butter. There is also a cheaper, vegetable-based ghee that is nasty. Clarified butter keeps better than regular but should be refrigerated once opened.

real butter—there are also vegetable oil imitations)

paneer (mild, white Indian cheese, similar to mozzarella)

yogurt

Groceries

Indian and Pakistani shops stock a delicious collection of **chutneys**, **pickles**, and more. If you like hot, you're really in luck. The Indian version of pickle is usually made from a citrus fruit, and the hot ones are blazing. The **cooking sauces** are generally pretty good and save a huge amount of time. Canned and/or frozen versions of Indian desserts and vegetables are also available.

chutneys: mango, cilantro, mint, eggplant, combos
cooking sauces: tandoori, rogan josh, korma, more
jaggery (unrefined sugar, sold in big hunks and often wrapped in burlap)
mustard oil (it will say, "for external use only"; this is because the FDA has decreed it may be a health risk)
orange blossom water
pickles: lime, lemon, mango, tamarind, combos,

Five Things to Do with Cilantro or Mint Chutney

1. Use it as a sandwich spread. (Mint chutney on leftover Thanksgiving turkey is divine.)

2. Serve as a dip (as is or mixed with sour cream or yogurt) for pita, pappadam, or vegetables.

3. Mix with mayo and use in tuna, chicken, potato, or egg salad.

4. Add it to salad dressings.

5. Heat and use as a sauce for fish or chicken.

everything but kosher dill!
rose water
varak (edible gold or silver in thin sheets; ask at the checkout—it's expensive)

Miscellaneous

Look to Indian and Pakistani shops when you want a new and different cocktail nibble. I've listed only a few of the many crunchy, salty, spicy snacks you'll find.

channa (spiced roasted chickpeas)

chivda (puffed rice)

sev (chickpea-noodle bits)

Indian ice cream called **kulfi** comes in exotic flavors, like saffron and rose. It also comes in individual-size containers. Just unmold on a dessert plate for a classy but instant dessert.

Stop by a sweet shop and pick up some **barfi**, the unfortunate name for Indian fudge. It comes in many flavors, such as ginger and cashew. You'll also find **ladoos**, which are big, sugary balls kind of like donuts, and cheese-sweets like **rosogollas**.

Finger-Lickin' Potatoes

(Makes 4 servings)

1-½ lb. red potatoes, boiled until tender, then peeled and cut into chunks

2 T. oil

2 T. butter

2 tsp. garlic-ginger paste (or use fresh)

2 to 4 tsp. chaat masala (to taste)

salt and pepper (to taste) lemon wedges for serving

This riff on Indian street food is addictive. Make sure you have good-quality, fresh chaat masala, with dried mango listed as one of the main ingredients. Alternately you can use amchoor powder, which is dried mango, and add other spices of your choosing. Think of these as slightly exotic hash browns, and feel free to improvise, adding tomato, onion, whatever.

Heat the vegetable oil and butter in a sauté pan. Add the ginger-garlic paste and stir. In 30 seconds add the chunks of potatoes and masala. Stir to combine, then leave to brown for 5 to 10 minutes. Turn with a spatula, scraping up the flavorful crust, and brown the other side. Adjust the seasoning. (You may not need salt and pepper.) Serve with wedges of lemon.

Cauliflower with Seeds, Indian Style

1 head cauliflower

2 T. oil

1 T. butter

2 tsp. panch phoron (Bengali five-spice mix: cumin seed, mustard seed, fennel seed, fenugreek seed, and nigella seed [kalonji] mixed in equal proportions)

1 T. ginger-garlic paste (or use fresh ginger and garlic)

1 tsp. ground cardamom

½ C. water

½ tsp. garam masala

salt and pepper to taste

hot sauce to taste (or add minced chiles when you add the ginger-garlic paste)

Wash the cauliflower and cut into 1-inch florets. Heat the oil and butter in a large sauté pan that has a cover. (Or use all ghee, if you have it on hand.) Add the panch phoron and let it sizzle a few seconds, until the mustard seeds pop (try to keep them in the pan by judicially applying the cover). Add the ginger-garlic paste. Cook for 30 seconds. Add the cauliflower florets. Stir to coat with the spices and cook for 2 or 3 minutes. Then add the water and the cardamom, stir to mix, cover, lower the heat, and cook 10 to 15 minutes, until the cauliflower is tender enough for you. Check occasionally to stir, and make sure it's not totally dry. Add a little water if it is. Uncover, season with salt and pepper, add the garam masala, and the hot sauce. The mixture should be fairly dry, so if there's too much water left, turn up the heat and let it evaporate. Serve hot or at room temperature.

India and Pakistan

Indian and Pakistani Stores

Awami Bazaar and Zabiha Meat
2350 W. Devon Ave.
773/274-9600

This is primarily a butcher shop (and a nice big one, too), but they do carry a modest selection of Indian groceries and spices.

Big Suchir
669 N. Cass Ave.
Westmont
630/920-0115

Big Suchir is quite small, but it's in a nifty mall that also features **Shree Mart**, listed later, as well as the Chinese market **Hunan** (p. 213), so if you're shopping in the neighborhood, it's a convenient place to pick up Indian supplies. (Don't miss **Westbrook Market** [p. 263] either, if you're doing the Cass Avenue/Westmont thing.)

Bismillah Meat and Grocery
2742 W. Devon Ave.
773/761-1700

This grocery features a butcher shop and the standard selection

of seasonings. It's at the western end of the shopping district where parking is often a bit easier.

Chicago Zabiha Halal Meat
2243 W. Devon Ave.
773/743-6934

And here is another butcher shop for **halal/zabiha lamb**, etc.

Farm City Meat and Farm Supermarket
2255–57 W. Devon Ave.
773/274-2255 (meat)
773/274-6355 (market)

These are two adjacent, connected stores. One is a very, very busy butcher shop that carries **beef** as well as **lamb**, **chicken**, etc. The grocery next door stocks **Middle Eastern specialties** as well as **Indian and Pakistani foods**. You'll find **pomegranate concentrate**, **giant limas**, **rose petal spread**, **grape leaves**, **cracked wheat**, **whole wheat**, and **bulgur**. They even have some **Mexican products**. Very ecumenical.

Fish Corner

6408 N. Campbell Ave.
773/262-7173

Just around the corner from Devon, this place carries all kinds of **frozen fish imported from Bangladesh, India, Thailand, and Pakistan**, among other places. There are reasonably priced **tiger shrimp** from Thailand, plus **frozen ruhu, pomfret, hilsa, poa, and surmai** (kingfish), to name a few.

Fresh Farms

2626 W. Devon Ave.
773/764-3557

This grocery probably has the biggest produce selection in the area. It's the place for **methi leaves** and **fresh turmeric**, as well as **every kind of green and fruit**. You'll find **green mangos, young coconuts, fresh young ginger**, and much more, depending on the season. Many products, like mangos, can be bought by the case.

They also carry **cheeses** (many kinds of **feta**), the usual **pickles, chutneys**, and **spices**, and many different kinds of **flatbread**, including **pita, naan**, and **chapati** from a variety of bakeries.

Jai Hind Plaza

2658 W. Devon Ave.
773/973-3400

The small selection of grocery items in this store is overshadowed by the wide array of equipment. There are **long wooden tongs, cutting boards with feet, Indian rolling pins, idli steamers** (used to steam the round cakes made of rice and dal), **flat tava steel skillets** (used for Indian flat breads), **stainless pots in many sizes**, serving dishes, and other interesting gadgets.

JK Grocers

2552 W. Devon Ave.
773/262-7600

Here is another grocery that carries the expected array of **dals, spices**, and **chutneys**. Many stores have the same products, and one reason is that their customers spend a lot of time comparison-price shopping. If you're purchasing in quantity, check sale prices. They vary from store to store on many of the most popular items.

Kamdar Plaza

2646 W. Devon Ave.
773/338-8100

Kamdar has been on Devon since the '70s and has grown

Cheater's Tandoori Chicken

(Makes 4 to 6 servings)

2 whole boneless, skinless chicken breasts, divided into 4 half-breast pieces

1 C. plain yogurt (preferably whole milk)

3 to 4 T. prepared Indian tandoori paste from a jar

A great weeknight grilling dish, if you can remember to put together the marinade in the morning or the night before.

Rinse off and clean the chicken and cut 2 or 3 shallow slits in each piece. For the marinade, mix together the yogurt and 3 to 4 tablespoons of tandoori paste (check the directions on the bottle). Slather it over the chicken, rubbing it into the slits. Refrigerate for at least 3 hours. Then remove from the marinade and grill about 5 minutes a side. Serve with wedges of lemon, basmati rice, pappadam, chutney, and a green veggie for a fast, yummy, but inauthentic Indian dinner.

with the street. There are aisles of **spices**, **dals**, **rice**, **pappadams**, and **chutneys**, but the **Indian fast foods and snacks** are where Kamdar really shines. All the foods served in the modest 48-seat snack bar are vegetarian and made on the premises. There are dozens of snack items sold by the pound, from popular **Indian snack mixes** to **roasted nuts** and **plantain chips**. A sweets counter is filled with colorful treats. Prices are very competitive. Kamdar is a good place to rest your feet and enjoy a snack and a mango lassi before you finish your shopping adventure.

Lawando's Grocery and Meat
2244 W. Devon Ave.
773/262-1222

It looks like an everyday supermarket, but Lawando's stocks Indian specialties as well as a

good selection of **Middle Eastern stuff**, like **sumac** and
grape leaves.

Madni Mart

2440 W. Devon Ave.
773/761-4626

Madni is located at the eastern
end of Devon and, like its many
neighbors, competes for the
Indian and Pakistani grocery business with good prices on the usual
spices, **dals**, and **chutneys**.

Mehrab Meat &
Grocery

2445 W. Devon Ave.
773/764-3737

As with many stores along Devon, this place is a butcher
shop in back with a grocery in
front. And like the rest, it offers
a decent selection of the usual
grocery items.

Mubarak Grocers
and Meat

2522 W. Devon Ave.
773/743-3889

Mubarak is nothing out of the
ordinary but offers most of the
basic groceries for Indian or
Pakistani cooking and a **ha-
lal/zabiha butcher shop**.

Julie's Extra Easy Cilantro Salmon

Simply smear some cilantro
(usually labeled "coriander")
chutney on a salmon steak,
then broil a few minutes,
until almost done. Crush
some good-quality potato
chips, and pat a thick layer
on top of the chutney. Broil
again, until cooked through.

Noor Meat Market

2505 W. Devon Ave.
773/274-6667
773/973-7860

Noor is primarily a butcher
shop, and I've purchased excellent **lamb** here. They also make
**their own Indian-style
pickles** and stock some equipment as well: **tava skillets**,
pots and pans, and gadgets.

Par Birdie Foods

2234 W. Devon Ave.
773/274-1750

This grocery has a golfer on the
sign leftover from who knows
when, hence the name Par
Birdie. It is now an all-purpose
grocery store with the emphasis
on **Indian and Pakistani as
well as Middle Eastern in-**

India and Pakistan

193

Perfumed Basmati

(Makes 8 servings)

2 C. basmati rice   2 green cardamom pods

2-½ C. water   2-inch cinnamon stick

pinch of salt

Rinse the rice in several changes of water, then soak in cold water for 30 minutes. Put the drained rice and other ingredients in a saucepan and bring to a boil. Then turn the heat very low, cover, and cook for 15 minutes. Turn off the heat and let it sit another 10 minutes. No peeking. Remove the spices, fluff with a fork, and serve.

If you are cooking more or less rice, you will have to adjust the amount of water, but it is NOT proportional. Try this trick: With the rice in a pan, add enough water to come up to the first knuckle on your index finger when you place your finger on top of the rice. I don't know why, but it works.

gredients. You'll find **dals**, **atta flour**, and **basmati**, plus **sumac**, **rose water**, and such. They do have **spices** and **chutneys**, but not as good a selection as at **Patel Brothers** and some others. You can pick up staples, like baby food and detergents, however.

Patel Brothers

2610 W. Devon Ave.
773/262-7777

2554 W. Devon Ave.
773/764-1857

This is the definitive Indian grocery store. The Patels were Devon Avenue pioneers and actually own a lot of Devon Avenue real estate, I'm told. They also have outposts in many other cities. The stores are clean, are well laid out, and have everything in the way of **spices, flours, dals, chut-**

neys, **pappadams** and other breads, and **canned goods**.

All the flours, like **atta, besan**, and **dokra**, are here, plus a modest assortment of cooking gear. The bigger store (at 2610) also carries a good selection of **Indian specialty produce**, like **tuvar and valor beans, fresh methi**, and **tindora**. Best of all, it has a center aisle filled with bins of bulk Indian snack items—more than 80 varieties—like **sev, channa**, and **boondi**, to name a few. You can mix and match as you like. Fun!

The Patel family also imports **spices, frozen Indian vegetables**, and a line of heat-and-serve foods in aseptic (nonrefrigerated) packages. The prepared items are actually quite good (no preservatives) and an easy way to add an Indian side dish to a weeknight meal. Swad and Raja brands are part of the Patel line.

The staff in both stores will try to answer questions or offer help if you look lost. Note that these stores are totally jammed on the weekend, with folks from all over the Midwest driving into Chicago to stock up. It's fun, but parking is problematic.

Breakfast at Zam Zam

To heck with the Egg McMuffin! Try breakfast at Zam Zam. This modest little diner at 2500 W. Devon makes what is probably my all-time favorite breakfast— halwa puri. This traditional Northern Indian–Pakistani breakfast combo includes puffy, freshly made puri bread, spicy chickpeas (chole), and halwa, which is a sweet cereal kind of like Cream of Wheat. Be prepared to return—this breakfast is very addictive! For a beverage, chai is recommended.

Shree Mart
683 N. Cass Ave.
Westmont
630/789-1200

A tiny Indian store in a mall tucked behind a Jewel-Osco, Shree Mart offers all the necessities for Indian cooking. It's not worth a trip unless you're in the vicinity or in desperate need of a Bollywood video.

Breads, Sweets, and Other Delights

Argo Georgian Bakery

2812 W. Devon Ave.
773/764-6322

OK, I'll admit this bakery doesn't belong in this chapter, being neither Indian nor Pakistani, but it is right on the Devon Avenue shopping strip. Not only does Argo make incredible bread, they make it right before your eyes in an enormous oven sunk into the middle of the floor. It's a beehive-shaped oven, like a tandoor, and bread is baked by sticking it onto the interior walls. Try to stop by when they're either starting or finishing so you can catch the action. In addition to bread, they offer pastries filled with cheese, apples, and other yummy stuff.

Sukhadia Sweets

2559 W. Devon Ave.
773/338-5400

I used to think Indian sweets were way too sugary and not my thing at all. Until I tried some good ones! Sukhadia makes all their sweets with pure ghee right on the premises. They happily offer samples and are very patient. (They are also always crowded, so you need to be patient, too.) **Pistachio barfi** is excellent as are the little **cumin cookies**, whose name now escapes me. One half of the store is sweets, and the other is devoted to snacks, which are really full meals and quite delish. Thankfully, you order from an illustrated menu.

The Pleasures of Pappadam

Pappadam is a round, cracker-thin Indian bread made of lentil flour. It comes in packages of 10 or more, either plain or flavored with garlic, pepper, or my favorite, ajowan. Most every store carries at least one brand.

Before serving pappadam, they need to be cooked to puff and crisp. The simplest way to do this is in the microwave.

Nuke at full power in a single layer for 15 to 30 seconds. When they curl a bit and color a little, they're ready.

Serve them with chutney as a cocktail snack, or try them as a base for a salad.

Cheese and Peas

(Makes 2 or 3 main course servings)

1 T. butter

1 T. olive oil

1 onion, chopped

½ sweet pepper, chopped (optional)

1 hot pepper, minced

2 cloves minced garlic

1 tsp. minced ginger

1 tsp. ground cumin

2 tsp. ground coriander

1 to 2 tsp. garam masala

1 can (14-½ oz.) diced tomatoes (preferably organic)

6 oz. white cheese (paneer or queso fresco)*

1 C. fresh or frozen peas

salt and pepper to taste

Melt the butter and oil in a sauté pan. (Or use just ghee, if you have it on hand.) Add the onion and peppers and cook until wilted. Add the garlic and ginger. Cook for a minute and then add the cumin, coriander, and garam masala. Stir them around for about 30 seconds and add the tomatoes. Cook for 10 minutes, until the tomatoes break down a bit. Add ½ cup of water if things seem too dry. Meanwhile, cut the cheese into small ½-inch cubes. Add the cheese and peas to the tomato mixture and cook another few minutes until flavors blend. Taste and adjust the seasoning.

*White cheese is fresh, unaged cheese that is fairly bland. The Indian version is paneer and is available in Indian and Middle Eastern stores. You'll find white cheese in most supermarkets near the cottage cheese. Feel free to substitute any bland cheese that won't melt. I tried smoked mozzarella once, and while it was yummy, it also got stringy.

India and Pakistan

Julie's Super Twangy Tamarind Pie
"Looks real ugly, tastes real pretty"

9-inch pie shell (store-bought is fine)

1-½ C. sugar

⅓ C. cornstarch

1-½ C. water

3 egg yolks, slightly beaten

2 tsp. lime peel (or more)

½ C. lime juice (or more)

2 to 3 T. tamarind concentrate (or more, depending on your twang tolerance)

3 egg whites

¼ tsp. cream of tartar

6 T. sugar

½ tsp. vanilla

Bake the pie shell and keep the oven at 400°.

Filling

Mix the sugar and cornstarch in a saucepan. Gradually stir in the water. Cook over medium heat, stirring constantly until mixture thickens and boils. Boil and stir 1 minute. Stir ⅓ to ½ of the hot mixture slowly into the egg yolks. Blend the tempered egg yolk mixture back into the saucepan. Boil and stir 1 more minute, until thick and creamy. Remove from the heat. Add the lime juice, lime peel, and tamarind (to taste, but it should be pretty sour, as the meringue will sweeten it up). Pour into the cooked shell.

Meringue

Beat the egg white and cream of tartar until foamy. Beat in the sugar, a tablespoon at a time. Continue beating until stiff. Beat in the vanilla. Spoon the meringue over the pie filling while still hot, spread to the edges of the crust, filling the cracks. Lightly touch and lift the meringue with a ladle or spoon to create cool shapes or bumps.

Bake 10 minutes or until the raised part of the meringue starts to brown. Cool thoroughly and serve.

Top 10 Indian and Pakistani Ingredients

1. red lentils* (p. 161)
2. basmati rice* (p. 194)
3. whole cardamom* (pp. 189 & 194)
4. chaat masala* (p. 188)
5. saffron* (p. 18)
6. tamarind concentrate* (p. 198)
7. tandoori paste* (p. 192)
8. pappadam* (p. 196)
9. mint and cilantro chutneys* (pp. 187 & 193)
10. ghee* (p. 186)

tip or recipe included

China

(tofu and dried mushrooms)

Chinese Ingredients

For many of us, Chinese was the first "foreign" meal we experienced. It was Chinese cooking American style, of course, and in most restaurants, it still is. We are more sophisticated now and understand there's a difference between Szechuan and Cantonese. But reading a really good authentic cookbook, like *The Chinese Kitchen*, by Eileen Yin-Fei Lo, makes you realize how little you know. Her recipes for what we consider Chinese classics (but have only tasted in hybrid form), like moo goo gai pan, are a revelation. I highly recommend it.

Chinese grocery stores seem both more foreign and more assimilated than other Asian stores. Many of the ingredients are familiar. They've been with us since Chung King first canned chop suey. On the other hand, nobody does the exotic better than the Chinese. You can pick up **shark fin**, **bird's nest**, **fish lips**, and **thousand-year-old eggs** on your shopping trip. Better yet, you can get higher quality staples, like **oyster sauce** (the brand does make a difference), as well as more sophisticated forms of old standbys. **Mushroom soy sauce**, for instance, is a wonderful addition to any cook's pantry.

If you've only visited the old Chinatown on the South Side, do try one of the bigger, newer markets elsewhere in the city. They don't have the atmosphere, but they do have the goods.

Fish and Seafood

Really fresh fish is alive. We all know this, but the Chinese markets act on it. Even some of the smaller ones will have tanks of swimming fish, and you can usually find **live crabs**, too. **Shrimp**, while not alive, are cheap and good and, best of all, easy to find uncooked and often with their heads on, which gives better flavor to sauces and soups.

Fresh Fish and Seafood:
clams
crabs, **live**: blue, Dungeness, others
eels
flounder
lobster
mackerel
octopus
oysters
shrimp, **head-on**
snails
squid
tilapia

China

Frozen Seafood:
crab legs
crabmeat
jellyfish
oyster meat
prawns
plus frozen versions of most
    fresh items

Dried Seafood:
abalone
anchovies
fish lips
fish maw (air bladder)
jellyfish
octopus
scallops (conpoy)
sea cucumber
shark fin
squid

Meat

In the Chinese kitchen meat most
often means pork. Poultry is important, and you'll find **good
whole chickens** as well as the
harder-to-find **quail**, **squabs**,
geese, and **ducks** (frozen).

chicken: including feet,
    gizzards
pork: including snouts,
    tails, backbones
quail eggs

Many groceries display prepared meats—**barbecued
chicken, duck, ribs, and
pieces of pork**—near their
fresh meat. This is a great way
to experience **Peking duck** or
soy sauce chicken without
going to the trouble of making
it. You'll also find **flattened
duck**, called dried duck, in the
refrigerated case or hanging
with his friends.

Produce

You will always find **plenty of
greens** and many members of
the **broccoli-cabbage family**
in Chinese stores. Don't be put
off by odd names or seeing
flowers on the greens. They are
mostly interchangeable with the
more familiar spinach, kale, and
regular broccoli. The standards
for judging them are the same,
too. Look for a bright color, no
wilting, and a perky leaf.

amaranth
baby bok choy
bitter melons
bok choy
bottle gourds
chives: yellow, flowering
choy sum (flowering cab-
    bage)
daikon
durian
eddo (taro)

China

Eddo and Eggplant

(Makes 4 servings)

6 small eddo (taro) (about 1 lb.), unpeeled but well scrubbed

2 long, thin Asian eggplants, peeled if you like, sliced into ½-inch coins

4 to 6 T. olive oil

3 T. ginger-garlic paste

1 to 2 T. hot sauce, preferably Caribbean papaya-habanero hot sauce

salt and pepper

lime wedges for serving

Poke a few holes in the eddoes with a fork and nuke at full power for 2 minutes, or until soft when squeezed. (Or bake in the oven.) Heat the oil in a sauté pan. Peel the eddoes and slice into ½-inch hunks. Add to the oil and cook until beginning to brown. Add the eggplant and ginger-garlic paste and toss to coat the vegetables. Add additional oil if needed to prevent scorching. Cook over medium heat until very brown. You want the vegetables to be crusted with the spices, so don't stir too often. Add hot sauce and correct the seasoning. Serve with lime wedges to squeeze on each serving.

gai choy (mustard cabbage)
gai lan (Chinese broccoli)
ginger, **young ginger**
horned water chestnut (water caltrop)
jicama
kabocha squash
kohlrabi
kumquats
kun choy (Chinese celery)
long beans
lotus root
luffa (silk squash)
lychees
mushrooms: enoki, oyster, shiitake
napa cabbage (Chinese cabbage)
pea shoots
rambutans
sprouts
tai goo choy (flat cabbage, tatsoi)
tsu goo (Chinese arrowhead)

China

Vietnamese spinach (slippery vegetable)
water chestnuts
winter melons

Spices and Seasonings

You will often find Southeast Asian ingredients, like **lemon grass** and **green papaya**, as well, especially in bigger stores.

bean sauce
black vinegar (Chinkiang)
char siu sauce (barbecue paste)
Chinese five-spice powder
fish sauce (most places)
hoisin sauce
lemon sauce
oyster sauce
pickled mudfish
plum sauce
rice vinegar
rock sugar
salted (preserved) black beans
sesame paste
sesame seeds
shrimp paste
soy sauce: dark, light, mushroom
Sriracha (Thai chili sauce—it's everywhere)
star anise
Szechuan peppercorns
XO sauce

zizyphus (jujube, Chinese red dates)

Carbs

Visit Chinese stores to stock up on all sorts of rice (usually in 10-pound or larger sacks), **every kind of noodle**, and lots of Cup O' Noodle–type products, too. Look in the refrigerated or frozen section for the fresh (not dried) noodles. They are a treat and also quicker than dried. Especially try the kind called fresh rice noodles (sometimes they are made with rice, sometimes wheat). They come in folded sheets, plastic wrapped. You then cut the sheets into noodles of whatever width you want.

bean thread noodles (cellophane noodles)
glutinous rice flour
jasmine rice
mein (wheat flour noodles), fresh or dried
potato starch (flour)
ramen
rice: black, glutinous rice (aka sticky or sweet), red
rice flour
rice flour, glutinous
rice noodles: fresh (chow fun), dried rice sticks, or vermicelli
soba (buckwheat noodles)
somen (wheat noodles)

China

Noodle Nests

Fried in hot oil, bean thread (cellophane) noodles puff up to a crunchy, tangled nest perfect for serving things.

1. Pull apart noodles and flatten into a disk shape. You may have to wet them with hot water to do this, but make sure they are completely dry before frying or you risk a splattering, fiery, dangerous mess.

2. Heat 2 inches of vegetable oil in a deep wok or other heavy pan until it shimmers.

3. Carefully place the noodle nests into the oil. In a matter of seconds, they will magically puff up and crisp.

4. Drain on paper towels and keep warm. Top with stir-fried vegetables or, my favorite, crab and spinach cooked briefly with garlic, ginger, and some soy sauce. Save stray noodle bits to sprinkle on top for garnish.

tapioca pearls
tapioca starch (flour)
udon noodles
water chestnut flour
wheat starch (nonglutinous flour)

Groceries

adzuki (red beans)
agar-agar
anchovies and other fish, dried
bird's nest (for soup)

black sesame seeds
chestnuts, dried
cloud ear fungus (black fungus, tree fungus)
ginger, crystallized
ginkgo nuts
hair vegetable (black moss)
jackfruit
jellyfish, dried
lily buds
longan
lotus root
lotus seeds
lychees
mock duck (wheat gluten)

China

mung beans
mushrooms, dried: black, shiitake, wood ear
persimmons, dried
pork floss (pork fu)
preserved plums
preserved vegetables: radishes, kohlrabi
rice papers
rice vinegar
sesame paste
shark fin
spring roll wrappers
water chestnuts
watermelon seeds
white fungus (silver fungus)
wonton wrappers

Magic Beans

Salted black beans, also called fermented or preserved black beans, are the original form of soy flavoring. You'll find them packed in plastic bags or jars. Once you take a whiff of their winey, magical aroma, you'll want to use them everywhere. They are delicious added to all kinds of stir-fries and work particularly well with vegetables. Just crush with some garlic and ginger and cook.

Soy Products

bean curd sheets
dried soybeans
fermented (preserved) bean curd
pressed bean curd
tofu, all forms, including fried and tofu pockets

Miscellaneous

exotic drinks: grass jelly, bird's nest, etc.
ginger candies
jellies: lychee, durian, etc.
rice candies (edible wrappers)

shrimp chips (crackers)
tea drinks, canned
teas, medicinal and otherwise

China

Chinese Stores

Chinatown

The original old Chinatown, at Cermak and Wentworth, is a great place to visit, especially with out-of-towners or kids in tow. If you've been spoiled by big Asian markets, though, the grocery stores at first seem a bit disappointing. They're small and usually crowded. But they also seem more authentic, and you can pick up most anything you'd need in one place or another. You'll find plenty of bakeries, herbal stores, and places to buy fancy chopsticks or porcelain rice bowls, not to mention great places to eat!

Sometimes the names of the stores change, so don't get hung up on finding the exact name listed. The nice thing about Chinatown is that it's a community, so even if one store closes, there's another to pick up the slack. Just wander up and down Wentworth and into the Chinatown Square Mall on Archer and you'll find everything you want and then some.

A & J Housewares
2125-A S. China Pl.
312/567-9908

This may belong under equipment, but it's not worth the trip unless you're in the area anyway. It's in the mall, across from **Mayflower Food** (p. 211). Among the usual souvenirs, you'll find **sauce dishes**, **rice cookers**, **tea pots**, **Benriner slicers**, **strainers**, **peelers**, and gadgets of all kinds.

Best Food Products, Inc.
2403 S. Wentworth Ave.
312/808-8878

This smallish store at the far south end of Wentworth proffers an excellent selection of **fish and seafood**. There are **live blue crabs**, of course, and also **oysters**, **whelks**, and **periwinkles**, as well as **live fish**. On my last visit there were also two bins of **live greenish frogs**. They were so cute I briefly considered kissing one. The groceries are limited but representative, and there is also a small selection of fresh produce.

China

Chicago Food Market

2245 S. Wentworth Ave.
312/842-4361

The emphasis here is on **fresh (live) fish**. Chicago Food Market only has a few aquariums, but they also display some fish on ice and have buckets filled with **live crabs** and such. They also carry some meat and a modest selection of groceries.

Chinatown Market

2121 S. Archer Ave.
312/881-0068

A relative newcomer to the Chinatown mix, this market is in the building that looks like one of those inflated bubble tennis courts (it's not) at the busy junction of Wentworth and Archer. Chinatown Market is a welcome addition. They offer a decent selection of produce and all the canned and packaged goods you could ask for, and they also have butcher shop and fish counter. Compared to Mayflower, the aisles are wide and there is almost room for the grocery carts that are provided. If you have questions or are searching for something, ask the friendly Amy, who is part of the family that owns the market and speaks perfect English.

Basic Asian Marinade

¼ C. soy sauce (mushroom is good)

3 cloves garlic, minced

1-inch piece of ginger, minced

2 T. oyster sauce

2 tsp. sesame oil

2 T. peanut or olive oil

3 T. red wine vinegar

freshly ground black pepper

Mix everything together and use to marinate steak, pork, or chicken. Particularly good on flank steak for the grill and pork tenderloin roast.

Dong Kee Company

2252 S. Wentworth Ave.
312/225-6340

This grocery and gift shop offers canned and dry goods; a decent assortment of **dried noodles**; **soy sauce**, **oyster sauce**, and other condiments; plus **fortune and almond cookies**. Two whole rooms are devoted to dishes, **woks**, cooking utensils, and souvenirs, including the **biggest, most hideously wonderful piggy banks** you've ever seen.

Goody Supermarket
211 W. 22nd Pl.
312/791-0300

You'll find this full-service market just west of Wentworth on the lower level of an ordinary-looking building. Goody stocks pretty much everything, including produce, a meat counter, some fish, and plenty of **candies**, **snacks**, and packaged goods. Oh, yeah, a bin full of **live turtles**, too.

Hong Kong Noodle Company
2350 S. Wentworth Ave.
312/842-0480

This **real noodle factory** has been a Chinatown fixture as long as I can remember. Luckily they sell retail, too. You can buy three sizes of **dried wheat noodles**, **fresh noodles** (only early in the day), and **fried chow mein noodles** like you get in the can, only lots fresher and better. These are so good that my daughter and I scarfed up a half pound right out of the bag before we got home. They'd probably be good sprinkled on things, too, if you don't eat them all first. This is a factory,

---

Quick, Easy Five-Spice Squash Rings

(Serves 4)

2 delicata (sweet potato) squash

1 to 2 T. olive oil

1 to 2 tsp. Chinese five-spice powder

salt and freshly ground black pepper to taste

Preheat the oven to 350°. Line a baking sheet with foil. Slice the squash into 1/2-inch thick rounds. Remove the pith and seeds. (Using a serrated grapefruit spoon makes this easy.) Lay rings on the foil and brush with oil. Sprinkle with the five-spice powder, salt, and pepper. Bake for 20 to 30 minutes.

China

not a store, so don't think you're in the wrong place when you walk in. You order by the pound at the service desk; the clerks are friendly and accommodating. **Egg roll and wonton wrappers** are also available, and everything is an amazing bargain.

Kwok Chiu Market

211 W. 23rd St.
(closed Wednesdays)

Kwok Chiu, a very clean, small meat market just off Wentworth, deals in **every kind of pork**, including **pork intestine** and **pork blood**, plus **Smithfield hams**, **ducks and geese with head and feet attached**, some **fresh and frozen fish**, **chicken**, **tripe**, and even some very fresh-looking vegetables. This is not a tourist stop.

Mayflower Food Company

2104 S. Archer Ave.
312/326-7440
312/326-7450

An always packed store with narrow aisles at the east end of Chinatown Square Mall, Mayflower recently expanded and added a large aisle of **frozen items (dumplings,** **fish balls, frozen shrimp, and fish)**, as well as more packaged goods. It smells a little funky when you first enter because there are bins of **dried shrimp and fish** right inside the door, as well as a mysterious collection of glass jars filled with dried **medicinal herbs**, like **angelica root**, **radix**, and **"semen euryales,"** whatever that is. Don't be deterred. This is a fun place, off the beaten tourist path.

You'll find meat, produce (including **fresh lotus root** and **long beans**), **fresh rice noodles**, a wide variety of frozen items, plus the usual groceries. Things seem to have high turnover here.

Check out **Yin Wall City** next door, too. It is a fascinating medicinal-herbal store. They offer every kind of **dried scallop and abalone** (some cost $600 per pound!), as well as **dried seahorse** and **deer antlers**.

Silver Star Food Company

2420 S. Wentworth Ave.
312/842-4163

Produce is the star in this narrow little shop. It's crammed with **greens**, **arrowroot**, **fresh water chestnuts**, **squash**, **lotus root**, **daikon**, etc. There's not much room to turn around, but the veggies look fresh and good.

Sunlight Kitchen and Hardware Supplies
2334 S. Wentworth Ave.
312/225-8388
See "Equipment" chapter (p. 54).

Tai Wah Grocery
2226 S. Wentworth Ave.
773/326-4120

Barbecued ducks and pork hang in the window of this crowded, tiny store that has almost everything. They have **fresh meat and live fish** (a modest selection), **live crabs**, all sorts of **dried fish and squid**, plus the usual canned goods and sauces and even some produce.

Ten Ren Tea
2247 S. Wentworth Ave.
312/842-1171
See "A Drink with That?" chapter (p. 266).

Wing Cheong Trading
2317 S. Wentworth Ave.
312/808-1199

Another small store, Wing Cheong is packed with a bit of everything, including **fresh (live) fish** and some meat, with a butcher to cut it for you. Last time I visited they had **live crabs**, **snails**, and **turtles**— fairly large ones. You'll find some produce and the obligatory assortment of **dried noodles** and canned goods.

Wing Lee Co.
2246 S. Wentworth Ave.
312/842-3376

I think of this as the no-name produce shop. The sign saying Wing Lee is in the front window and is sometimes obscured by various things. This small, two-aisle store is always busy ringing up sales of all kinds of produce to Chinese shoppers. They have a huge selection of **greens**, **fresh water chestnuts**, **burdock**, **lychee** (in season), and much more. This is the freshest, best produce I've found in Chinatown, and the Chinese guys behind the cash register are generous with recipes and cooking tips. If you see a tray full of fat mushrooms near the checkout, ask for some **king oyster mushrooms**.

China

These are the most delicious mushrooms I've ever encountered. Based on the recipe given me by the clerk. I stir-fried them with fresh sliced ginger and nothing more ("NO GARLIC!!" the cashier said emphatically), and they received raves by everyone who tasted them. Oh, yes, the **ginger** here is the most fragrant and freshest around, too.

Woks 'n' Things

2234 S. Wentworth Ave.
312/842-0701
See "Equipment" chapter (p. 56).

Elsewhere

Food Harbor

1421 W. Lake St.
Addison
630/629-1700
See "Multiethnic" chapter (p. 259).

Hunan Market, Inc.

673 N. Cass Ave.
Westmont
630/321-9383

Tucked away in a strip mall that also features Indian groceries (see **Big Suchir**, p. 190), Hunan

---

Four Non-Asian Ways to Use Asian Wraps

1. Use round wonton skins to make ravioli.

2. Stuff wonton skins into greased mini muffin tins and bake, then fill for hors d'oeuvres.

3. Cut into strips and deep-fry for garnishing soup or salad.

4. Wrap a fish fillet in rice paper and bake until crisp.

Market is small and clean and offers a complete array of Chinese ingredients. There are all the usual **sauces**, **marinades**, and **canned ingredients**. A freezer case holds **pot stickers**, **Chinese buns**, and **frozen seafood**. There is a decent selection of fresh produce, including **gai lan**, **daikon**, and such. The fish and meat counter in back really packs in a big choice in a small space. There are even **live fish** in an aquarium. Meats include **pork rib belly**, **pork liver**, and **kidney**. English is spoken, and the proprietor is happy to answer questions and provide information.

China

International Club

4000 W. 40th St.
773/927-0100 Ext. 410

Oh, my! This is an amazing place—sort of like Sam's Club, only for Asian food. It is located in the midst of an industrial corridor just south of I-55 on Pulaski Road (which is 4000 west). You'll see a huge sign on your right as you travel southbound over the hill by the ComEd plant on Pulaski. It says "Five Continents International Club." Turn at the Burger King. There is a small parking lot in front that is often crowded with trucks. It used to be a membership store that required a yearly fee, but no more. Now it's open to the public, though International Club still sells **cartons of noodles and drinks**, **institutional-size tins of oil**, **huge sacks of dried mushrooms**, and the like to the restaurants around town.

There are smaller sizes of everything, too, so don't freak when you first enter. I can happily wander the aisles for hours and always find something new. They carry dozens of brands of **soy sauce**, **fish sauce**, **canned water chestnuts**, and **bamboo shoots** that are superior to the poor dusty things you find in the supermarket. The prices are very good, even on small quantities. They have sections devoted to

Latin American, Japanese, Thai, African, and even Jamaican cooking**, though selections are limited.

The **drink variety** alone is good for 30 minutes of browsing. There are **bird's nest drinks**, **every kind of tea in a can**, and little paper **juice boxes in exotic flavors**, like tamarind and lychee. They also have **Jarritos drinks** from Mexico, **Coco Rico coconut soda** (my fave), and **Ting**, a Jamaican grapefruit soda that is a cult favorite.

After you've wandered the grocery aisles and loaded your cart, you come to the fresh produce. Pick up bok choy, yu choy, or fresh water chestnuts. There are also big self-serve bins of sprouts and bamboo shoots (both summer and winter kind). At first I thought these were fresh shoots. They're not. They're just sold by the pound instead of in a can. Fresh bamboo shoots are sometimes available and look like, no surprise, fat green pointed shoots, but they have to be peeled and boiled for quite a while to eliminate prussic acid.

On the other side of one of those "doors" made of strips of hanging plastic, you'll find more produce, as well as a **full-service butcher shop and fish market**. It's a large bright room filled with dozens of aquariums that are home to many kinds of

China

214

live seafood. There is always **tilapia, crab, lobster, catfish**, and whatever else is seasonal.

I guess because this is a discount warehouse, you have to bag your own groceries, so don't be shocked when they hand you a bunch of plastic bags and send you on your way. I am always amazed at how much stuff I bought for how little money, so I don't mind doing some work.

Richwell Market
1835 S. Canal St.
312/492-7030

This full-service market is about a mile from Chinatown, near Lawrence Fisheries (with a parking lot!). Grab a mango smoothie from the attached juice bar while you shop.

You'll find a **serve-yourself candy selection** in bins (fun for the kids). There are prepared foods, mainly **barbecued pork, barbecued duck**, and **pressed duck**. A butcher shop offers **every part of the pig, whole chicken**, and **chicken feet**, and the seafood department consists of four **well-stocked fish tanks**, plus **live snails, crabs**, and **clams**.

Ginseng and **dried abalone** are available in the (expensive) medicinal section up front. In the small but com-

plete produce department, you'll find **durian, lychee**, and **silk squash**. The grocery assortment includes **Vietnamese items** and some **Filipino products**, too, like **coco vinegar** and **palm vinegar**.

Breads, Sweets, and Other Delights

Aji Ichiban
2117-A S. China Pl.
312/328-9998

This **Asian candy** store is a real treat. Most things are sold by the pound, and there are plenty of free samples. The choices are exotic—dozens of kinds of **preserved plums**, including one called **preserved thinking milk plum**. Nobody could explain the name, but it tasted good. You can also try **dried kumquats, star fruit, and guava; fish and shrimp candies**; and many **exotic flavors of marshmallows**.

St. Anna Bakery & Cafe
2158 S. Archer Ave.
312/225-3168

Chinese buns for breakfast are just about perfect—high carb, a

China

bit sweet, a little bland. This bakery has excellent **custard and coconut buns**, along with many, many other choices. Or perhaps you'd pre- fer **congee**, a Chinese rice gruel that is real Asian comfort food. St. Anna is always crowded, but they are welcoming and will help you make your selections.

Fresh Rice Noodles

(Serves 6)

1 package fresh rice noodles

3 T. peanut oil

1 T. each minced garlic and ginger

1 bunch green onions, chopped, including green parts

2 C. quick-cooking vegetables (Asian greens, thin asparagus, small

pieces of broccoli, or a combination)

meat (chicken, pork, or beef), in small pieces (optional)

¼ C. soy sauce (mushroom is nice)

2 T. oyster sauce or hot bean paste

1 tsp. sesame oil

½ C. bean sprouts

Cut the noodles into strips, without unfolding. Make the strips as narrow or wide as you like. Half an inch works well. Place in a colander and pour boiling water over to loosen them. (Skip this step if they are very fresh and have not been refrigerated.)

Stir-fry the garlic and ginger in 1 tablespoon of peanut oil. Add the meat and cook until almost done. Remove and reserve the meat, then add 2 tablespoons of peanut oil and veggies (slowest cooking first), and stir-fry until crisp tender. Add the noodles and soy sauce, oyster sauce, and sesame oil. Stir-fry, separating noodles. Add the bean sprouts. Adjust the seasoning (adding the hot sauce, more soy sauce, or a squeeze of lemon) and serve.

China

Top **10** Chinese Ingredients

1. salted (fermented) black beans* (p. 207)
2. oyster sauce* (pp. 209 & 216)
3. mushroom soy sauce* (pp. 209 & 216)
4. Shaoxing wine
5. chili paste with garlic
6. greens, especially gai lan (Chinese broccoli) and others in the broccoli-cabbage family
7. five-spice powder* (p. 210)
8. fresh noodles, especially rice noodles* (p. 216)
9. wonton wrappers* (p. 213)
10. bean thread (cellophane) noodles* (p. 206)

tip or recipe included

Southeast Asia

(spring roll wrappers and kaffir lime leaves)

Southeast Asian Ingredients

We are very lucky to have such a wealth of Vietnamese and Thai markets in Chicagoland. Not only do these folks love food, they love freshness. You'll find great produce, fish, and meat in markets in which the ambiance runs the gamut from somewhat seedy to very posh.

Fish and Seafood

Vietnamese and Thai markets are great places to go for fish in all forms. From a simple **fillet of sole** to **live crabs** to **frozen sea squirt**, if it swims, floats, or crawls on the bottom, chances are they have it. This is handy when you're looking for a good price on something mainstream, like **crab legs**, or when you need exotica, like **sea urchin roe**.

There's often a bewildering array of **fresh fish on ice**, right out in the open so you can pick your own. You are also expected to choose your own **crabs** or **shellfish**. (Do like the natives and grab the ones that are the liveliest.) This is sometimes a bit daunting if the names of the fish are not in English. Be forewarned that fish is not cleaned the way we're used to, either. After all, the

head and the liver are delicacies in these cultures. Many kinds of **dried fish** and a huge selection of canned items that include all sorts of **smoked and seasoned sardines, mackerel, and shellfish** are also on hand.

Fresh Fish and Seafood:
butterfish
clams, live
crab legs
crabmeat
crabs, live
eel
mackerel
mussels, live
oysters, live
pomfret
sea bass
skate
snails
sole
squid
tilefish
and many more

Frozen Seafood:
cuttlefish
jellyfish
kingfish
octopus
oysters
periwinkles
prawns, head-on

sea cucumber
sea urchin
shrimp, head-on
squid

Dried Seafood:
anchovies
eel
mackerel
shrimp

Meat

At Southeast Asian stores the meat is a trifle mysterious. **Organ meats** from organs you never thought about before are displayed next to normal cuts. Good buys are available especially on **pork items**, like **tenderloin**, **whole pork shoulder with the skin on**, **fresh hams**, and **hocks**. Many places obviously butcher their meat on the premises.

beef: blood—often frozen—
   sometimes in chunks
   (don't ask), tendon, liver,
   tripe
chicken: feet, gizzards,
   other parts
pork: tongue, kidney, heart,
   uterus, spleen, trotters
quail eggs

Produce

Shop these markets for **Asian greens** in abundance and many **fresh herbs**. Vietnamese meals feature a **table salad** that is mostly fresh herbs. Identifying things is not always easy, especially since the names are different depending on language, dialect, and, if you're lucky enough to find something in English, the whim of a translator. Availability depends on the season, too. I've had good luck asking other shoppers. Even if they don't speak much English, they'll point to what they think is tasty and try to communicate with you. It's actually hard to go wrong. Sniffing tells you a lot. Don't wait till you have a Southeast Asian menu in mind either; most greens can be used in any stir-fry or side dish. When in doubt, sauté in oil with garlic.

amaranth
banana flowers
bitter melons
bok choy
chive flowers
daikon
dragon fruit
durian
fuzzy squash (melon)
gai choy (mustard cabbage)
gai lan (Chinese broccoli)
galangal

gau ma (Vietnamese spinach)
ginger: regular, young, or
   stem ginger
green papaya
herbs, fresh: Vietnamese
   cilantro, holy basil, Thai
   (anise) basil, mint
kaffir lime leaves
lemon grass
lily bulbs
long beans
longan
lotus root
luffa
opo squash
pandan leaves
pomelo
water chestnuts
water spinach (ong choy,
   kangkong)
wing beans
young coconuts
yu choy (flowering cabbage)

Spices and Seasonings

Fish sauce rules! There are many brands and styles. Southeast Asian cooks also use a fabulous chili sauce called **Sriracha**, which has a rooster on the label. It is hot and sweet and works with anything from stir-fries to roasted veggies. Still it is only one of a dizzying array of **chili sauces and pastes** available. Ditto **soy sauces and vinegars**.

chili-garlic sauce: Sriracha
   and others
crab paste
fish paste
fish sauce
soy sauce: dark, light, citrus
tamarind concentrate
vinegars: coconut, lemon,
   Chinkiang

Storage Tip

Lemon grass and kaffir lime leaves freeze well. (There is a change in texture, but not in flavor.) So don't hesitate to buy more than you need immediately. It is also easy to root lemon grass. Just put fresh stems in water. Plant in a pot once roots appear. Keep in a warm place.

Carbs

Noodles and **wraps** are ubiquitous, and most stores carry not only the Southeast Asian things, like **rice paper**, but also Pan-Asian items, like **soba** and **gyoza skins**.

You'll find **flour of all kinds** and a collection of **ready-to-use mixes for crêpes, dumplings**, and other fare.

Julie's Roasted Veggies with Sriracha

1 part Sriracha

2 parts olive oil

1-inch chunks of sweet potato and carrot (peeled or not—your choice)

Mix together the Sriracha and oil. Add the veggies and toss to coat. Bake at 400° until done (about 30 to 40 minutes). Hot, sweet, spicy, yummy!

tapioca starch noodles
wheat noodles: soba (buckwheat), somen, udon
yam (sweet potato) **noodles**

Groceries

All sorts of **tropical fruits** are readily found in cans at these groceries, including many you've probably never heard of before, like **palm fruit**. Personally I think they mostly taste sickeningly sweet, but they sure can turn a fruit salad into a conversation piece. **Pickled items** present an array of martini garnishes you won't find elsewhere. There are aisles devoted to **seaweed** and **dried vegetables**.

panko (bread crumbs)
rice:
brown, glutinous (aka sticky or sweet)
white, glutinous (aka sticky or sweet)
jasmine sweet brown
rice flour: rice flour, glutinous (aka sweet, called mochiko in Japanese)
rice noodles: fresh (gway tiaow in Thai), rice stick, rice vermicelli, jantaboon noodles (wide rice stick)
rice papers
roasted rice powder
tapioca pearls
tapioca starch

banana buds, pickled or plain
daikon, pickled
flavorings: pandanus (bai toey), rose water
fried shallots, onions
halo halo (Filipino fruit salad)
jackfruit
lychee
longan
loquat
MSG
palm fruit
peppers, pickled
preserved (1,000-year-old) **eggs**

Southeast Asia

Chef Tim's
Vietnamese-Style Pork Tenderloin
(Serves 6)

3 lb. pork tenderloin

Marinade:

1 C. sugar

¼ C. water

additional ¼ C. water

4 tsp. soy sauce

4 tsp. fish sauce

¼ C. vegetable oil

Make caramel with the sugar and water by heating in a heavy pan without stirring. (You can also purchase ready-made caramel sauce in a Southeast Asian store.) Let cool slightly and stir in the other ingredients. Marinate the meat for several hours or overnight. Grill.

The use of caramel with meat is traditional and scrumptious. For more recipes using Vietnamese-style caramel, an explanation of its culinary history and use, and detailed instructions on making it, visit the excellent Viet World Kitchen Web site (www.vietworldkitchen.com).

Dipping Sauce:

1-½ T. chili-garlic sauce

1 tsp. minced garlic

¼ C. rice vinegar

⅓ C. sugar

½ tsp. salt

1 T. cornstarch dissolved in ⅓ C. water

2 T. chopped cilantro

Mix together everything but the cilantro. Heat until thickened, then add the cilantro.

Serve at room temperature. Drizzle some dipping sauce over the meat and greens. Serve extra on the side.

224

rock sugar
seaweed: wakame, nori
wheat gluten

Soy Products

edamame (soybeans), fresh
   or frozen
fermented bean curd
soy milk
tofu, every kind

Miscellaneous

coffee drinks, all kinds
ginger, crystallized
jellies: litchi and others
Poky cookies (YUM!)
teas, medicinal and others

Equipment

bamboo steamers
clay pots
cleavers
stone mortars, large
strainers
sushi rolling mats
woks

Green Papaya Salad

(Serves 4 to 6)

1 medium green papaya

¼ C. frozen French-cut green beans, thawed

2 hot peppers, in tiny slivers

3 cloves garlic, minced

3 T. fish sauce

3 T. sugar

juice of 2 limes

¼ C. roasted peanuts

I adore this stuff. It is hot and sweet and crunchy and sour and chewy and refreshing. So I whittled the recipe down to an easy version that is halfway between Thai and Vietnamese. If you are really lazy, buy precut papaya, which saves even more time.

Cut the papaya in half vertically, scrape out the seeds, and peel. Shred in a food processor. Combine with the green beans and peppers. Whisk together everything else, except the peanuts, and mix in. Serve topped with peanuts.

Southeast Asian Stores

The area around Argyle and Broadway is sometimes called the new Chinatown. It isn't Chinese at all, of course, but Southeast Asian. This is a wonderful place to come to eat and shop. You'll find everything you've been dreaming of in terms of Thai and Vietnamese ingredients, not to mention many things you'd never dream up.

Plan on spending time exploring. While the area around the L-stop on Argyle is on the seedy side, the stores are delightful. You can get a delicious (and cheap) bowl of noodles at dozens of places. Check out the great Thai food and gorgeous pastries at **Thai Pastry** (4925 N. Broadway, 773/784-5399). And stop at one of the many butcher shop–delis to pick up a soy-cooked chicken or roasted duck to go so you don't have to cook when you get home exhausted after your adventure. **Vinh Phat BBQ** (4940 N. Sheridan, 773/878-8688) is legendary (and closed on Thursdays).

Golden Pacific

5353 N. Broadway St.
773/334-6688

This relative newcomer to the area is slightly north of the Argyle-Broadway corridor but is a most welcome addition to the neighborhood. It is very clean and well stocked with Southeast Asian basics. There is a decent selection of fresh produce, and all of it looks fresh and is nicely arrayed. Plenty of **Sriracha**, **fish sauce**, and **canned Asian fruits and veggies** are lined up neatly on the shelves. The frozen food selection includes pretty much anything that swims, crawls, or wiggles in the sea. A small fresh meat and fish counter in the back displays a limited, but lovely, selection of pork, beef, and seafood. Owner Jimmy Wong speaks English and is anxious to help in any way he can. (I got a free sample of Sriracha sauce and a recipe for pad see eiw on my visit.) Go there! (Did I mention it's very CLEAN?)

Hoa Nam Grocery

1101–03 W. Argyle St.
773/275-9157

This is one of the smaller groceries on Argyle. They proffer **all things Vietnamese**, plus lots of **Thai ingredients** (**green papaya**), **fresh Asian greens**, and a smattering of **Chinese, Filipino, and Japanese products**.

Mien-Hoa Market
1108 W. Argyle St.
773/334-8393

This narrow little store has a small but excellent selection of produce. This is where I first found **dragon fruit**, that wild-looking cactus fruit that belongs in a Dr. Seuss book.

Sea World Food Market
1130 W. Argyle St.
773/334-5335
See "Fish and Seafood" chapter (p. 33).

Tai Nam Market
4925 N. Broadway St.
773/275-5666

Tai Nam, located in the Thai Mall, is a very clean, big supermarket with excellent produce and greens, although most are plastic-wrapped and hard to sniff. Choose from a large assortment of **fresh Vietnamese herbs and vegetables**, including **rau ma** (pennywort) and **ong choy** (water spinach), a narrow-leafed green with crunchy stems that a fellow shopper turned me on to. Quite tasty. Some vegetables are even labeled in English.

The fresh fish selection is ex-

tensive and easy to examine, as it's all laid out on ice. Some prepared food is also available, especially bakery goods, which come in gorgeous, garish colors. Look for a decent selection of equipment, including **rice cookers**, **V-slicers**, etc., and crossover **Chinese, Filipino, and Japanese products**, too.

Thai Grocery
5014 N. Broadway St.
773/769-0800
773/561-5345

One of the original Thai stores in the neighborhood and the model for the truly wonderful book *The Asian Grocery Store Demystified*, by Linda Bladholm, Thai Grocery is smaller than most but is packed with groceries, produce, **fresh fish**, and meat. The nicest **green papaya** you'll find is here, and there's a deli section in back featuring **prepared Thai foods**. The staff is extremely helpful and even introduced me to an imported gadget that's designed to shred green papaya.

Thaong Xa My A
(Broadway Supermarket)
4879 N. Broadway St.
773/334-3838

A nice big market in a mall with parking (provided the lot's not full), Broadway Supermarket has a varied assortment of food-stuffs and is a fun place to browse. Cases full of **unusual frozen food** (**dragon fruit** and more) share the aisles with a wide-ranging choice of produce. They carry many **exotic fruits**, even **durian**, along with **greens** and **herbs**, plus a **good selection of fish—live tilapia**, **clams**, **oysters**, and much more, including a fairly large offering of **Japanese products** (such as **panko** and **wasabi**), as well as some **Chinese and Filipino** ones.

This must be the place where a lot of restaurants shop, as they have a huge variety of equipment, serving dishes, and institutional sizes of products. **Woks**, **bamboo steamers**, **rice cookers**, **clay pots**, **fish scalers**, and **stone mortars** are among the delights for sale.

Trung Viet Supermarket

4936–42 N. Sheridan Rd.
773/561-0042
773/561-0131

On Sheridan Road, just south of Argyle, this store is easy to miss. It has a parking lot directly in front. (Don't get too excited; the parking lot is small and usually full.) While the junk-filled windows make it look most unpromising from outside, inside

the store is fairly clean and rather large. They offer very good prices on the usual items and have a wide selection of **sauces**, **rice papers**, and **frozen foods**. Lots of **frozen fish** are available along with a good selection of **fresh, including flounder and crabs**. The butcher shop even carries **skin-on pork shoulder**, which is hard to find.

Trung Viet has **green papaya already shredded** in a self-serve barrel to purchase by the pound, as well as **whole papayas**. Many **herbs**, like **saw-leaf herb** and **basil**, are well priced even in January. Another great find here is **fresh garlic**, the kind you get in spring at the farmers market, with the greens still attached (and a lot of the dirt, too). It looks like an overgrown green onion, but one smell and you'll recognize it. Delicious!

Viet Hoa Plaza

1051 W. Argyle St.
(no phone listed)

Viet Hoa is very similar to **Hoa Nam** (p. 226), which is just to the west on Argyle, but bigger and with a more supermarket-y feel. While perusing their good selection of **greens**, groceries, **noodles**, and **fish**, I actually came upon **fresh sea cucumber** here (quite startling!), as well as **live snails and clams**. They have a large offering of **Filipino ingredients** (such as **banana sauce** and **halo halo**) and some equipment, too, including **clay pots**, **V-slicers**, and the ubiquitous (in Asian stores at least) **ice shavers**.

The grocery is conveniently located very close to the Argyle L-stop on the red line.

Whole Grain Fresh Market

665 Pasquinelli Dr.
Westmont
630/323-8180

This big Asian market used to be called Diho. It is still in the same space but has new owners and has become more focused on Southeast Asian products than Chinese. You'll still find all the Asian staples, such as dozens of sorts of **rice**, **soy sauce**, and **Asian greens**. In addition, though, there are **Vietnamese herbs**, **fuzzy squash**, and many brands of **fish sauce**. There's a **butcher**, **lots of fish** (some of it alive), **fresh bamboo shoots**, **galangal**, and something I haven't seen very many places—**edible lily bulbs**. Pan-Asian items include **tapioca pearls**, **Malaysian dried guava**, **ground cassava**, Ko-

rean **pancake mix**, **umeshi plum wine**, and **lychee ice cream**.

There seems to be a good representation of **Filipino ingredients**, too. I spotted **screwpine leaves**, **purple yam jam**, **bibinka** (rice cake mix), **mung bean starch**, and more.

There is a Yin Wall medicinal-herbal store right next door, and the mall has a small Asian food court as well.

Breads, Sweets, and Other Delights

Ba Le Vietnamese French Bakery

5018 N. Broadway St.
773/561-4424

Pâté and **crusty baguettes** are made on the premises, but Ba Le is most famous, justifiably, for their Vietnamese sandwiches, which are topped with a fabulous **carrot-radish salad/relish**. (It doesn't sound like much, but trust me.)

Ba Le also offers **shrimp cakes**, **pickled ham**, **head cheese**, **spring rolls**, **steamed cakes**, and **exotic desserts** made with coconut milk, jackfruit, lotus seeds, and more. The bakery is tiny, and most of their business is take-out. I always expect to see Phuong from *The Quiet American* walk in the door.

Thai Pastry

4925 N. Broadway St.
773/784-5399

This lovely Thai restaurant is frequently listed as a great place to dine, and it most certainly is, but there's a reason the word *pastry* is part of the name. The gorgeous goodies on display include beautiful **miniature candy fruits and veggies**. They look like marzipan but are actually made with bean paste and agar-agar.

Chicken Bites That Bite Back

(Serves 4 to 6)

2 whole boneless, skinless chicken breasts

1 C. plain yogurt (full fat)

¼ C. Sriracha

flour (and cornmeal, optional)

salt and pepper

chili powder (optional)

olive or vegetable oil for frying

Cut the chicken into nugget-size pieces. Mix together the yogurt and Sriracha. Pour over the chicken, coating thoroughly. Marinate, refrigerated, for at least an hour and up to 10 hours.

Prepare a plate with flour or a cornmeal-flour mix for dusting. Season it generously with salt and pepper. Add a bit of chili powder if you want extra spicy.

Heat a wide skillet. Add oil to a depth of 1/8 inch. (If you prefer, these can also be deep-fried.)

Remove the chicken pieces from the marinade; shake off the excess. Roll in flour to coat lightly. Fry until golden and cooked through. Keep warm in a low oven until ready to serve.

Pomelo Crab Salad

(Serves 3 to 4)

1 pomelo

1 can lump crabmeat

1 T. finely chopped cilantro

1 small hot chile, finely minced

oil for frying

2 small or 1 large shallot, peeled

1-½ T. fish sauce

1 tsp. sugar

2 T. lime juice

lettuce leaves and/or rice papers for serving (optional)

Peel the pomelo. Section the fruit, removing all of the white membrane. The easiest way to do this is to cut off an end and stand the fruit up. Cut out individual sections, leaving behind the white membrane in between. Pull off any remaining membrane. Break the flesh up into shreds and place in a medium bowl. Squeeze any juice remaining in the pomelo "carcass" into the bowl. Add the crabmeat, picking it over to remove bits of shell. Toss in the cilantro and chile and gently combine.

Heat at least an inch of oil in a heavy pan. Slice the shallots crosswise into very thin rings. When the oil is medium hot (300 to 325°), fry the shallots for about 5 minutes, until they turn golden brown. Watch carefully—they are easy to burn. Drain on paper towels while you prepare the dressing.

Combine the fish sauce and sugar in a small bowl or screw-top jar. Stir to dissolve the sugar. Add the lime juice and whisk or shake to combine. Add to the pomelo-crab mixture; stir gently. Top with fried shallots. If you like, serve with lettuce leaves and/or softened rice papers to roll around portions of the salad.

Top 10 Southeast Asian Ingredients

1. Sriracha sauce* (pp. 223 & 230)
2. lemon grass* (p. 222)
3. fresh greens and herbs* (p. 231)
4. fish sauce* (pp. 224, 225, & 231)
5. rice papers
6. frozen shredded coconut
7. fresh fish
8. green papaya* (p. 225)
9. prepared curry paste
10. canned coconut milk

*tip or recipe included

Knowing Your Noodles

The choice of noodles in an Asian store is overwhelming. While I've never met a noodle I didn't like, it helps to have an idea of the commonest types on your shopping trips. English spelling is idiosyncratic at best. Noodle names are made even more arcane by virtue of different languages (and different dialects!) that may each have more than one word to describe the same basic noodle.

Sometimes noodles are even labeled "alimentary paste." This really threw me the first time I saw it. Then I read that it is a holdover from an old U.S. law forbidding any product without egg to be called a noodle. Go figure.

The following list is far from definitive. But it's a starting place to help you begin to untangle the many strands of noodle cookery. In addition to the wheat and rice noodles mentioned here, there are also noodles made from mung beans, cornstarch, tofu, yams, and potatoes, among other edibles.

The photos that follow are all life-size to give you an idea of the look of different kinds of noodles. Don't take them too literally, though, since the hundreds of real-world noodles don't always conform to these nice, neat categories.

For further explanation and helpful drawings, consult *The Asian Grocery Store Demystified*, by Linda Bladholm (see the bibliography, p. 276).

Noodles Made from Wheat

Chinese mein (also spelled mian)

Flat or round, fresh or dried noodles made with or without egg. They are sold in bundles or arranged in nests.

Japanese somen

Thin, dried noodles made from wheat flour and oil. They are usually sold tied in neat-looking bundles with ribbon or paper tape.

Japanese udon

Round or flat noodles of various widths made of wheat flour and water. They are sold dry or fresh, often with a packet of seasoning mix to make soup.

Japanese soba, Korean buckwheat (naengmyon)

Noodles made from buckwheat and some regular wheat flour. The unique, nutty flavor works well in cold dishes. The Korean version is chewier. (See recipe on p. 247.)

Ramen or chuka soba

Curly nests of instant noodles familiar to all from Cup O' Noodles. They are usually sold in single-serving sizes with seasoning packets in a multitude of flavors.

Noodles Made from Rice

Rice sticks

Flat or round, fat or skinny, fresh or dried noodles. These pale, almost see-through noodles are particularly popular in Southeast Asian cuisines. They are used in pad thai and Vietnamese pho.

Fresh rice noodles

Also called chow fun (Chinese), gway tiaow (Thai), or river rice noodles. These very perishable noodles come folded up in (usually) uncut sheets. You'll find them in the refrigerated case, stocked near the cashier in some groceries (unrefrigerated), or in Asian bakeries. (See recipe on p. 216.)

Fresh Noodles

Cantonese egg noodles (mein)

fresh rice noodles

Wheat Noodles

yacamein

soba

somen

wheat
vermicelli

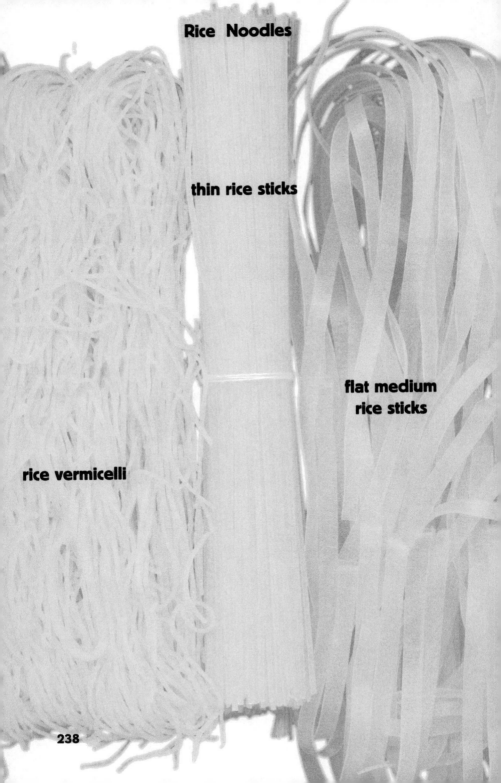

Rice Noodles

thin rice sticks

flat medium
rice sticks

rice vermicelli

238

Japan, Korea, and the Philippines

(octopus and lotus root)

Japanese, Korean, and Filipino Ingredients

Lumping these three cuisines together is convenient and arbitrary. They are together because many ingredients are common to all three and also because they tend to carry at least some of each other's specialties (though this is less true of Filipino stores).

The Korean shopping scene in Chicago was a revelation to me, who knew next to nothing about the culture or the food. You'll find huge supermarkets to get lost in. Some have "salad bars" of ingredients that are sold by the pound and are totally unrecognizable. There are often **sacks of red pepper** so huge it would take two big guys to carry them. The **fish is impeccably fresh**, and the produce is gorgeous and varied. Sure, they have **kimchee** (dozens of kinds), but there is so much more! And perhaps because it is a highly developed cuisine that we are less familiar with, a trip to a Korean market feels like a foreign vacation that you don't have to leave the city to experience.

As for Japanese groceries, some items can be found at health food stores or gourmet markets (**seaweeds**, **nori**, **wasabi**, and other mainstream items). To find a real Japanese supermarket, you have to go to Arlington Heights (at least to the best of my knowledge).

There is a fairly large Filipino population in Chicago, though much of it is assimilated, so there aren't as many strictly Filipino groceries as there are Korean. Filipino food is fascinating and worth seeking out because it is a blend of so many influences, from Spanish (with a little Mexican thrown in) to Southeast Asian, with side trips through China and India.

Fish and Seafood

All three types of stores have an excellent selection of seafood. Japanese products are the most cleaned and prepped (and the most expensive).

Fresh Fish and Seafood:
clams
crabs, live
flounder
mackerel
octopus
oysters

240

pomfret
shrimp
squid
tilapia, live

Japanese Specialties:
baby octopus
eels
pollack roe
salmon roe
scallops in the shell
sushi fish: including uni,
    eel, clams, octopus
tobikko (flying fish roe)
tuna
uni (sea urchin roe)

Frozen Seafood:
beltfish
clam meat
crabmeat
croaker
milkfish
octopus
oyster meat
pollack
rex sole
sand dab
sea cucumber
sea snails
sea squirt
skate

Dried Seafood:
anchovies
cuttlefish
jellyfish
sardines
squid
tilefish

Meat

Small but interesting selections of meat can be found in all of these stores. The Japanese cuts are exquisite, beautifully and symmetrically arranged. Koreans have **very good beef**, because they use it for tableside barbecue, among other things. This list doesn't include the stuff you can get anywhere, like chicken, which is also available.

beef feet
beef tendons (shins)
flank steak
longaniza (Filipino
    sausage)
oxtail
pampana (Filipino sausage)
sukiyaki—beef and pork
    (Japanese)
tripe
various bones and offal

Korean Specialties:
beef bulgogi meat (usu-
    ally sirloin)
beef ribs (kalbi)
sliced pork belly

Produce

All these stores carry a good selection of fresh produce. The Japanese is the most beautiful and most expensive. There are greens of all kinds, of course, and exotic fruits in season. If you want to be sure to get a particular ingredient for an ethnic dish, it's better to go to the appropriate store, but there are certain things they all carry, like **Asian eggplants**, **daikon**, and **assorted mushrooms**.

banana flowers
bitter melons
daikon
edamame (soybeans)
ginkgo nuts
gobo (burdock)
jute leaves
kabocha (pumpkinlike squash)
Korean melons (delicious)
long beans
lotus root
luffa (silk squash)
mitsuba (trefoil)
mushrooms: enoki, oyster, nametake, shiitake
myoga (ginger buds)
naga-imo (mountain yam)
pea shoots
perilla (shiso) **leaves**
persimmons
sata-imo (taro)
shungiko (chrysanthemum leaves)
sprouts
ume (green plums, pickled to make umeboshi)

Spices and Seasonings

rice vinegar
sea salt
soybean paste
soy sauce: light, dark, mushroom
Sriracha sauce

Japanese Specialties:
furikake (seasoning blends)
ichimi togarashi (dried ground red chiles)
memmi (noodle-dipping sauce)
mirin
ponzu (citrus soy dipping sauce)
sansho (Japanese pepper)
shabu shabu sauce

Wasabi Mayo

1 T. wasabi   ¼ C. mayo

Mix together the wasabi and mayo. Adjust amounts to taste.

Wasabi mayo can be used anywhere you'd use regular mayo. It really perks up a tuna salad and is also a great dip for crudités. Try it as a coating for fish—sprinkle with bread crumbs and bake or broil.

shichimi (seven-spice seasoning, shichimi togarashi)
tamari
tonkatsu sauce
wasabi

Korean Specialties:
brown rice vinegar
bulgogi sauce
denjang (soybean paste)
fish sauce
gochujang (hot pepper paste)
grape vinegar
perilla (shiso) **oil**
persimmon vinegar
red pepper powder

Filipino Specialties:
banana sauce
cane vinegar
kecap manis (the name for this tomato-based condiment is the origin of our word "ketchup")
nipa sap (coconut palm vinegar)
toyomansi (soy sauce)

Carbs

bean thread noodles
harusume sai fun noodles (potato starch noodles)
pancit noodles (Filipino noodles)
rice (all kinds)
rice flour
rice flour, glutinous (aka sweet, sticky or mochiko in Japanese)
rice noodles: fresh, rice stick, vermicelli
shirataki noodles (gelatin noodles for using in sukiyaki)
wheat noodles: chukasoba (ramen), soba (buckwheat), somen
yam noodles (Korean)

A Rice Primer

Short-grain rice. Japanese and Korean "sushi rice," sticks together, but is not the same as glutinous (aka sweet or sticky rice).

Medium-grain rice. All purpose (Calrose, Nishiki).

Long-grain rice. Chinese and Thai, fluffy, separate grains, jasmine or regular American.

Sweet rice. Sticky or glutinous rice, short grain, used in sweets and as table rice in northern Thailand.

243

Groceries

Most Japanese items are carried by Korean stores (and vice versa, but less so). Filipino stores are probably closer to Southeast Asian in this category.

adzuki (red beans)
barley, pressed
bean cakes
daikon, pickled
dashi (soup) mix
fish, pickled
fish cakes
garlic, pickled
ginger, pickled
katsuobushi (bonito flakes)
kimchee
konyaku (yam cakes)
mugwort flour
mushrooms, dried
panko (bread crumbs)
red bean paste
seaweed: nori, wakame, hijiki, kombu
tapioca pearls
tempura mix
umeboshi (pickled plum)
veggies, pickled, all kinds

Filipino Specialties:
acorn starch
annatto
baitop shell, canned
coconut, frozen shredded
coconut milk, canned
cod intestines
ginseng
green bean starch sheets
halo halo (fruit dessert)
jackfruit
lumpia, frozen
lumpia wrappers
palm fruit, canned
purple yam jam
purple yam powder
red eggs, preserved
taro stems, dried
tuna, canned with red pepper

Soy Products

atsuage (fried tofu)
miso: akamiso (brown), mamemiso (soybean), shiromiso (white)
natto (fermented beans)
nigari (the coagulant used to make tofu)
soybean powder, fermented
soybean powder, roasted
soy milk
tofu, all kinds
tofu "pockets"
yuba (bean curd skin)

Miscellaneous

The snacks and sweets available in these markets are fascinating,

Miso Misconceptions

1. Miso is just soybeans.

WRONG! In fact, only mamemiso is all soybeans. The others categories include komemiso, which is rice based, and mugimiso, which is made with barley.

2. Miso is all alike.

WRONG! There are dozens of variations, including genmai (brown rice) miso and akamiso, which is made of barley or rice and is the most popular variety in Japan. The darker the miso, the saltier and more pungent it is. Shiromiso (white miso, made from rice and soybeans) is the sweetest and mildest.

3. Miso is just for soup.

WRONG! Add miso to marinades, salad dressings, sauces, and stir-fries for a deep, rich flavor (and good nutrition). You must add it at the end of the cooking time, or it can break (the oil separates out; not harmful, just not pretty).

usually more interesting looking than good tasting, although I'm seriously considering trying to get a mainstream U.S. distributorship for **Poky cookies**. These luscious little sticks coated with chocolate or chocolate and nuts are eaten up instantly at our house. I suspect they would look good doing duty as fancy garnishes for desserts, too, but we keep eating them before I can try it.

The larger Korean stores stock **drinks of all kinds**. (And we thought the idea of putting herbs and protein in a can of soda was new!) There are **medicinals** that promise energy or weight loss, and there are even "sexy" drinks. But the Japanese **Pocari Sweat** wins the prize for unappetizing name. It's a Gatorade-type drink.

cinnamon punch
citron tea
ginkgo nut tea
honey tea
Korean drinks: crushed pear drink, mulberry drink, pine bud drink, pumpkin gruel, "sexy drink"
Morning Rice drink
Poky cookies
rice cracker snack mixes
shrimp crackers
wasabi peas

Equipment

The bigger stores have a pretty good assortment of cooking tools. Japanese shops tend to be more expensive (and perhaps offer higher quality), and you can also pick up amusing children's dishes decorated with characters from Japanese animated TV series there.

bamboo strainers and steamers
chopsticks
clay pots
crocks (for pickling, etc.)

rectangular skillets
(Japanese omelet pans)
rice cookers
suribachi and surikogi
(Japanese mortar and pestle)
sushi mats

Sushi Mats Aren't Just for Sushi

A sushi mat makes a great device for rolling up all kinds of things, such as spinach.

Blanch and season spinach, squeeze out most of the water, and then roll it into a cylinder in a mat lined with plastic wrap. You'll get a neat, dense spinach roll you can slice into pretty serving-size pieces. You can even roll it around a filling of chopped, sautéed mushrooms.

Cold and Spicy Soba Noodles

(Serves 6)

Soba noodles are the brown buckwheat kind that in Japan are often served on a slatted bamboo dish with a dipping sauce on the side. They have a nice nutty flavor on their own but are great paired with hot chili paste and lots of garlic. For this recipe I took the liberty of combining the noodles with a sauce instead of serving it separately. It's no longer very Japanese, I suppose, but it's very tasty. (And you don't have to wash as many dishes.)

1 lb. dried soba (buckwheat noodles)

2 shallots, sliced, or 1 bunch green onions, sliced (the white and most of the green part)

¼ C. soy sauce

¼ C. rice vinegar

1-½ T. (about 8 cloves) minced garlic

1 T. minced fresh ginger

3 tsp. sesame oil

3 tsp. chili-garlic paste

1 T. sake (optional)

Cook the noodles in lots of rapidly boiling water until done but not mushy, about 4 minutes. Consult package directions if in English, but don't trust them as they often give too long a time. Drain and rinse in cool water.

Combine the rest of the ingredients and mix with the cooled noodles. Refrigerate at least several hours or even overnight. These go great with grilled meats of all kinds, and they're not bad for breakfast either.

Pickled Pink

(Quick Pickled Turnips in Ume Vinegar)

⅓ C. ume (Japanese pickled plum) vinegar

⅓ C. rice wine vinegar

⅔ C. water

1 tsp. sugar

1 T. pink peppercorns

1 T. white peppercorns

4 to 5 small turnips, peeled, and cut into bite-size wedges (no more than ½ inch thick)

3 whole cloves garlic

2 to 3 small whole hot peppers

(This pickling brine works well on other white vegetables, like cauliflower, too.)

Combine the vinegar, water, sugar, and peppercorns in a saucepan and heat to a simmer. Arrange the turnips in a nonreactive (e.g., glass or stainless) container, tucking the garlic cloves and hot peppers around and between. Pour the hot liquid over the turnips (it must cover them completely) and let cool to room temperature. You will probably need to use a weight (like a plate or pot cover) to keep the veggies submerged.

After they cool, refrigerate for at least 24 hours. Flavor and color will improve over the next several days. Serve with grilled or roasted meats or as a cocktail nibble.

Japanese Stores

Mitsuwa Marketplace

100 E. Algonquin Rd.
Arlington Heights
847/956-6699

You'll see the Asian-style roof peeking out from behind the parking lot at the corner of Algonquin and Arlington Heights roads. Mitsuwa used to be called Yaohan. It is an all-under-one-roof Japanese shopping center and not to be missed. Plan on spending the entire morning or afternoon.

As you enter, there is a shop with Japanese serving ware on your left. A **liquor store** next to it offers a wide selection of **sake**, **plum wine**, and other goodies.

On your right, you enter the supermarket through an **amazing produce section**, featuring everything Japanese, including the more esoteric, like **fresh ume**. (The kind pickled to make umeboshi. Don't try to eat them raw, like I did. They're supposedly poisonous, although fortunately they are also inedible!) This is where you will find **fresh wasabi**. (It was $60 a pound on my last visit.) In season they also stock **myoga** (ginger buds). This is the place to get **fresh mushrooms**

(**beech, oyster, enoki**), **shungiku** (chrysanthemum leaves), and **gobo** (burdock).

Miso and **tofu** come in more brands and varieties than you'll see anywhere else. If you like **pickled things**, you've come to the right place. A special deli case displays a jewel-like array of **pickled eggplant, carrot, and burdock, as well as dozens of flavors of pickled daikon**. If it's a weekend, you may even be treated to samples.

The back of the store is lined with refrigerator and freezer cases loaded with **impeccable fish and meat**. All the **ingredients for sushi** are here: **octopus, surf clams, tobikko** (the bright orange flying fish roe used in California rolls), **unagi** (grilled eel), and more.

The cooking equipment includes some items that made me smile. Pick up a **Hello Kitty waffle iron or toaster** or a **special attachment to add a bidet function** to your toilet. There are also more practical things, like **sushi mats** and pots and pans.

When you're through shopping—and please allow plenty of time to peruse the many aisles of **noodles, rice, sea-**

weed, and sauces—visit the food court for lunch. Go for sushi or a bowl of udon. There's even a bakery, amusingly named Hippo, that sells **Japanese croissants**.

Sea Ranch

518 Dempster St.
Evanston
847/492-8340

Sea Ranch Market

3223 Lake St.
Wilmette
847/256-7010

Sea Ranch Market is the grocery store located across the parking lot in the same mall with the original Sea Ranch seafood store in Wilmette. Sea Ranch specializes in **fresh fish** and **prepared sushi**. (You'll find more information in the "Fish and Seafood" chapter p. 33.) Sea Ranch Market manages to cram a lot into a limited space. You'll find Japanese groceries, including **seaweed**, **panko**, **soba noodles**, **furikake seasoning blends**, and **tempura mixes**. There is a representative, but very small, selection of produce, as well as refrigerated **miso**, **tofu**, and the like.

True World Market

3 S. Arlington Heights Rd.
Elk Grove Village
847/806-1200

Somewhat smaller than **Mitsuwa**, True World (on Arlington Heights Road at Higgins) is still a full-service Japanese supermarket. They also do a booming carryout business in sushi and sashimi.

You'll find pretty much the same stuff as at Mitsuwa in terms of produce, groceries, and meat. There's just a little less of it, which can be a good thing if you're short of time.

They carry **equipment**, too, including a lot of **Japanese kid stuff**, like **Sailor Moon chopsticks**. I picked up cute **porcelain soup spoons** decorated with Japanese writing and cartoon vegetables.

Korean Stores

Arirang Supermarket
4017 W. Lawrence Ave.
773/777-2400

I almost drove away from this place, thinking it was closed down since the burglar gates were up over the windows. Glad I didn't. Inside it's big and clean.

Arirang offers a comprehensive selection of **all things Korean**, even **liquor** and **medicinals**. There is a **"salad bar"** (with lots of kinds of **kimchee** and many unrecognizable things), as well as a deli with prepared items, but there's no place to eat.

Asia Super Market
9800 N. Milwaukee Ave.
Des Plaines
847/297-4949

34–36 E. Golf Rd.
Schaumburg
847/781-0289

These full-service Korean groceries offer the usual array of **kimchees**, **bulgogi sauces**, and **hot pepper pastes**. Groceries also include many **grains**, **teas**, **seaweed**, and **flours**, including **carrot flour** and **beet flour**. (A quick look at the ingredients shows that these are wheat flour flavored and colored with the vegetables, not flour totally made from them.) A small assortment of produce and a **decent selection of fish and meat** are offered as well. As with most Korean markets, there is an interesting collection of gadgets (need an **eggplant corer**?) and cooking utensils, too.

Chicago Food Corporation
3333 N. Kimball Ave.
773/478-5566

This definitive Korean supermarket is being discovered by non-Koreans, especially on weekends. They come for the good prices as much as the authentic food, I suspect. It's located almost on the Kimball off-ramp of the Kennedy. You'll see the big sign in Korean and English. The small parking lot is in front and usually jammed, but they often have attendants to direct traffic.

Everything Korean is here, and **most things Japanese**. The outside walk is jammed with **huge bags of rice** and **cartons of fruit**. A selection of **sweets**, including the yummy **maltose-sesame candy**, greets you on entering.

The produce department offers good buys on **garlic**, **shallots**, **herbs**, and **Asian greens**. **Peeled garlic cloves** are a real time-saver! Be sure to try **Korean melons** in season and the very crunchy **wet white pears** when they're around.

An awesome selection of **fresh and frozen seafood** tempts with good prices on ordinary things and a world of exotic offerings. There is an entire aisle of different **seaweeds**, another with **sauces** and **condiments**, and much more.

You'll find two refrigerators full of various kinds of **kimchee**, as well as a **"salad bar"** that allows you to take small portions of strange-looking prepared dishes. An adjoining room is filled with dishes, cookware, and gadgets. You'll find **Benriner slicers**, big **ceramic crocks** to make kimchee (or whatever you want), dishes, **mortars and pestles**, **sushi rolling mats**, and cute little **plastic Japanese-style lunch boxes** with badly translated English on them.

Toward the rear is a small eating area with an open kitchen and a picture menu on the wall. Try pibimpap, a rice and vegetable dish with an egg on top.

Kimchee, 160 Different Ways

As I stood paralyzed with indecision in front of a refrigerator full of jars of different kinds of kimchee, a kind fellow shopper pointed me to basic cabbage kimchee and warned me that the green onion kind is the hottest. Although there are labels, names are spelled many ways. Just look at the ingredients and take your chances.

Here are a few of the more than 160 kinds, from a book by the Korean tourist organization:

T'ongbaecch'u kimchee
whole cabbage

Oisobaegi kimchee
stuffed cucumber

Kkaktugi kimchee
diced radish (daikon)

Nabak kimchee
radish and cabbage

The spelling varies wildly—I just call it bim-bam-bop, and they seem to understand.

Clark Market

Albany Park Mall
4853–55 N. Kedzie Ave.
(no phone listed)

Clark Market is large, but not as huge as **Chicago Food Corp**. All the Korean necessities are here— **hot bean paste, pickled garlic**, and **kimchee**—as well as a good assortment of **Japanese ingredients**. This is where I found an amazing convenience product—**cooked rice in aseptic (nonrefrigerated) packs**. It was not bad and sure beat Minute Rice in terms of flavor (easier, too).

Hyundai Supermarket

2837 Pfingston Rd.
Glenview
847/559-1618

In a mall at the corner of Willow and Pfingston roads, this good-size market carries produce, meat, and fish and has a large deli offering prepared foods.

Kimball Food

3445 N. Kimball Ave.
773/539-5553

Hidden away on an industrial side street, this market is quite near to **Chicago Food Corp**. Kimball Foods isn't as big, but it has a **very nice butcher shop–fish market**, as well as

decent produce and good prices. It also has the **best selection of bizarre drinks**. Pick up a six-pack of "**sexy drink**" for a bachelor(ette) party.

Lawrence Fruit Market

3318 W. Bryn Mawr Ave.
773/279-8020

This small, older place in the heart of the Korean neighborhood offers a representative selection of Korean foods. Offerings are mostly packaged goods with a few produce items. It's the kind of mom-and-pop shop that used to be in every city neighborhood.

Song Do Market

282 E. Golf Rd.
Arlington Heights
847/718-1010
847/718-1919

Song Do Market is a smallish Korean grocery near the big Japanese stores in Arlington Heights. Expect to find the usual **sweet potato noodles** and **kimchee**. There is a fairly extensive deli featuring **Korean pancakes, vegetable dishes**, and other specialties to take out. When I visited they also had barrels of seaweedlike stuff displayed in the back, which I didn't recognize.

Filipino Stores

Uni-Mart

5845 N. Clark St.
773/271-8676

1038 W. Golf Rd.
Hoffman Estates
874/755-1082

7315 W. Dempster St.
Niles
847/663-8388

2457 W. 75th St.
Woodridge
630/910-6386

Located in a strip mall on busy Clark Street, the Chicago store is not huge, but it is packed with merchandise. The grocery on Dempster is a bit larger and very similar in terms of merchandise. **Bakery goods** abound and tempt the shopper with unusual-looking cakes, cookies, and breads. The small, exotic produce department carried (when I was there) **fresh jute leaves**, **taro leaves**, and **banana flowers**, as well as the usual **taro**, **bitter melon**, and **long beans**.

There is a selection of **fresh fish on ice—silverfish** (these look like noodles with eyes), **squid**, **butterfish**, **sap-sap**, **hasa-hasa**, **baka**, and more. The butcher case offers **pork belly**, **stomach**, and other cuts. Aisles are filled with **Filipino noodles** (**pancit**), **sauces** (toyomansi), and **canned tropical fruit treats**, including **halo halo** and the gorgeous **purple yam jam**, which unfortunately doesn't really taste like much. You can purchase **atchara** (pickled papaya), **longanisa** (sausage), **tocino** (bacon), **beef blood**, and, of course, **lumpia** in the refrigerator or freezer case.

Both the Clark and Dempster stores carry an array of prepared foods and **will fry fish to order** for takeouts. (I didn't visit Woodridge or Hoffman Estates.)

The Wonders of Banana Sauce

It is bright red and has the consistency of ketchup. It even tastes like ketchup without the vinegar, but it's made from bananas!

Chicken Adobo Style

(Serves 4)

1 whole chicken, cut up	**2 C. water**
1 C. palm or cane vinegar	**8 cloves garlic**
1 C. soy sauce	**1 T. whole black peppercorns**

Put the chicken in a nonreactive pan or plastic zip-top bag. Mix together the vinegar, soy sauce, water, garlic, and peppercorns and pour the marinade over the chicken. Cover and marinate in the refrigerator for 2 to 6 hours.

Pour the chicken and marinade into a wide pan with a cover. Simmer, covered, until the chicken is almost cooked through (about 15 minutes). Remove the chicken and turn the heat to high to reduce the marinade by about half and make a sauce. Meanwhile, finish the chicken pieces on a grill or under a broiler until browned and done (2 to 3 minutes a side). Strain the reduced marinade-sauce and serve with the chicken. Rice or couscous is a good accompaniment.

Japan, Korea, and the Philippines

Top 10 Japanese, Korean, and Filipino Ingredients

1. wasabi* (p. 240)
2. panko bread crumbs
3. short-grain Japanese rice* (p. 241)
4. miso* (p. 243)
5. soba noodles* (p. 245)
6. citrus (yuzu) soy
7. furikake seasoning blends
8. Korean melon
9. kimchee* (p. 250)
10. banana sauce* (p. 252)

tip or recipe included

Multiethnic Stores

(assorted carbs, spreads, and snacks)

Multiethnic Stores

It's so American—shopping for Lithuanian sausage, Oaxacan tamales, Thai fish sauce, and Indian mango chutney while pushing a behemoth cart down wide aisles, listening to conversations in Spanish, Russian, Arabic, and Polish with Muzak blasting soft rock. I just returned from an afternoon spent checking out various supermarkets and have decided to add this chapter to the book to accommodate those places that don't fit into one specific ethnic category but, rather, serve many of them.

It's always a slippery proposition categorizing a store—not unlike deciding what ethnicity we ourselves fit. I remember my mom, who is of English–Irish–early American ancestry, preaching to me that an American is an American, not a Lithuanian or an Irishman or whatever. (Hey, we lived in a Lithuanian neighborhood, and she was probably one of the few residents who didn't speak the not-so-native language.) We are a nation of immigrants, and this makes for some very good eating and shopping. I'm happy to report that there are more markets every day that cater most profitably to a mixed crowd. Since I do many food demos

promoting Chicago's ethnic diversity, these stores are a godsend to me. They represent one-stop shopping for everything from green papaya to purple yam. Sure beats running from neighborhood to neighborhood.

I've taken to asking checkout clerks how many languages they speak when I'm in one of these joints. The answer is usually three languages, at least, and they are not easy ones. Often the lowly clerk, who probably makes minimum wage, knows a wild geographic assortment of tongues—Arabic, Armenian, Spanish, and English, for instance. I don't know about you, but I find this very humbling.

A & G International Fresh Market
5630 W. Belmont Ave.
773/777-4480

The display of breads just inside the entrance of A & G is enough to get a rise out of anyone. It seems every Eastern European bakery is represented, as well as most Italian and Middle Eastern ones—and there are tortillas, too. Amazingly enough, A & G, in the spirit of true diversity, also stocks Wonder Bread. The produce aisles seem to go on forever. Here are all the **Mexican veggies** you've dreamed of, including **Mexican chayote** (the spiny kind), **habaneros**, **tuna** (cactus fruit), **epazote**, **verdolaga**, and more. You'll find **fresh shiitake and oyster mushrooms**, as well as the usual button and **portobello**. There are **greens, lettuces, malanga, taro**, and, in season, **fresh olives** to marinate at home.

Grocery shelves are arranged according to ethnicity. There is a huge **Polish assortment** of packaged goods—all those **pickled mushrooms** and **plum jams**. **Middle Eastern products** include **chickpea flour**, **cracked wheat**, **tahini**, and such. **Mexican comestibles** are well represented, and there is an **Asian section**, although it's a bit disappointing compared to the scope of the store. Among the meat offerings are some **choice beef**, **lamb tripe**, and **chicken feet**. There is **frozen goose** and **capon**. The deli and adjoining deli cases supply **Polish bacon**, **Bobak sausages**, **chorizo made on the premises**, and lots more.

Several aisles are devoted to nothing but **bulk bins of nuts, European candies, trail mixes, and other dry**

goods. The dairy department is comprehensive, with many brands of **Greek yogurt**, **kefir**, and a mind-boggling assortment of **European-style butter**, including one imported from Italy and made with the cream left over after producing **Reggiano Parmesan**.

A & G is a delightful store with only one serious fault—a small, badly laid-out parking lot.

Food Harbor

1421 W. Lake St.
Addison
630/629-1700

This store is the suburban cousin of **International Club** (p. 214). They are both Asian oriented but multiethnic. The Addison store offers a bit wider array of international items. **Fresh fish** is the main attraction at Food Harbor (hence the name, of course). They have a room full of aquariums (like International Club) with **live crabs, eels, lobster, catfish, bass, tilapia**, etc. Pick your favorite finster and they'll kill and clean it. **Octopus, shrimp with heads, cuttlefish**, and other sea creatures are displayed on ice.

The produce selection is incredibly wide ranging and well priced. Be careful, though—some things are cheap for a reason. All the **Asian greens** are here, as well as **green papaya** (ripe ones, too), **tropical tubers** (including **cush-cush yams**, which are labeled "yampi"), **lychees** in season, **durian**, and more. Grocery aisles are heavy on the **soy and fish sauce**, but there is a reasonable selection of **Hispanic and Filipino items**.

Marketplace on Oakton

4817 W. Oakton Ave.
Skokie
847/677-9330

This is a truly multicultural, international supermarket and one I frequent regularly. The produce selection is amazing. There are **Asian greens** that go way beyond **bok choy** and include **Chinese flowering chives**, **gai lan**, and **water spinach** (aka kangkong, ong choy). **Tropical tubers**, like **yucca**, nestle next to **lotus root** and **green papaya**. There is always a good selection of fresh **shiitake, oyster, and portobello mushrooms**. You can easily find **burdock root** (gobo), two varieties of **bitter melon**, **methi leaves**, and every kind of fresh pepper you've ever heard of. In season, Marketplace also stocks esoterica like **fresh dates** (mild and delicious!) and **fresh lychees**.

While the emphasis is on produce, Marketplace also has a **full-service butcher shop**, **fresh fish**, and an enormous offering of packaged goods from almost everywhere. You name it, they've got it: **Quail**? Sure. **Mastic**? Yup. **Ajvar**? At least six brands. **Ghee**? Of course! Probably the only thing you CAN'T buy at Marketplace is Wonder Bread, although I'm not sure about that either. Oh, yeah, the prices are very good, too. This one is worth a detour.

Nature's Best

257 N. Cass Ave.
Westmont
630/769-0004

This market probably shouldn't be listed, since it's not very big and it's out in the boonies. I happened upon it while journeying from Westbrook Market over to the Indian shops on Cass (p. 195). It's here because I just loved it (and this after a long day of heavy-duty cart pushing). The produce is beautiful and includes pretty much everything: **bok choy**, **tomatillos**, **tindora**, and **fresh herbs**, to name a few. The butcher shop makes excellent **chorizo**, and the butchers are friendly and accommodating. The narrow aisles are neatly packed with **Polish, Middle Eastern, and Asian prod-**

ucts. Maybe it was just the refreshing coziness after the wide-open spaces of Westbrook, but Nature's Best has good vibes.

Produce World

8325 W. Lawrence Ave.
Harwood Heights
708/452-7400

8800 Waukegan Rd.
Morton Grove
847/581-1029

The Harwood Heights store is the bigger of the two markets, and the merchandise has a slightly different skew—a bit more **Balkan and Italian**, I'd say. There's a selection of **baked goods from a multitude of Polish and Italian bakeries**. Produce hits all the bases—**jalapeños, cardoon, boniato, bok choy**. The deli offers **Bobak's sausages, Hungarian sausages, Middle Eastern cheeses**, and **basturma**. There's a small butcher shop with **baby lamb** and **goat** as well as more ordinary stuff and an even smaller fish counter. The aisles skip gaily from **Latin Goya products** to **Polish jam** to **Greek herbs** still on the stem. I counted five kinds of **sherry vinegar**, and there was a bigger selection of **Italian tuna packed in oil** than I've seen anywhere (still not cheap, un-

fortunately). The **wine department** has bottles from Romania and Croatia, as well as the regular California swill.

Produce World in Morton Grove offers a wide assortment of all the standard items, too. They stock some **Asian, Middle Eastern, and Mexican produce** (**daikon, cactus fruit**). There are tons of **greens**—among them, several kinds of **chard** and **dandelion**, as well as enough different **lettuces** to drive a bunny bonkers. A deli and meat market feature a good selection, including some hard-to-find cuts, such as **lamb liver**. They are (or they say they are!) famous for **Greek shish kebab** marinated and ready to grill. The place is crammed with **ethnic sausages and breads** from Chicago brands like **Bobak's** and the **Georgian Bakery**. Dry goods include **Greek and Polish specialties** as well as awesome **house-prepared veggie chips**.

(Super) Tony's Finer Foods

2099 N. Mannheim Rd.
Melrose Park
708/345-4700

This is part of a chain of stores that are **Latino oriented**. (Other non-super Tony's are listed in the "Latin America" chapter [p. 96].) Super Tony's is definitely schizophrenic in the nicest possible way. It is a huge market with wide aisles and Italian murals on the walls. Certainly **anything Mexican, Puerto Rican, or Central American** is available. Tony's has all the different brands of **tortillas** and a deli that offers **Oaxacan tamales**, **carnitas**, and **pizzas** by the pie or the slice. Produce is gorgeous. The fat **rutabagas** sit next to very fresh-looking **malanga** and **guinea banana**. There is fresh **mamey**, **xoconostle**, **fuzzy squash**, and **bitter melon**. **Herbs** are plentiful and include **culantro** (there's **cilantro**, too, though it's not the same thing), **chamomile**, **Thai basil**, and more. Sections of ethnic goodies feature **Polish and Indian specialties**, as well as **tropical Mexican drinks**, **Polish juices**, and a wide assortment of **Italian sodas**.

The **butcher shop** is huge and neatly arranged. You'll find **beef** and **pork** in every incarnation, including preseasoned for tacos. There is **chicken** displayed on ice instead of shrink-wrapped, not to mention **fresh goat meat**. Amazingly enough, there seemed to be absolutely NO lamb, however, when I was there. A decent-size **fish department** displayed **calamari**, **octopus**, **skate**, and several sizes of **raw shrimp**.

Tony's has a fair-size **liquor department** and a freezer case with **tropical fruit purees** (moro, mamey, passion fruit), **prepared tostones**, and other **Puerto Rican products**, as well as all-American stuff. There is also a garden supply section, which was closed for the winter when I visited but looked big enough to be interesting.

Valli Produce

450 E. Golf Rd.
Arlington Heights
847/439-9700

850 Roselle Rd.
Hoffman Estates
847/252-7200

Valli bills itself as "an international marketplace." The Golf Road store that I visited lives up to its name. It's not huge, but it is jam-packed. The produce seems fresh, and there's anything you could wish in the way of Mexican (**chayote**, **tuna**, **yucca**), Indian (**methi leaves**, **taro leaves**), and Asian (**chive flowers**, **bok choy**, **pea tips**). **Italian goods** are very well represented, too—not a surprise, since the owners are Italian. This is the only place I've seen what I think was fresh **puntarella**, a kind of chicory or dandelion (labeled "cinecicoria" in the store). I purchased **panforté** from Sienna, and at Christmastime they had at least half a dozen brands of imported **panettone**, too. I was very impressed (I'm a connoisseur) with the wide selection of **anchovies, including salt-packed**. There are aisles devoted to **Middle Eastern, Greek, Polish, and Indian packaged goods**. The customers look just as ethnically diverse as the merchandise. There's a huge deli and a butcher counter. I saw **veal brains** and **tongue** in the meat case, and even cleaned **hog casings** for making sausage.

Westbrook Market

10 W. 63rd St.
Westmont
630/737-1400

An enormous supermarket located pretty far out in the southwestern boonies (Cass Road and 63rd Street), this one is worth a trip. The produce selection is quite global and covers the **Latin American, Asian, Eastern European, and Indian** bases and then some. It's the only place I've seen what is labeled "calamase," but which I believe to be the Filipino **calamansi**, a lime-like citrus fruit. There are **fresh water chestnuts, ong choy, methi, pomelo, escarole,** and **long beans. Frozen fish** cases are loaded with everything from **Brazilian lobster** tail and **Indian mackerel** to **squid tubes** and all-American **fish sticks**. Grocery aisles are labeled according to ethnicity. The Mexican aisle has everything you'd expect, and the Polish aisle includes the largest offering of **Lithuanian products** I've encountered anywhere. There is **Lithuanian honey, bilberry jam, candies**, and more. Greece, the Middle East, and India are all well represented, too. You'll find **grape molasses, tamarind paste, grape leaves, lentils, bulgur wheat**, etc., etc. The butchers are behind a glass partition, and the meat is all shrink-wrapped, which I found kind of creepy and sterile, but the **beef was choice grade** and the selection was good.

A freezer case holds **green bean ice cream bars** (not a good idea), various **fish balls, grated purple yam**, and Eggo frozen waffles. Oh, yes, there are good prices on many **Polish beers and several Lithuanian ones**, too. If you go to Westbrook, bring an appetite—and an empty trunk.

See also the following stores in other chapters:

Andy's Fruit Ranch (p. 4)

Berwyn Fruit Market (p. 4)

Fresh Farms (p. 191)

International Club (p. 214)

Pete's Fresh Market (p. 96)

A Drink with That?

(filters, corks, and corkscrew)

A Drink with That?

Coffee and Tea

Coffee is easy to find these days. The few shops listed here are the real local specialists. Don't forget the ethnic stores for coffee and tea, either. Polish and Asian markets are great resources for **herbal and medicinal teas**. Latino stores carry **espresso** and **South American coffees**. Vietnamese stores have **French Market–style coffee with chicory** (the French influence, I guess). **Canned coffee and tea drinks** are also available in most Asian stores and a nice change from AriZona Iced Tea.

Coffee and Tea Exchange

3311 N. Broadway St.
773/528-2241
www.coffeeandtea.com

These guys have been roasting and selling dozens of blends of coffee and tea to Chicagoans, to restaurants, and by mail order since 1978, long before the coffee boom.

Intelligentsia

3123 N. Broadway St.
773/348-8058

53 W. Jackson Blvd.
312/253-0594
(weekdays only)
www.intelligentsiacoffee.com

Intelligentsia roasts its own coffee and does its own tea blending and will even roast to order. It's where many local restaurants and gourmet stores acquire their house blends.

Ten Ren Tea

2247 S. Wentworth Ave.
312/842-1171

This Chinatown store devoted to imported teas has a small tea room for tasting, lots of packaged teas, and hundreds of varieties by the pound. Ten Ren's "bubble teas," which are flavored tea drinks with tapioca pearls added for texture, are some of the tastiest. You can also purchase the tapioca pearls here to brew your own. (They'll give you instructions, too.)

Todd & Holland
Tea Merchants

7311 Madison St.
Forest Park
708/488-1136
www.todd-holland.com

Tea is the story at Todd & Holland. They are knowledgeable and friendly and have an enormous selection of whole leaf tea, plus pots, cozies, and other tea-related ware.

Brewing and
Winemaking

These retailers carry all the chemicals and hardware necessary for making wine or for home-brewing. You'll also find the "mother" you need to start your own batch of vinegar fermenting.

See also the listing for **Chiarugi Hardware** in the "Equipment" chapter (p. 49).

Bev Art Brewer and
Winemaker Supply

10033 S. Western Ave.
773/233-7579
www.bev-art.com

Bev Art sells a full panoply of equipment and ingredients and also teaches tons of classes on subjects ranging from brewing

mead to advanced wine making. Many classes are on-site, and the wine that you make is fermented in Bev Art's temperature-controlled cellar. They also sponsor trips to Michigan for grape picking and other events related to brewing and wine making. In fact, Bev Art traditionally brews up a special beer every year for folks to sample during the South Side St. Patrick's Day parade.

Chicagoland
Winemakers

689 W. North Ave.
Elmhurst
800/226-BREW
www.cwinemaker.com

A mail-order source as well as a retail store, Chicagoland Winemakers offers special package deals for beginners who wish to try their hand at making wine or beer. In addition, you can order what you need in terms of equipment or ingredients. They also carry soft drink flavor extracts.

Wine Stores

This is a far from definitive listing of some of Chicago's wine shops. New ones seem to be opening up daily. All these establishments offer everyday wines, plus access to more interesting bottles. And whether big (**Sam's** at 33,000 square feet) or small (**Howard's Wine Cellar** at 1,000 square feet), they all offer tastings, information, and a knowledgeable staff to assist you. If you're serious about wine, finding a merchant you trust and who understands your taste is invaluable. (Kind of like having a great butcher.) There are times when a big warehouse store is just fine, like the time I needed enough champagne to fill a champagne fountain for a party. For personal service, though, go to a smaller place. They have the advantage of more easily dealing with small producers and of getting to know you. They all offer many choices for every pocketbook and will not look down their nose at you if you're seeking a good wine for less than $20. (For less than $5, see **Trader Joe's**.)

The Artisan Cellar

222 Merchandise Mart Plaza
Suite 116
312/527-5810

The ambiance is European in this wine shop cum gourmet deli. There are more than 1,000 carefully selected bottles, including unusual varietals from around the world. The champagne selection avoids big names and focuses on small French producers. Among the deli items, you'll find oils, cheeses, and charcuterie.

Bin 36

339 N. Dearborn St.
(Marina City)
312/755-9463

This is a combination restaurant, wine bar, and retail store.

Binny's Beverage Depot

3000 N. Clark St.
773/935-9400

213 W. Grand Ave Ave.
312/332-0012

Also in Niles, Skokie, Schaumburg, Highland Park, Elmwood Park, and Buffalo Grove
www.binnys.com
See "Gourmet" chapter (p. 3).

Chalet Wine and Cheese

40 E. Delaware Pl.
312/787-8555
See "Gourmet" chapter (p. 3).

Chicago Wine School

2001 S. Halsted St.
312/266-9463
www.wineschool.com

This is not a store, but a school that features everything from one-night seminars to comprehensive five-week courses. Owner Patrick Fegan believes in wine education without intimidation. Their Web site has a great wine lover's vocabulary section that covers everything from the difference between acetic and acidic to yeasty and provides some handy adjectives to throw at wine-snob friends.

Fine Wine Brokers

4621 N. Lincoln Ave.
773/989-8166
www.fwbchicago.com

This shop has the same owners and philosophy as the **Artisan Cellar**, listed earlier.

House of Glunz

1206 N. Wells St.
312/642-3000
www.houseofglunz.com

The city's oldest wine seller, the House of Glunz has been operating from the same address since 1888. Wine appreciation classes are held monthly.

Howard's Wine Cellar

1244 W. Belmont Ave.
773/248-3766

This small shop is packed with interesting wines selected by owner Howard Silverman from every wine-producing country and in all price ranges.

Kafka Wine Co.

3325 N. Halsted St.
773/975-9463
www.kafkawine.com

A newcomer to the market, this small shop's specialty is wine priced at less than $15 a bottle. They stock more than 250 of them. Wine is arranged by flavor (toasty, earthy, floral, etc.), instead of country of origin or grape variety.

Randolph Wine Cellars

1415 W. Randolph St.
312/942-1212

While Randolph Wine Cellars is staffed by certified sommeliers and is committed to carrying some of the great classic wines of the world, they also stock dozens of bottles that retail for less than $10 apiece. The Tasting Room, an adjoining wine bar, lets you try before you buy and offers food, including cheese flights (assorted cheeses chosen to go with appropriate wines).

Sam's Wine and Spirits

1720 N. Marcey St.
312/664-4394

2010 Butterfield Rd.
Downers Grove
630/705-9463
www.samswine.com

One of the first warehouse-style wine stores, Sam's also houses a gourmet store, the **Marcey Street Market** (p. 5).

Schaefer's Wines, Foods and Spirits

9965 Gross Point Rd.
Skokie
847/673-5711
www.schaefers.com

Schaefer's has a well-attended tasting of wine and food every Saturday. In addition to wine, they sell more than 100 varieties of cheese, homemade dips, pâtés, and sausages in their Signature Market.

Wine Discount Center

1826 N. Elston Ave.
773/489-3454

Also in Buffalo Grove, Forest Park, and Highland Park
www.winediscountcenter.com

This warehouse-style discount store offers good prices on a huge selection of vino.

Delicious Day Trips

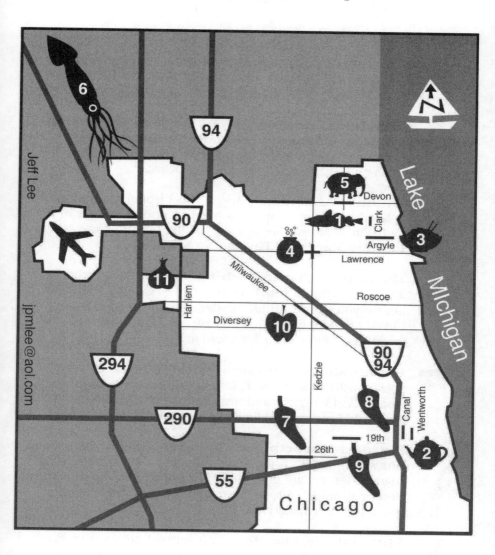

Spend the day in a foreign country without leaving town. Shop, gawk, eat, and learn a little of the language without spending much money.

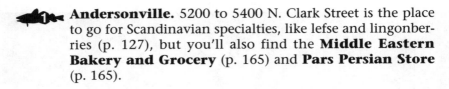 **Andersonville.** 5200 to 5400 N. Clark Street is the place to go for Scandinavian specialties, like lefse and lingonberries (p. 127), but you'll also find the **Middle Eastern Bakery and Grocery** (p. 165) and **Pars Persian Store** (p. 165).

Chinatown. Make sure to visit **Ten Ren Tea** shop (p. 266) and the **Hong Kong Noodle Company** (p. 210) on Wentworth Avenue. Don't miss the "modern" mall at the north end. It has good, less touristy stores.

Southeast Asia. Wander Argyle Street from Broadway east to Sheridan Road. Stop for a bowl of noodles. Then head south on Broadway to visit one of the big supermarkets— **Tai Nam Market** or **Thaong Xa My A**. (p. 227).

The Kedzie-Lawrence melting pot. For exotic produce, don't miss **Andy's Fruit Ranch** (p. 41). On the east side of Kedzie you'll find Middle Eastern shops and restaurants. **Clark Market** (p. 253) is Korean and **Lindo Michoacán** (p. 94) can supply Latin American ingredients.

Little India. Devon Avenue from 2200 to 2600 west is packed with Indian and Pakistani grocers, spice shops, sari stores, halal butchers, and restaurants (pp. 190–195), as well as Jewish, Russian, Middle Eastern, and Balkan spots, too.

Mitsuwa Marketplace. (Arlington Heights) It's only one store, but it's a Japanese shopping center. Among its many offerings are groceries, fish, booze, and equipment. Best of all there's a food court that features sushi, noodles, and a Japanese bakery. (p. 249)

Little Village. This Mexican neighborhood, which runs from 3200 to 3500 west on 26th Street, is centered around a pink welcome arch at 26th and Albany Avenue. You'll find supermarkets, restaurants, nightclubs, and, on summer weekends, a fiesta mood. (pp. 88–93)

Maxwell Street. This open-air flea market sets up on Canal between Roosevelt and S. 18th Street every Sunday from 7 A.M. to 3 P.M. It's a little like visiting Tijuana on the near South Side. (p. 94)

Pilsen. The neighborhood is rapidly gentrifying, but Pilsen still offers authentic Mexican markets (pp. 88–99), fast-food style tamale and carnitas shops, and the wonderful **Bombon Bakery** (p. 99). Don't miss the Mexican Fine Arts Center Museum, at 1852 W. 19th Street.

Milwaukee Avenue. Blending old and new establishments, this Polish shopping neighborhood stretches from Diversey to Roscoe. Discover great sausage, bacon, and beer. When hunger hits, head to the famous **Czerwone Jabluszko** ("Red Apple"; 3123 N. Milwaukee) for an overflowing buffet of Polish specialties. (pp. 111–117)

Pasta and Polish. Explore North Harlem between Fullerton and Lawrence by car. **Caputo's** (p. 137) is the quintessential Italian market. Across the street, **Mercato del Pesce** (p. 32) offers calamari, octopi, and more. **Rich's Foods and Liquors** (p. 117) is Polish sausage heaven. Then, if you have the stamina, head east on Belmont to **A & G International Fresh Market** (p. 258) for a true multicultural finish to your shopping experience.

Leftovers
(bibliography and indexes)

Bibliography

References

Bladholm, Linda. *The Asian Grocery Store Demystified*. Los Angeles: Renaissance Books, 2000.

———. *The Indian Grocery Store Demystified*. Los Angeles: Renaissance Books, 2000.

———. *Latin & Caribbean Grocery Stores Demystified*. Los Angeles: Renaissance Books, 2001.

Cost, Bruce. *Asian Ingredients*. New York: HarperCollins Publishers, Quill, 2000.

Davidson, Alan. *Fruit: A Connoisseur's Guide and Cookbook*. New York: Simon & Schuster, 1991.

———. *The Oxford Companion to Food*. Oxford, England: Oxford University Press, 1999.

Garfunkel, Trudy. *Kosher for Everybody*. San Francisco: Jossey-Bass, 2004.

Gibson, Kelly, and Portia Belloc Lowndes. *The Slow Food Guide to Chicago Restaurants, Markets, Bars*. White River Junction, Vermont: Chelsea Green Publishing, 2004.

Grigson, Jane, and Charlotte Knox. *Exotic Fruits and Vegetables*. New York: Henry Holt, 1986.

Grigson, Sophie. *Gourmet Ingredients*. New York: Van Nostrand Reinhold, 1991.

Haddix, Carol Mighton, editor. *Ethnic Chicago Cookbook*. Lincolnwood, Illinois: NTC/Contemporary Publishing Group, Contemporary Books, 1999.

Haddix, Carol Mighton, and Sherman Kaplan. *Cook's Marketplace Chicago*. San Francisco: 101 Productions, 1996.

Herbst, Sharon Tyler. *Food Lover's Companion*. New York: Barron's Educational Series, 1995.

Jaffrey, Madhur. *World Vegetarian*. New York: Clarkson Potter, 1999.

Larkcom, Joy. *Oriental Vegetables*. Tokyo: Kodansha International, 1991.

Lindberg, Richard. *Ethnic Chicago: A Complete Guide to the Many Faces and Cultures of Chicago*. Lincolnwood: NTC/Contemporary Publishing Company, Passport Books, 1997.

Morgan, Lane. *The Ethnic Market Food Guide*. New York: Penguin Putnam, Berkley Publishing Company, 1977.

Norman, Jill. *The Complete Book of Spices*. London: Viking Studio Books, 1990.

Passmore, Jacki. *The Encyclopedia of Asian Food and Cooking*. New York: William Morrow, 1991.

Ross, Rosa Lo San. *Beyond Bok Choy*. New York: Workman Publishing Company, Inc., Artisan, 1996.

Schneider, Elizabeth. *Uncommon Fruits and Vegetables: A Commonsense Guide*. New York: William Morrow and Co., 1986.

———. *Vegetables from Amaranth to Zucchini*. New York: William Morrow, 2001.

Werle, Loukie, and Jill Cox. *Ingredients*. Cologne, Germany: Konemann Verlagsgesellschaft, 2000.

Whiteman, Kate. *A Cook's Guide to Italian Ingredients*. New York: Annex Publishing, Lorenz Books, 2000.

Wood, Rebecca. *The New Whole Foods Encyclopedia*. New York: Penguin Putnam, 1999.

Ethnic Cookbooks

Asian—

Brennan, Jennifer. *The Original Thai Cookbook*. New York: Berkley Publishing, 1981.

Coultrip-Davis, Deborah, and Young Sook Ramsay. *Flavors of Korea: Delicious Vegetarian Cuisine*. Summertown, Tennessee: Book Publishing Co., 1998.

Lo, Eileen Yin-Fei. *The Chinese Kitchen*. New York: William Morrow, 1999.

Loha-Unchit, Kasma. *It Rains Fishes: Legends, Traditions and the Joys of Thai Cooking*. Rohnert Park, California: Pomegranate Artbooks, 1994.

Shimbo, Hiroko. *The Japanese Kitchen*. Boston: Harvard Common Press, 2000.

Trang, Corinne. *Authentic Vietnamese Cooking*. New York: Simon & Schuster, 1999.

Caribbean/African—

Harris, Jessica B. *Iron Pots & Wooden Spoons*. New York: A Fireside Book, Simon & Schuster, 1989.

Ortiz, Elizabeth Lambert. *The Complete Book of Caribbean Cooking*. New York: M. Evans & Co., 1973.

Indian—

Devi, Yamuna. *The Art of Indian Vegetarian Cooking*. London: Leopard, 1995.

Jaffrey, Madhur. *Flavors of India*. Seattle: West 175 Publishing, 1995.

———. *Indian Cooking*. New York: Barron's Educational Series, 1982.

————. *Spice Kitchen*. New York: Carol Southern Books, 1993.

Latin American—

Bayless, Rick. *The Mexican Kitchen*. New York: Scribner, 1996.

————. *Mexico One Plate at a Time*. New York: Scribner, 2000.

Kennedy, Diana. *From My Mexican Kitchen*. New York: Clarkson Potter, 2003.

Kijac, Maria. *The South American Table*. Boston: Harvard Common Press, 2003.

Ortiz, Elisabeth Lambert. *The Book of Latin American Cooking*. New York: Knopf, 1979.

————. *The Complete Book of Mexican Cooking*. New York: M. Evans & Co., 1967.

Zaslavsky, Nancy. *A Cook's Tour of Mexico*. New York: St. Martin's Press, 1995.

Mediterranean/Middle Eastern—

Hazan, Marcella. *The Classic Italian Cookbook*. New York: Ballantine Books, 1973.

Jaffrey, Madhur. *World of the East Vegetarian Cooking*. New York: Alfred A. Knopf, 1981.

LaPlace, Viana, and Evan Kleiman. *Cucina Rustica*. New York: William Morrow and Co., 1990.

Roden, Claudia. *A Book of Middle Eastern Food*. New York: Vintage Books, A Division of Random House, 1968.

Recipe Index

ajvar ideas, 147
ancho pepper dip, 93
artichokes, baby, using, 141
Asian marinade, basic, 209
Asian wraps, using, 213

baby artichokes, using, 141
barbacoa, using, 88
basmati rice, perfumed, 194
beet salad, Lithuanian-style, 121
black beans, fermented, using, 207
borscht, 72
breakfast plantains, 178
broccoli raab and polenta, 136

cabbage, stuffed, 123
candied kumquats, 44
Caprese salad, 134
carnitas, using, 88
cauliflower with seeds, Indian-
    style, 189
cham-polski, 110
cheater's tamales, 98
cheater's tandoori chicken, 192
cheese crisps (frico), 131
cheese and peas, 197
chicken, cheater's tandoori, 192
chicken, pomegranate, 163
chicken adobo style, 255
chicken bites that bite back, 230
chickpea nibbles, 165
chips, persimmon, 40
chips, vegetable, 48
chips, whole wheat pita, 168
chutney, cilantro or mint, using,
    187
chutney, double-ginger rhubarb, 40
chutney and pappadam, 196
cilantro chutney, using, 187
cilantro salmon, 193
coffee, flavored, 13
cold and spicy soba noodles, 247

coo coo, using 173
crab salad, pomelo, 231

dessert plantains, 178
dip, ancho pepper, 93
dip, walnut-pomegranate (ma-
    hamorrah), 168
double-ginger rhubarb chutney, 40

eddo and eggplant, 204
eggs, scrambled, the best in the
    world, 119

fermented (salted, preserved) black
    beans, using, 207
finger-lickin' potatoes, 188
five-spice squash rings, 210
frico (cheese crisps), 131
fu fu, using, 173

ghee, using, 186
gigandes with giant flavor, 150
green papaya salad, 225
gruzdis, 115
guava products, using, 175

herb butter, 17
herbs, dried, 17
hibiscus drink (jamaica), 87

Indian-style cauliflower with seeds,
    189

jam, 38–39
jamaica (hibiscus drink), 87

kaffir lime leaves, storing, 222
kolackys, 113
kosher salt, in recipes, 70
kumquats, candied, 44

labna, using, 160

lemon grass, storing, 222
lentil (red) and tomato soup, 161
lita (calabacita), using, 83
Lithuanian potato gratin, 109
Lithuanian-style beet salad, 121

mahamorrah (walnut-pomegranate
    dip), 168
mango salsa, simple, 87
Marilyn's mojo, 84
marinade, basic Asian, 209
mayo, wasabi, 242
meatball pocket sandwich, 165
mint chutney, using, 187
mushroom-stuffed spinach roll,
    244

nutmeg ideas, 12
noodle nests, 206
noodles, rice, fresh, 216
noodles, soba, cold and spicy, 245
noodles, tips on using, 233–235

papaya salad, green, 225
pappadam, in microwave, 196
peas and cheese, 197
pennycakes, 122
perfumed basmati rice, 194
persimmon chips, 40
pesto, saving as ice cubes, 17
phyllo, using, 148
phyllo triangles, spinach-cheese,
    153
pickled pink turnips, 248
pie, super twangy tamarind, 198
pita chips, whole wheat, 168
plantains, 178
polenta and broccoli raab, 136
pomegranate chicken, 163
pomegranate-walnut dip (ma-
    hamorrah), 168
pomelo crab salad, 231
pork tenderloin, Vietnamese-style,
    224
potato gratin, Lithuanian, 109
potatoes, finger lickin', 188

rhubarb chutney, double-ginger, 40
rice, perfumed basmati, 194
rice noodles, fresh, 216
risotto, spinach, 135
roasted veggies with Sriracha, 223

saffron-pistachio biscotti, 18
saganaki, 152
salad, beet, Lithuanian-style, 121
salad, Caprese, 134
salad, green papaya, 225
salad, pomelo crab, 231
salmon, cilantro, 193
salsa, simple mango, 87
salt, kosher, in recipes, 70
sandwich, meatball pocket, 166
scrambled eggs, the best in the
    world, 119
snacks, chickpea, 165
soba noodles, cold and spicy, 247
soup, tomato–red lentil, 161
spinach-cheese phyllo triangles,
    153
spinach risotto, 135
spinach roll, 246
squash rings, five-spice, 210
Sriracha roasted veggies, 223
stuffed cabbage, 123
Swiss chard and pasta, 37

tamales, cheater's, 98
tamarind pie, super twangy, 198
tandoori chicken, cheater's, 192
tomato–red lentil soup, 161
trout meunière, 29
tubers, tropical, tips on using,
    101–102
turnips, pickled pink, 246

vegetable chips, 48
veggies, roasted with Sriracha, 223
Vietnamese-style pork tenderloin,
    224

walnut-pomegranate dip (ma-
    hamorrah), 168

wasabi mayo, 242
whole wheat pita chips, 168
wraps, Asian, using, 213

yogurt raita, 167
yucca with Marilyn's mojo, 84

Stores, Clubs, and Organizations Index

A & G International Fresh Market, 41, 258–259, 273
A & J Housewares, 208
A & T International, 111
Abyssinia Market & Coffee, 176
A-J Meats, 111
Aji Ichiban, 215
Al-Bayan Grocery, 162
Al-Khyam Bakery and Grocery, 162
Alliance Paper and Food Service, 49
American Institute of Wine and Food, 77
Andy's Deli & Bakery and Mikola-jczyk Sausage Shop, 111
Andy's Fruit Ranch, 41–42, 149, 264, 272
Angelic Organics, 37
Ann Sather's, 127
Arax Foods, 149, 162–162
Argo Georgian Bakery, 196
Arirang Supermarket, 251
Armando's Finer Foods, 88
Armitage Produce, 88, 172
Artisan Cellar, The, 3, 268
Asia Super Market, 251
Athens Grocery, 149
Awami Bazaar and Zabiha Meat, 190

Ba Le Vietnamese French Bakery, 229–230
Bagat Bros. Sharp Knife Service, 58
Baltic Bakery, 120
Bari Foods, 137
Bed, Bath & Beyond, 57
Belmont Produce, 88
Berwyn Fruit Market, 42, 149, 264
Best Food Products, Inc., 208
Best Turkish Foods, 149

Bev Art Brewer and Winemaker Supply, 267
Big Suchir, 190
Bin 36, 268
Binny's Beverage Depot, 3, 268
Biodynamic Farming and Garden-ing Association, 37
Bismillah Meat and Grocery, 190
Blommer Chocolate Company, 8
Bobak's Sausage Company, 111–112
Bombon Bakery, 99, 273
Bonné Sante, 63
Brazil Legal, 89
Brillakis, 149–151
Broadway Supermarket (Thaong Xa My A), 227–228
Burbank Deli, 112
Burhop's Seafood, 30

Calphalon Culinary Center, 74
Captain Alex Seafood, 30
Caputo Cheese Market, 137
Caputo's, 137–138, 273
Caribbean American Bakery, 178
Carnicería Guanajuato, 89
Carnicería Jimenez, 89
Carrot Top, 42
CB2, 50
Chaim's Kosher Bakery and Deli, 69
Chalet Wine and Cheese, 3–4, 268
Cheese Stands Alone, The, 4
Chef's Catalog, 49
Chefwear, 49
Chez Madelaine, 74
Chiarugi Hardware, 49, 267
Chicago Cooks, 77
Chicago Food Corporation, 28, 251–252

Chicago Food Market, 209
Chicago Game and Gourmet, 21
Chicago Live Poultry, 25
Chicago Produce, 90
Chicago Wine School, 269
Chicago Zabiha Halal Meat, 190
Chicagoland Winemakers, 267
ChicaGourmets, 77
Chinatown Market, 209
Chopping Block, The, 74–75
City of Chicago farmers markets, 36
City Fresh Market, 151
City Noor Meat Market, 21, 164
Clark Market, 251, 272
Coachouse Gourmet, 75
Coffee and Tea Exchange, 264
Collins Caviar, 28, 30, 34
Columbus Meat Market, 21
community-supported agriculture, 36–37
Conte di Savoia, 138
Convito Italiano, 138–139
Cooking with the Best Chefs, 77
Corner Cooks, 75
Cost Plus World Market, 50
Crate and Barrel, 50–51
Culinary Historians of Chicago, The, 77
Czerwone Jabluszko (Red Apple), 273

D'Amato's Bakery, 142
D'Andrea Italian Market, 139
Devon Market, 151
Di Cola's Seafood, 30
Dirk's Fish and Gourmet Shop, 31
Don Outlet Store, 51
Dong Kee Company, 209–210
Dulcelandia, 99
Dunajec Bakery and Deli, 112

E & J Sausage, 112–113
Ebner Kosher Meat Market, 69
Edgewater Produce, 90
El Guero Supermarket, 90–91

El Mercado Food Mart, 91
El Milagro, 99
El Popocatepetl, 99
Erickson's Delicatessen, 127
Eurostyle Deli, Inc., 114

Family Euro Deli, 114
Family Fruit Market, 42
Farm City Meat and Farm Super-market, 190
Farm Meat Market, 22, 164
farmers markets, City of Chicago, 36
Ferrara, Inc., "Original", 142
Fertile Garden, 16
Fiesta Market, 91
Fine Wine Brokers, 269
Fish Corner, 191
Fish Guy Market, The, 31
Flavour Cooking School, 75
Food Harbor, 31, 213, 259–260
Foodstuffs, 4
Fox & Obel Food Market, 4–5, 14
Fresh Farms, 191, 264
Frugal Muse, The, 78
Fruitful Yield, 63

Gene's Sausage Shop and Deli, 114–116
Gepperth's Meat Market, 22
Gethsemane Garden Center, 16
GFS Marketplace, 51–52
Gilmart, 116
Gino's Italian Imports, 139
Gold Brothers, 52
Golden Pacific, 226
Good Morgan Kosher Fish Market, 31, 69
Goody Supermarket, 210
Grandpa's Bakery & Deli, 116
Greek Islands, 154
Green City Market, 36

Hagen's Fish Market, 32
Halsted Packing, 22
Harrison's Poultry Farm, Inc., 22

Hoa Nam Grocery, 226
Holy Land Bakery and Grocery, 164
Home Economist, The, 14
Homeland Food Market, 176
Hong Kong Noodle Company,
  210–211, 272
House of Glunz, 269
Howard's Wine Cellar, 269
Hunan Market, Inc., 213
Hungarian Kosher Foods, 69–70
Hyundai Supermarket, 253

Illinois Fresh, 37
Intelligentsia, 266
International Club, 28, 214–215,
  264
Isaacson L and Stein Fish Co., 32

Jai Hind Plaza, 191
J.B. Sanfilippo & Sons Thrift Stores,
  14–15
Jerry and John's Quality Meats,
  22–23
Jerry's Fruit and Garden Center, 43
JK Grocers, 191
Joe & Frank's Homemade Sausage,
  116–117
Joe's Food and Liquor, 91
John's Live Poultry and Egg Market,
  25
Joseph's Food Market, 139–140

Kafka Wine Co., 269
Kamdar Plaza, 191–192
Kay's Treasured Books, 78–79
Kendall College, 75
Kimball Food, 253
Kol Touhy Kosher Foods, 70
Kol Tuv Kosher Foods, 70–71
Krasny Supply, 52
Kurowski Sausage Shop/Rich's Bak-
  ery, 117
Kwok Chiu Market, 211

L'Appetito, 140
La Casa Del Pueblo, 91–92

La Chiquita, 92
La Fruitería, 176
La Guadalupana, 92
La Justica, 93
La Unica Foodmart, 93–94, 172
Lalich Delicatessen, 151–152
Lawando's Grocery and Meat,
  192–193
Lawrence Fruit Market, 253
Lietuvele, 120
Lincolnwood Produce, 43, 152
Lindo Michoacán, 94, 272
Linens-n-Things, 57
Little Treasures, 79

Madni Mart, 193
Maestranzi Sharp Knife Service, 58
Marc Bakery Equipment, 52
Marcey St. Market, 5, 270
Marketplace on Oakton, 28, 41,
  152, 260
Marlinn Restaurant Supply, 52–53
Marshall Field's Marketplace, 7, 57
Maxwell Street Market, 94–95, 273
Mayflower Food Company, 211
Mediterranean Plus, 164–165
Mehrab Meat & Grocery, 193
Mercato del Pesce, 32, 140, 273
Meyer's Delicatessen, 126–127
Middle East Bakery and Grocery,
  165, 272
Mien-Hoa Market, 227
Mikolajczyk Sausage Shop, 111
Minelli Brothers Italian Specialties,
  140
Mitsuwa Marketplace, 28, 249–250,
  272
Mubarak Grocers and Meat, 193
Mulica's Deli, 117

Nature's Best, 260–261
New York Kosher, 71
Nicholas Quality Meats, 23
Ninevah Grocery and Meat Market,
  165
Noor Meat Market, 193

Northeastern Fruit, 43
Northshore Cookery, 75–76
Northwestern Cutlery, 53, 58–59
Nottoli & Son Sausage Shop, 140
Nuts on Clark, 65

Oak Mill Bakery, 120
Old World Market, 177
Olympic Meat Packers, 23
Olympic Store Fixtures, 53
Organic Food Network, The, 37
"Original" Ferrara, Inc., 142

Pan-Hellenic Pastry Shop, 154
Par Birdie Foods, 193–194
Pars Persian Store, 127, 165–167, 272
Pasta Shoppe, Inc., The, 140
Pastoral, 5
Patel Brothers, 194–195
Paulina Market, 23
Penzey's Spices, 14, 16
People's Market, 63
Peoria Packing, 23–24
Pesche's, 17
Pete's Fresh Market, 96, 262
pick-your-own farms, 37
Pierce Chef Mart, 53
Platt Hill Nursery, 17
Prairie Crossing, 37
Produce World, 152, 261

Racine Bakery, 120
Ramar Supply, 53
Randolph Wine Cellars, 270
Red Apple (Czerwone Jabluszko), 273
Reza's, 127
Ricci & Company, 65
Rich's Bakery, 117
Rich's Deli, 117
Rich's Food and Liquors, 117–118, 271
Richwell Market, 215
Riviera Market, 141
Roberts Fish, 33, 71

Rogers Park Fruit Market, 43, 177
Romanian Kosher Sausage Company, 71
Rubino's Seafood, 33

Sabina's Food Products, Inc., 99
Sam's Wine and Spirits, 5, 270
Santa Maria Lacteos, 96
Savoring Chicago, 78
Schaefer's Wines, Foods and Spirits, 6, 270
Schmeisser's Meats, 24
Schweppe Foodservice Equipment, 54
Sea Ranch, 33, 250
Sea Ranch Market, 250
Sea World Food Market, 33, 227
Sherwyn's Health Food Shop, 64
Shree Mart, 195
Silver Star Food Company, 211–212
Slow Food, 78
Something's Cooking, 47, 54
Song Do Market, 253
Southtown Health Foods, 64
Spice House, The, 15, 16
Spice Merchant and Tea Room, The, 15
St. Anna Bakery & Cafe, 215–216
Stanley's Fruits and Vegetables, 43–44
Sukhadia Sweets, 182, 196
Sunlight Kitchen and Hardware Supplies, 54, 212
(Super) Tony's Finer Foods, 96, 261–262
Superior Nut & Candy Company, 65
Superior Products Mfg. Company, 54–55
Supreme Lobster and Seafood, 33
Sur La Table, 55, 59
Sustainable Agriculture Research and Education (SARE), 37
Swedish Bakery, 127

Tai Nam Market, 227, 272

Tai Wah Grocery, 212
Ted's Fruit Market, 152
Ted's Greenhouse, 17
Ten Ren Tea, 212, 266, 272
Thai Grocery, 227
Thai Pastry, 226, 230
Thaong Xa My A (Broadway Super-
    market), 227–228, 272
Three Sister's Delicatessen, 28, 118
Todd & Holland Tea Merchants,
    267
Tony's Finer Foods, 96–97
Trader Joe's, 6–7, 41
Treasure Island, 7, 28
Trotter's To Go, 7
True World Market, 250
Trung Viet Supermarket, 228

Ukrainian Village Grocery, 118
Uni-Mart (Philippine Plaza), 254

Valli Produce, 262–263
Viet Hoa Plaza, 228–229
Vinh Phat BBQ, 226

Wally's International Market, 28,
    118–119
Westbrook Market, 41, 263
Whole Foods, 8, 28, 41, 64
Whole Grain Fresh Market, 229
Wikstrom's Gourmet Food, 128
Wild Oats Natural Marketplace, 41,
    64
Williams-Sonoma, 55–56
Wilton Homewares, 56
Wilton School of Cake Decorating
    and Confectionary Arts, 76
Wine Discount Center, 270
Wing Cheong Trading, 212
Wing Lee Co., 212–213
Winston's Market, 127
Wok's 'n' Things, 56–57, 213
Wooden Spoon, The, 76
World Fresh Market, 167
World Kitchen, 76

Zam Zam, 195

Equipment and Supplies Index

All-Clad products, 49, 55, 56, 57
appliances
    large, 47, 53, 54
        Gaggenau, 54
        Garland, 54
        Sub-Zero, 54
        Traulsen, 54
        Viking, 47, 54
    small, 49, 51, 57
        Cuisinart, 49, 51
        Hobart, 53
        KitchenAid, 7, 49, 51, 56
aprons, professional, 49, 52
Ateco pastry tips, 52

baking equipment and supplies, 46,
    47, 51, 52, 53, 56, 56, 57, 60
    cake decorating equipment, 56
    sheet pans, 46, 47, 52, 53, 60
    silicon/silicone baking sheets,
        47, 60
    Silpat, 47
baking sheets. See sheet pans
bamboo
    plates, 50
    steamers, 225, 228, 246
    strainers, 246
bar supplies, 52
barrels, winemaking, 49
barstools, 47
baskets, 50
beermaking supplies, 267
Benriner slicers, 208, 252
biscuit cutters, 50
blenders
    hand, 47, 49, 60
    professional, 47
brewing supplies, 267
brushes, pastry, 47

butane torches, 46, 56, 60
butcher block tables, 47, 48
    John Boos, 48

cake decorating equipment, 56. See
    also pastry making supplies
    Wilton, 51, 52, 56
cake pans, 56
Calphalon products, 7, 49, 51, 56,
    57
candy making supplies, 56
canning equipment
    jars, 50
    Weck, 55
cappuccino machines, 56
carts, 47
cast-iron cookware, Le Creuset, 55
catering supplies, 46, 54
cavatelli makers, 49, 139
cedar planks, 31
chafing dishes, 46, 54
chef aprons, 49, 54
chef coats, 49, 54
chef hats, 49, 54
chef pants, 49, 54, 60
chef shoes, 49
chemicals, winemaking, 49
Chinese food cartons, 46
chocolate frothers (molinillos), 86
chopsticks, 208, 246
    Sailor Moon, 250
clay pots, 225, 228, 229, 246
cleavers, 56, 220
coffee brewers, 47
    cappuccino machines, 56
    espresso machines, 139
coffee urns, 47
colanders, 54
    enormous, 46

comales (griddles), 86
cookbooks, 7, 51, 56, 76, 78–79
cookware, 50, 51, 52, 54, 55, 56,
    57, 58, 76, 193, 249, 252
    All-Clad, 49, 55, 56, 57
    Calphalon, 7, 49, 51, 56, 57
    clay pots, 225, 228, 229, 246
    copper, 55, 75
    Emeril's, 51, 52
    garlic pots, Provencal, 55
    Le Creuset, 55
    madeleine pans, 50
    quality at reasonable prices, 46
    racks, 47, 48
    rice cookers, 182, 208, 246
    sauté pans, commercial, 53
    stainless steel, 191
    stock pots, 47, 52, 53
    tarte tatin, copper, 55
copper cookware, 55, 75
corer, eggplant, 251
corks (for winemaking), 49
couscoussières, 55
crocks, 246
    ceramic, 252
cruets, 50
Cuisinart products, 49, 51
cutlery, 51, 53
cutters
    biscuit, 50
    tiny, 52–53
    vegetable, 56
cutting boards, 46, 52
    with feet, 191

deep fryers, 47, 49
    used, 53
dehydrators, 64
dipping (sauce) dishes, 208
dishes. See serving dishes
dishes, Chinese, 209

eggplant corer, 251
electronics. See appliances, small
Emeril's line, 51, 52
escargot plates, 52

espresso machines, 139

fish scalers, 228
fish tweezers, 51
food coloring, paste, 56
food processors, 49
    professional, 47
food storage containers, 46, 55, 60
Forschner knives, 58
French rolling pins, 47
furniture
    bar stools, 47
    restaurant, 52

gadgets, miscellaneous, 46, 50, 51,
    52, 56, 57, 58, 76, 191, 193, 208,
    210, 251, 252. See also specific
    names of gadgets
    restaurant, used, 53
Gaggenau appliances, 54
Garland appliances, 54
garlic pots, Provencal, 55
garnishing tools, 47, 52, 56
glassware, 50, 51, 52
gloves, steel, 47
graters, 46
    Microplane, 51, 56, 60, 75
    nutmeg, 47
    wasabi, 7
green papaya shredder, 227
griddles (comales), 86
grill equipment, 50
grinders, large Italian, 139

hand blenders, 47
Hello Kitty appliances, 249
Henckels knives, 49, 55, 56, 58
Hobart mixers, 53
hookahs, 165, 167

ice shavers, 229
idli steamers, 191
Indian cooking equipment, 191,
    193
    idli steamers, 191
    rolling pins, 191

tava skillets, 191, 193
Irish dishware, 127
Italian equipment, 139

Japanese kidstuff, 250, 252
Japanese knives, 58, 75
Japanese omelet pans (rectangular skillets), 246
John Boos butcher-block tables, 48
juicers, 64

KitchenAid products, 7, 49, 51
    mixers, 56
knife sharpening, 58–59
knives, 49, 52, 55, 56, 58
    cleavers, 56, 220
    Forschner, 58
    Henckels, 49, 55, 56, 58
    Japanese brands, 58, 75
    odd/large sizes, 52
    oyster, 31, 47
    Wüsthof, 7, 49, 56
Kuhn Rikon pressure cookers, 55

ladles, 47, 54, 55
    odd sizes, 46, 54
Latin American cooking equipment, 86
    comales (griddles), 86
    lime squeezers, 86
    molcajetes (lava mortars), 86
    molinillos (chocolate frothers), 86
    tortilla presses, 48, 86
Le Creuset cast-iron cookware, 55
lime squeezers, 86
linens, 50, 56, 127
lunchboxes, Japanese, 150

madeleine pans, 50
mandolines, 7, 47, 48, 54, 56, 60.
    See also V-slicers
marble rolling pins, 47
melon balers, 46, 47
Metro shelving, 48
Microplane graters, 51, 56, 60, 75

mixers
    Hobart, 53
    Kitchen Aid, 56
    professional, 47
molcajetes (mortars), 86
molds, 56
molinillos (chocolate frothers), 86
mortars and pestles, 86, 225, 228, 246, 252
    molcajetes (lava mortars), 86
    stone, 225, 228
    suribachi and surikogi (Japanese), 246
napkin holders, 53
nutmeg graters, 47

oyster knives, 31, 47

paper goods, 46, 49, 51, 52, 53
parchment paper, 47, 49, 60
pasta machines, 49, 56, 139
    cavatelli makers, 49, 139
    ravioli presses, 49
pasta serving dishes, imported, 139
paste food coloring, 56
pastry brushes, 47
pastry making supplies, 47, 52
    Ateco tips, 52
    bags and tips, 47, 52, 53, 56
peelers, 208
peels, pizza, 47, 54
pepper mills, 53
piggy banks, 210
piñatas, 99
pizza peels, 47, 54
pizza stones, 47
plastic goods, 52, 53
popcorn machines, used, 53
porcelain rice bowls, 208
porcelain soup spoons, 250
pot and pan racks, 47, 48
pots and pans. See cookware
prep tables, 47–48, 55
    John Boos, 48
    stainless steel, 47
pressure cookers, 51, 182

pressure cookers (continued)
    Kuhn Rikon, 55
professional equipment, 47, 51
Provencal garlic pots, 55

racks, pot and pan, 47, 48
ramekins, 46, 47, 54
ranges. *See also* appliances, large
    Viking, 47, 54
ravioli presses, 49
rectangular skillets (Japanese
    omelet pans), 246
refrigerators. *See also* appliances
    large glass-door, 53
restaurant dishes, 54
restaurant equipment, used, 52, 53
restaurant equipment and supplies,
    47, 52, 54
    deep fryers, 47, 49, 53
    Viking ranges, 47, 54
restaurant furniture, 52
restaurant-sized goods, 49
rice bowls, porcelain, 208
rice cookers, 182, 208, 246
rolling pins, 47, 52
    French, 47
    Indian, 191
    marble, 47

sauce dishes. *See* dipping dishes
sauce strainers, 47
sauté pans, commercial, 53
scales, 47
serving dishes, 50, 51, 52, 54
    Chinese, 209
    Indian, 191
    Irish, 127
    Korean, 252
    pasta, 139
    Southeast Asian, 228
sheet pans, 46, 47, 52, 53, 60
shelving, 47
    Metro, 48
    wire, 48
shredder, green papaya, 227
silicon/silicone baking sheets, 47,
60
Silpat, 47
silverware. *See* cutlery
skillets
    rectangular, 246
    tava, 191, 193
skimmers, 47, 54, 56
slicers
    Benriner slicers, 208, 252
    mandolines, 7, 47, 48, 54, 56, 60
    professional, 47
    V-slicers, 47, 52, 60, 229
spaetzle maker, 127
spatulas, heat-proof, 46, 47, 52, 53,
    60
spoons, porcelain soup, 250
spoons, wooden, 76
springerle pan, 127
squirt bottles, 47, 60
stainless steel cookware, 191
stainless steel prep tables, 47
steamers, 54, 56
    bamboo, 225, 228, 246
    idli, 191
steel gloves, 47
stock pots, 47, 52, 53
stone mortars, 225, 228
stones, pizza, 47
strainers, 50, 54, 55, 56, 60, 208,
    225
    bamboo, 246
    sauce, 47
    Vittorio, 49, 140
straws, drinking, 46
Sub-Zero appliances, 54
suribachi and surikogi (Japanese
    mortar and pestle), 246
sushi rolling mats, 31, 48, 225, 246,
    249, 252

tables
    butcher block, 47, 48
    stainless steel prep, 47–48
tagines, Moroccan, 55
tamis, 47
tart pans, 52

tarte tatin pans, 55
tava skillets, 191, 193
tea cozies, 265
tea pots, 208, 267
thermometers, 47, 53, 60
toasters
    Hello Kitty, 249
    professional, 47
"to-go" containers, 46
tongs, 47, 53, 54, 60
    wooden, 191
torchietto spremi, 140
tortilla presses, 48, 86
Traulsen appliances, 54

urns, coffee, 47
utensils, cooking. *See* gadgets

V-slicers, 47, 52, 60, 229. *See also*
    mandolines
vegetable cutters, 56
Viking appliances, 47, 54
Vittorio strainers, 49, 140

waffle irons, Hello Kitty, 249
wasabi graters, 7
Weck canning equipment, 55
wedding cake equipment, 56
whisks, 47
Wilton cake decorating equipment,
    51, 52, 56
wine presses, 49, 140
winemaking equipment and sup-
    plies, 49, 267
wire shelving, 48
woks, 50, 54, 56, 209, 225, 228
wooden spoons, 76
Wüsthof knives, 7, 49, 56

Ingredients Index

1,000-year-old eggs. *See* preserved eggs

abalone, dried, 203, 211, 215
achiote, 173. *See also* annatto
  paste, 83
  seeds, 10, 83
ackee, canned, 174
acorn starch, 244
adobo, 83
adzuki (red beans), 206, 244
African ingredients and products, 172–179, 214
agar-agar, 206
aji amarillo paste, 91
ajowan (carom), 10, 184, 196
ajvar (eggplant-pepper dip), 42, 43, 147, 151, 152, 155, 260
akamiso (brown miso), 244
Aleppo pepper, 10, 15
Al-Khyam's best whole wheat pita, 162
Alsatian wine, 127
alfalfa seeds, 62
allspice, 10, 173, 184
  whole, 10
almond
  butter, 62
  cookies, 133, 209
  syrup, 132, 147, 159
almonds, 65, 147
  Jordan (candy-coated), 148, 160
  marcona, 2, 7
alum, 15
amaranth, 62, 183, 203, 221
  flour, 64
amardine (dried apricot sheets), 160, 167
amaretti, 133
amaretto, 133
amchoor (mango powder), 159, 184

ammonium carbonate. *See* baker's ammonia
Anaheim peppers, 83
American sturgeon caviar, 3
anardana (pomegranate seeds), 184
ancho peppers, 83, 93, 95, 100
  powdered, 89
anchovies, 130, 139, 263
  dried, 203, 206, 221, 241
  salt-packed, 263
  tinned, 130
  white, 7
angelica root, 159, 211
annatto, 173, 244. *See also* achiote
anise (Thai) basil, 222, 262
anise seed (saunf), 184
antipasti, 139
apple slices, 116
apricot, dried sheets. *See* amardine
apricots, 146
  dried, 167. *See also* amardine
Arabian ingredients and products, 164. *See also* Middle Eastern products and ingredients
Aranchiata, 133
arbol peppers, 83
Arborio rice, 132, 135, 139, 140, 143
arepas, 94
Argentinian ingredients and products, 91. *See also* Latin American ingredients and products
Armenian ingredients and products, 114, 163. *See also* Middle Eastern ingredients and products
aronia jam, 109, 114
artichoke
  paste, 132
  tapenade, 2
artichokes, baby, 42, 132, 138, 141, 143
arugula, 132

asafoetida, powdered (hing), 184
Asiago, 133, 136
Asian duck sauce, 69
Asian ingredients and products, 4,
     43, 64, 138, 151, 226, 259, 260,
     261, 262, 263. *See also* specific
     ethnicities
asparagus beans. *See* long beans
Assyrian ingredients and products,
     165. *See also* Middle Eastern in-
     gredients and products
atchara (pickled papaya), 254
atsuage (fried tofu), 244
atta flour, 186, 194, 195
attieké (couscous de manioc). *See*
     cassava couscous
avocado oil, 62
avocados, 82

baby vegetables, 42, 132, 138, 141,
     143, 203
bacalao. *See* cod, dried
baccalà. *See* cod, dried
bacon, 108, 254
     Filipino (tocino), 254
     house-cured/smoked, 116, 124
     pancetta, 3, 130
     Polish, 259, 273
bacon buns, 111
bagels, 69
baharat, 159
bai toey. *See* pandanus
baitop shell, canned, 244
bajri (Indian millet flour), 186
baka (fish), 254
baker's ammonia (ammonium car-
     bonate), 15, 147
bakery goods. *See also* breads; cook-
     ies; specific types
     Bennison's (Evanston), 5
     Caribbean, 178
     Chinese, 215–216
     Eastern European, 109, 111, 114,
          116, 118, 120, 261
     Greek, 148, 154
     Filipino, 254

Indian sweets, 188, 196
Italian, 142, 261
Japanese, 250, 272
kosher, 69, 71
Mexican sweets, 99, 273
Middle Eastern, 148, 154, 163,
     165
Southeast Asian, 226, 227, 229
baking chocolate, 8
baking supplies, 15
baklava, 148, 154
Balkan ingredients and products,
     42, 43, 146–155, 162, 261, 272.
     See also Eastern European ingre-
     dients and products
balsamic vinegars, 2, 4, 5, 132, 134,
     136, 138, 139, 143
balti (Indian cooking sauce), 185
Baltic Bakery products, 109, 120
bamboo shoots, fresh, 214, 229
banana
     blossoms, 183
     buds, 223
     flowers, 221, 242, 254
     leaves, frozen, 174
     sauce, 229, 243, 254, 255
bananas, guinea, 262
bangers (sausages), 127
Bangladeshi ingredients and prod-
     ucts, 191. *See also* Indian ingredi-
     ents and products
barbacoa, 20, 88, 89, 100
barfi (Indian fudge), 188, 196
barley, 62, 109, 117, 118, 151
     flour, 93
     pressed, 244
basil, 10, 16, 17, 130, 132, 134,
     135, 143, 228
     holy, 222
     plants, 139
     Thai (anise), 222, 262
basmati rice, 62, 147, 159, 186,
     194, 199
     brown, 186
     Dehraduni, 186
     Patna, 186

bass, live, 259
basturma, 146, 149, 158, 261
batatas (Cuban sweet potatoes). *See* boniato
bay leaf, Indonesian (salam leaf), 184
Bayless, Rick, products, 5. *See also* Frontera products
bean
    cakes, 244
    curd. *See* tofu
    flour, 93
    sauce, 205
    sprouts, 214, 216
    thread (cellophane) noodles, 205, 206, 217, 243
beans, 85, 89, 91, 92
    adzuki (red), 206, 244
    black, 85
        salted (fermented), 205, 207, 217
    borlotti, 132
    brown, 147, 160
    canary, 85
    cannellini, 132
    coba, 85
    fava (broad), 85, 132, 147, 151, 160, 162, 164
    green, French-cut, 225
    guajes, 83, 92, 94, 97
    habas. *See* fava
    kidney, 85
    limas, giant (gigandes), 147
    long, 183, 204, 211, 222, 242, 254, 263
    lupini, 132
    mung, 185, 207
    oil, 177
    pink, 85
    pinto, 85
    refried, 85
    Swedish brown, 128
    tuvar, 184, 195
    valor, 184, 195
    white, 85
    wing, 222

beech mushrooms, 249
beef, 21, 23, 112, 190, 221, 241, 262. *See also* cow feet
    aged, in-house, 5, 8, 22, 23, 24
    barbacoa, 20, 88, 89, 100
    basturma, 146, 149, 158, 261
    blood, 221, 254
    bresaola, 130
    bulgogi, 241
    calf liver, 108
    caul fat, 21
    choice grade, 88, 259, 263
    corned, 127
    flank steak, 91, 241
    flanken, 72
    ground, 23
    kosher cuts, 71
    liver, 23, 71, 221
    ribs, 241
    round, 23
    short ribs, 23
    skirt steak, 20, 23
    smoked, 151
    sukiyaki, 241
    t-bones, 23
    tendons, 221, 241
    tongue, 82
    tripe, 221
    veal, 20, 130, 263
    whole loin, 21
beer. *See also* brewing supplies
    Eastern European, 116, 117
    German, 127
    Latin American, 94
    Lithuanian, 117, 118, 263
    Polish, 116, 118, 263, 273
beet flour, 251
beets, 48, 72, 112, 121
Bel Paese, 133
Bella Romana products, 138
beltfish, 241
beluga lentils, 64
bergamot jam, 148
besan (Indian gram/chickpea flour), 186, 195
betel leaves (paan leaves), 183

bibinka (rice cake mix), 229
bilberry jam, 263
biodynamic farming, 37
bird's nest, 202, 206
bird's nest drink, 207, 214
biscotti, 133
bitter melon (karela), 42, 151, 183, 203, 221, 242, 254, 260, 262
bitter orange preserves, 148, 160
bitter oranges, 177
bitterleaf, 177
black
  beans, 85
    salted (fermented), 205, 207, 217
  cumin. *See* kala jeera
  currant
    Georgian vodka, 114
    juice, boxed, 114
    syrup, 110
  fungus (tree fungus). *See* cloud ear fungus
  lentils (urad dal), 185
  moss. *See* hair vegetable
  mushrooms, dried, 207
  onion seed. *See* charnuska
  rice, 205
  salt (kala namak), 13, 184
  sesame seeds, 206
  vinegar (Chinkiang), 205, 222
Black Forest ham, 126
blackberry jam, 114
blackstrap molasses, 62
blinis (mix for), 120
blintzes, 114
blood, beef, 221, 254
blood oranges, 8
blood sausage, 126
blue cornmeal, 62
blueberries, wild, dried, 6
blueberry pierogis, 112
bocconcini, 134
bok choy, 203, 214, 221, 260, 261, 262
baby bok choy, 203
boletus. *See* porcini, dried

bologna, veal, 126
bones, 108, 241
boniato (batatas, Cuban sweet potatoes), 83, 91, 102, 104, 172, 179, 261
bonito flakes. *See* katsuobushi
boondi, 195
borage, 16
borlotti beans, 132
borscht, 112, 117, 118
bottle gourds, 183, 203
bouillon cubes, 83
boxed fruit drinks, 110, 114, 151, 214
brains, veal, 263
bratwurst, 24
  Sheboygan, 126
  veal, 126
Brazilian ingredients and products, 89, 174, 263. *See also* Latin American ingredients and products
bread crumbs, Japanese (panko), 223, 228, 244, 250, 255
bread mixes, 93
breadfruit, 88, 172, 176
breads. *See also* bakery goods; flours
  bacon buns, 111
  Baltic Bakery, 109, 120
  chapatti, 185, 191
  Eastern European, 116, 117, 120, 124, 151, 258, 261
  focaccia, 132
  French, 229
  Georgian, 196, 261
  hardo, 178
  Indian, 185, 186, 191
  injera, 176
  Irish soda, 127
  Italian, 138, 142, 258, 261
  lavosh, 148, 160
  Lithuanian, 109, 120
  Middle Eastern flatbreads, 152, 164, 258
  naan, 185, 191
  pita, 148, 151, 152, 158, 160, 162, 164, 165, 168, 169, 191

breads *(continued)*
  Polish, 118, 119, 120, 261
  pumpernickel, 109
  rye, 109, 111, 120, 152
  Scandinavian flatbreads, 127,
    128
  Starapolski, 119
  sourdough, 109, 111
  Vietnamese, 229
  whole wheat, 142, 162
bresaola (cured raw beef), 130
brewing supplies, 267
broad beans. *See* fava beans
broccoli, 203
broccoli raab (rapini), 132, 136, 143
brown
  beans, 147, 160
    Swedish, 128
  lentils, 147, 159
  miso. *See* akamiso
  rice, 62, 223
    basmati, 186
    glutinous, 223
    jasmine, 223
  rice vinegar, 62, 243
  sugar, 86, 86, 173
bubble teas, 266
buckwheat, 117, 151
  flour, 64
  groats. *See* kasha
  noodles. *See* naengmyon; soba
buffalo, 21
buffalo milk mozzarella, 133
bulgogi beef, 241
bulgogi sauce, 243, 251
bulgur wheat, 147, 151, 159, 162,
    164, 165, 169, 190, 263
  dark, 162
  pilaf, 149
bulk items
  candy, 15, 65, 99, 215, 259
  chocolate, 8
  grains, 63, 64, 162, 164
  herbs, dried, 14–15
  lentils, 15
  nuts, 15, 63, 65, 162, 163, 167,

    192, 259
  seeds, 167
  snack mixes, 15, 163, 192, 259
  spices, 14–15,
  teas, 15, 164
bull penis, 21
burdock (gobo), 212, 242, 249, 260
  pickled, 249
butcher shops/counters, 4, 5, 7, 8,
    20, 21–24, 42, 63, 88, 91, 92, 94,
    112, 114, 116, 117, 151, 162,
    167, 176, 190, 193, 209, 210,
    214, 226, 229, 253, 254, 260,
    261, 262, 272. *See also* meats
  halal/zabiha, 68, 158, 162, 165,
    183, 190, 193
  kosher, 68, 69, 71
butter
  European (high-fat), 2, 5, 110,
    117, 124, 259
  ghee (Indian clarified), 186, 199,
    260
  Polish, 110
butterfish (pomfret), 183, 191, 220,
    241, 254

cabbage, 123, 151, 203. *See also*
    kimchee; sauerkraut
caciocavallo, 133
cactus
  fruit (tuna), 42, 42, 83, 259, 261,
    262
  paddles (nopales), 83, 97, 177
cajeta, 86, 96
calabaza, 83, 90
calamansi, 263
calamari. *See* squid
calf liver, 108
callaloo, 174
calzones, 132
Campari, 133
canary beans, 85
candy. *See also* chocolate; marsh-
    mallows
  Asian, 210, 215, 230, 252
  bulk, 15, 65, 99, 215, 259

chocolate-covered cherries in booze, 110
chocolate-covered coffee beans, 65
European, 110, 114, 120, 127, 259, 263
fish and shrimp, 215
ginger, 8, 207
hard, 110
Irish, 127
Jordan almonds, 148, 160
maltose-sesame, 252
Mexican, 99
rice (edible wrappers), 207
sesame, 160, 252
tamarind, 99
cane sugar, 173
cane syrup/juice, 174
cane vinegar, 243, 255
canela (Mexican/soft-stick cinnamon), 83, 173
canned coffee/tea drinks, 207, 214, 225, 245, 266
canned goods,
Chinese, 209, 210, 212, 213
Greek, 149, 263
Indian/Pakistani, 195, 195, 263
Italian, 137, 138, 139, 140, 141
kosher, 70, 71
Latin American, 91, 93
Middle Eastern, 43, 162, 164, 263
restaurant sizes, 49
Southeast Asian, 223, 226
cannellini beans, 132
cannoli shells, 132
cannolis, 142
Cantonese egg noodles. See mein
caper berries, 2, 132, 147
capers, 2, 132, 147
capons, 259
carambola (star fruit), 183
dried, 215
caramel
corn, 65
sauces

cajeta, 86, 96
dulce de leche, 86, 91
caraway, 184
cardamom, 10, 12, 147, 159, 182, 189, 194, 199
black, 184
green, 10, 184
cardi. See cardoons
cardoons (cardi), 132, 261
Caribbean ingredients and products, 172–179
Carnaroli rice, 132, 139
carnitas, 20, 82, 88, 89, 94, 96, 97, 100, 262, 273
carob
chips, 62
molasses, 147, 160, 167
carom. See ajowan
carrot
flour, 251
juice, boxed, 110
carrots, pickled, 249
cashew butter, 62
cashews, 147, 160, 182
cassareep (concentrated cassava juice), 173, 177
cassava. See yucca
cassava
couscous (attiéké, couscous de manioc), 174
flour. See gari
meal, 174, 229
cassia. See cinnamon
cassia leaf, 184
catfish, live, 215, 259
caul fat, 21
cauliflower, 189
caviar, 2, 3, 28, 30, 31, 34, 118, 146, 241
citron, 34
American sturgeon, 3
cod, smoked, 146
Collins Caviar, 3, 30, 34
lumpfish, 34
pollack, 241
salmon, 3, 28, 34, 241

caviar (continued)
  sea urchin (uni), 220, 241
  smoked golden, 34
  sturgeon
    American, 3
    Hackelback, 34
  taramasalata, 146
  tobikko (flying fish roe), 3, 34, 241, 249
  wasabi, 34
  whitefish, 3, 28, 34
cayenne, 10
ceci beans. *See* chickpeas
celery seed, 184
cellophane noodles. *See* bean thread noodles
Central American ingredients and products, 91, 93, 94, 262. *See also* Latin American ingredients and products
cèpes. *See* porcini, dried
cereals. *See* grains
chaat masala, 185, 188, 199
chamomile, 83, 262
  tea, 110
champagne, 268
cham-polksi, 110
channa dal, 185, 188, 195
chanterelles, 7, 42
  pickled, 109
chapatti, 185, 191
char siu sauce (barbecue paste), 205
chard (Swiss chard), 37, 136, 261
charnuska (nigella, kalonji, black onion seed), 10, 14, 184, 189
chayotes (christophenes, mirli-tons), 42, 83, 172
  spiny (Mexican), 42, 259, 262
cheese, 2, 3, 4, 5, 43, 89, 91, 92, 93, 126, 127, 133, 137, 138, 191, 268, 270
  artisanal, 2, 4, 5, 7
  Asiago, 133, 136
  Balkan, 148, 162
  Bel Paese, 133
  caciocavallo, 133

farmer's cheese, 109–110, 114, 116, 118, 119, 122, 124, 138, 153
feta, 149, 153, 155, 158, 160, 191
Fontina, 133
Gorgonzola, 133
gouda, 127
Grana Padano, 133
Greek, 148
halloumi, 148, 152, 155
havarti, 127
Italian, 133, 137, 139
kashkaval, 148, 155
kasseri, 148, 149, 152, 155, 160
kefalotiri, 148
kosher, 70, 71
Limburger, 126
Manchego, 137
manouri, 148
mascarpone, 133
Mexican, 86, 91, 92, 93, 96. *See also* queso
Middle Eastern, 162, 163, 164, 261
montasio, 131, 133
mozzarella, 133, 137, 139, 143
myzithra, 148
paneer, 187, 197
Parmesan, 37, 136
  Reggiano, 133, 135, 139, 140, 143, 259
Pecorino Romano, 133
Polish, 110
quark (glumse), 126
ricotta, 133, 137, 139, 153
scamorza, 133
Scandinavian, 110
Stracchino, 133
sustainable agriculture, 36
Taleggio, 133
touloum, 160
Turkish, 149
cheese spreads, 118
chefs'/restaurants' lines of prod-ucts, 7
  Bayless, Rick/Frontera, 3, 4, 5

Flay, Bobby, 5
Trotter, Charlie, 7
Vong, 4, 5
cherimoya, 42, 83
cherry
  boxed juice, 110, 114
  syrup (morello), 110
chestnut flour, 64, 132
chestnuts, 132
  canned, 138
  dried, 206
Chicago ethnic spice blends, 15
chicharrónes (fried pork skins), 82,
  86, 93, 95, 96, 172
chicken, 21, 25, 190, 203, 211, 215,
  221, 262
  barbecued, 203, 226
  breasts, seasoned, 22
  breasts, stuffed with kishke, 71
  feet, 82, 203, 215, 221, 259
  gizzards, 108, 203, 221
  grain raised without antibiotics
    or hormones, 22
  kosher, 68, 69, 71
  live, 25
  smoked, 108
  soy-cooked, 203, 226
  whole, 108, 203
chickpeas (ceci beans), 160, 162,
  165, 169
  Jordan (candy-coated), 160
  channa dal, 185, 188
  fresh, 83, 94, 183
  flour, 132, 147, 159, 259
    besan, 186, 195
chicory, 132
chilaca peppers, 95
chile con limón, 83
chile paste, yellow (aji amarillo), 91
chile-bean paste, 216, 253
chile-garlic paste/sauce, 217, 222,
  224, 247. See also Sriracha
chiles, chile peppers, 10, 83, 87, 89,
  90, 92, 93, 94, 95, 96, 100, 172,
  184, 231. See also specific types
  dried, 82, 83, 89, 92, 94, 95, 100,

184, 230
Chinese
  arrowhead. See tsu goo
  broccoli. See gai lan
  buns, 213, 215, 216
  cabbage. See napa
  celery. See kun choy
  dumplings, 211, 222
  five-spice powder, 40, 205, 210,
    217
  red dates (jujube). See zizyphus
Chinese ingredients and products,
  202–217, 226, 227, 228, 229,
  272. See also Asian ingredients
  and products
Chinkiang. See black vinegar
Chino, 133
chipotle peppers
  in adobo, 85
  brown (mecos), 83, 95, 100
  red (moritas, colorados), 83, 95,
    100
chipotle powder, 10
chips (plantain, taro, yucca), 93,
  192
chitterlings, 23
chivda (Indian puffed rice), 188
chive flowers, 221, 262
chives, 16
  flowering, 203, 260
  yellow, 203
chocolate
  baking, 8
  Belgian, 7
  bulk, 8
  covered cherries in booze, 110
  covered coffee beans, 65
  European, 127
  high cocoa content, 2
  high-fat Dutch cocoa, 8
  kefir, 118
  Mexican, 86, 100
chocolate sauce, restaurant size, 52
chocolate-covered items, 8, 65, 100
choice-grade meats, 20, 21, 22, 23,
  82, 88, 89, 259, 263

chorizo (sausage), 24, 82, 89
  homemade on premises, 259, 260
chow fun. *See* rice noodles, fresh
chow mein noodles, 210
choy sum (flowering cabbage), 203
christophenes (mirlitons). *See* chayotes
chrysanthemum leaves (shungiko), 242, 249
chubs, smoked, 32
chufas (tiger nuts, earth chestnuts), 85, 177
chuka soba. *See* ramen noodles
chutneys, 187, 191, 192, 193, 194, 195, 199
cilantro/coriander, 187, 193, 199
  eggplant, 187
  green mango (kuchela), 173
  mango, 187
  mint, 187, 199
cider vinegar, 62
cilantro, 17, 83, 84, 87, 93, 224, 231, 262
  chutney, 187, 193, 199
  Vietnamese, 222
cinnamon (cassia), 10, 12, 14, 182, 184, 194
cinnamon (Mexican/soft-stick). *See* canela
cinnamon punch, 245
citric acid, 15, 49, 108, 147, 159
citrus olive oil, 4, 138
clam meat, 241
clams, 32, 82, 130, 202, 220, 240, 241
  live, 33, 215, 228, 229
  surf, 249
  for sushi, 241, 249
cloud ear (black, tree) fungus, 206
cloves, 184
coba beans, 85
cockerel, tinned, 93
coconut
  buns (Chinese), 216
  cakes (totoes), 178

jam, 91, 174
milk, 232, 244
shredded, frozen, 151, 232, 244
soda (Coco Rico), 214
vinegar, 215, 222
  nipa sap, 243
coconuts, 179
green, 83, 177
young, 42, 184, 191, 222
cocoyam. *See* malanga
cod, 82
  dried (bacalao, baccalà), 82, 130. *See also* lutefisk
  intestines, 244
  paste, 127, 128
  roe, smoked, 146
  salt, 146
coffee, 133, 152, 266
  espresso beans, 133, 266
  extract, 15
  French Market style, 266
  house-roasted, 266
  South American, 266
  Turkish, 149
coffee beans, chocolate-covered, 65
coffee drinks, canned, 225, 266
coffee extract, 15
coffee, flavored, 12
cognac, 300-year-old, 3
cold cuts, homemade, 119. *See also* deli meats
Collins Caviar, 3, 30, 34
colorados. *See* chipotle peppers, red
conch, frozen, 172
condiments, 50. *See also* mustards; oils; salsas; sauces; vinegars
  African, 177
  Asian, 252
  Caribbean, 176, 177
  gourmet, 2, 3, 4
  Middle Eastern, 164
  restaurant size, 54
congee, 216
coo coo, 173
cookies
  almond, 133, 209

European, 110, 120
fortune, 209
Greek butter (kouambeithes), 154
Indian cumin, 196
Italian, 133, 142, 262, 263
kolackys, 110, 120
pizzelle, 133
Poky, 225, 245
coriander, 166, 184, 197
corn
    dried, 91
    flour, 174, 186
    purple, 91
    grits, 173, 174
    ground toasted, 91
    hominy, 85, 100
    husks, 85, 90, 98
    mote blanco, 85
    polenta, 130, 132, 136, 143, 173
    Peruvian popping, 91
    smut. *See* huitlachoche
corned beef, 127
cornichons, 2, 3
cornmeal, 174, 179
    blue, 62
    masa (for tamales, tortillas), 91, 92, 97, 99, 100
cornstarch, noodles, 233
couscous, 147, 151, 159, 165, 167, 169
cassava (attieké, de manioc), 174
    Israeli, 147, 159
    whole wheat, 64
cow feet, 82, 89, 93, 167, 172, 176, 241
crab
    cakes, 30, 31
    legs, 203, 220
    meat, 203, 220, 231, 241
    paste, 222
crabs, 228
    blue, 202, 208
    Dungeness, 202
    live, 202, 208, 209, 212, 215, 215, 220, 240, 259

softshell, fresh, 28
cracked wheat, 151, 159, 190, 259
cream of tartar, 198
crema (Mexican sour cream), 86, 96
crème fraîche, 2, 5
criolla (Jamaican) sauces, 177
criolla seasonings, 173
croaker, 241
Croatian wine, 261
Crodino, 133
crostini, 133
crullers, 120
crushed pear drink, 245
Cuban ingredients and products, 93. *See also* Caribbean; Latin American ingredients and products
Cuban sweet potatoes (batatas). *See* boniato
cucumbers, pickled wild, 162
cucumbers, stuffed, kimchee, 252
culantro, 262
cultured milk, 110
cumin, 166, 168, 184, 197
    cookies (Indian), 196
    flavoring water, 167
    seed, 189
cured meats, 130. *See also* deli meats
    basturma, 146, 149, 158, 261
    bresaola, 130
    pancetta, 3, 130
    pastrami, 69
    prosciutto, 2, 4, 130, 137, 138, 139, 143
    soprasetta, 3
currant
    boxed drink, 110
    syrup, 110
curry leaves, 183
curry pastes
    Indian, 182, 184
    Thai, 4, 232
curry powder, West Indian, 173, 176
cush-cush yams (yampi), 260

custard
  buns (Chinese), 216
  wrapped in phyllo, 154
cuttlefish, 220, 259
  dried, 241
Cynar, 138

Dahlia Exotic Flavoring Pastes, 3
daikon (mooli), 42, 43, 167, 183,
    203, 213, 221, 242, 261
  pickled, 223, 244, 249
  kimchee, 252
dairy products, 5, 96, 117, 133,
    148, 160, 259. *See also* specific
    types
  organic, 63
  kosher, 70
dals, 185, 191, 192, 193, 194, 195.
    See also beans; lentils; specific
    types
dandelion, 132, 167, 261
Danish smoked salt, 13
dasheen (eddo). *See* taro
dashi (soup) mix, 244
date
  honey, 148, 160
  molasses, 160, 162
dates, 146, 158, 169
  fresh, 260
decorating sprinkles and sugars, 15
deer
  antlers, dried, 211
  meat. *See* venison
Dehraduni basmati rice, 186
deli. *See* prepared foods
deli meats, 3, 24, 69, 108, 111, 126,
    130, 137, 140, 141, 229, 268. *See
    also* cured meats
delicata (sweet potato) squash, 210
dende (palm oil), 174, 177, 179
denjang. *See* soybean paste
Dijon mustard, 37
dill, 42, 108, 167
  seed, 184
diples, 154
dokra (Indian besan and rice flour

mix) flour, 186, 195
dragon fruit (pithaya), 221, 227,
    228
  juice, boxed, 114
dried fruit. *See* fruit, dried
dried vegetables. *See* vegetables,
    dried
dry-aged meats, in-house, 5, 8, 22,
    23, 24
duck, 23, 25, 112, 203, 211
  barbecued, 203, 212, 215, 226
  breasts, 7, 23
  dried (flattened), 203
  kosher, 71
  live, 25
  mock (wheat gluten), 206
  Peking, 203
  pressed, 215
  roasted, 226
  sauce, 69
  smoked, 7
dulce de leche, 86, 91
Dungeness crab, 202
durian, 203, 215, 221, 228, 260
  jelly, 207

earth chestnuts (tiger nuts). *See*
    chufas
Eastern European ingredients and
    products, 42, 43, 108–124, 151,
    258, 263. *See also* Balkan ingredi-
    ents and products; specific eth-
    nicities
edamame (soybeans), 225, 242
eddo. *See* taro
eel, 202, 220, 241
  dried, 221
  grilled for sushi (unagi), 249
  live, 259
egg roll wrappers, 211
egg whites, powdered, 62
eggplant, 146, 151
  Asian, 204, 242
  chutney, 187
  exotic varieties, 36, 41, 43
  pickled, 249

eggplant dips. *See* ajvar; ikra
eggs
    fresh, 22, 23, 25
    red, preserved, 244
    organic, 37
    preserved (1,000-year-old) eggs,
      202, 223
    quail, 203, 221
egusi (squash) seeds, 173
Egyptian ingredients and products,
    160, 163. *See also* Middle Eastern
    ingredients and products
empanada
    dough, frozen, 89
    wraps, 85, 97
empanadas, 91
Empire kosher poultry products,
    69, 71
enoki, 204, 242, 249
epazote, 10, 83, 91, 92, 94, 96, 97,
    177, 259
escabèche sauce, 177
escarole, 132, 138, 263
espresso beans, 133, 266
Ethiopian ingredients and prod-
    ucts, 176. *See also* African ingre-
    dients and products
extracts, 15

fagara. *See* Szechuan pepper
falafel mix, 160
farinha. *See* gari
farmer's cheese, 109–110, 114, 116,
    118, 119, 122, 124, 138, 153
farmers markets, 36, 41
farofa, 173
farro. *See* spelt
fava (broad) beans (habas), 85, 132,
    147, 151, 160, 162, 164
    Egyptian (foule mudammas),
      160
    spicy, 86
fava flour, 91
fennel (finocchio), 132
fennel pollen, 15
fennel seed, 184, 189

fenugreek (methi), 10, 147, 159,
    167, 183, 184, 191, 195, 260,
    262, 263
    seed, 189
feta, 149, 153, 155, 158, 160, 191
fiddlehead ferns, 8
fig
    preserves, 148, 151, 160
    trees, 139
figs, 138, 147, 158
filé (gumbo filé, sassafras), 10, 173
Filipino ingredients and products,
    215, 223, 226, 227, 228, 229,
    240–244, 254–256, 260, 263. *See
    also* Asian; Southeast Asian in-
    gredients and products
Filipino noodles. *See* pancit
filo. *See* phyllo
finocchio. *See* fennel
fish, 28–34, 63, 130, 137, 146, 183,
    191, 202, 208, 209, 210, 214,
    226, 227, 228, 240, 249, 251,
    253, 262, 263, 272. *See also*
    seafood
    abalone, 203, 211, 215
    anchovies, 7, 130, 139, 203, 206,
      221, 241, 263
    baka, 254
    bass, 259
    beltfish, 241
    butterfish (pomfret), 183, 191,
      220, 241, 254
    catfish, 215, 259
    chubs, 32
    cockerel, 93
    cod, 82, 130, 146, 244
    croaker, 241
    flounder, 202, 228, 240
    gefilte, 69, 70
    grouper, 32
    hasa-hasa, 254
    herring, 108, 116, 126
    hilsa, 183, 191
    kingfish (surmai), 183, 191, 220
    mackerel, 202, 220, 221, 240,
      263

fish (continued)
  smoked and seasoned, 220
  milkfish, 241
  monkfish, 28, 31, 32
  mudfish, 205
  poa, 191
  pollack, 241
  rex sole, 241
  ruhu, 183, 191
  sable, 32
  salmon, 32, 69, 108, 122, 151
  sand dab, 241
  sap-sap, 254
  sardines, 114, 130, 220, 241
  sea bass, 82, 220
  silverfish, 254
  skate, 31, 32, 220, 241, 262
  snapper, 82
  sole, 28, 220
  sprats, 114
  sturgeon, 32
  sushi/sashimi, 4, 31, 33, 241,
    249, 250, 272,
  tilapia, 151, 202, 215, 228, 241,
    259
  tilefish, 220, 241
  trout, 28, 108
  tuna, 241, 244, 261
  whitefish, 28, 32, 108
fish balls, 211, 263
fish, canned/tinned/jarred, 93, 114,
  118, 130
fish, dried, 172, 176, 177, 206, 211,
  212, 220, 241
  abalone, 203, 211, 215
  anchovies, 203, 206, 221, 241
  cod (bacalao, baccalà), 82, 130.
    See also lutefisk
  mackerel, 221
  sardines, 241
  tilefish, 241
fish, filleted to order, 5, 32
fish, fresh, 5, 8, 28–34, 97, 211,
  220, 227, 232, 240, 250, 254,
  259, 260
fish, fried to order, 254

fish, ground (for gefilte fish), 69
fish, kosher, 31, 33, 69, 71
fish lips, 202
  dried, 203
fish, live, 33, 208, 209, 212, 213,
  214, 215, 220, 228, 229, 259
fish maw (air bladder), dried, 203
fish pastes, 222. See also specific
  types
fish, pickled, 116, 244
fish sauce, 205, 214, 222, 224, 225,
  226, 229, 231, 232, 243
fish, seasoned and breaded, 4
fish and shrimp candies, 215
fish, smoked, 2, 28, 114, 118, 120,
  124, 172, 176, 220
  chubs, 32
  in-house, 5
  mackerel, 220
  sable, 32
  salmon, 32, 108, 122, 151
    lox, 69
  sardines, 220
  sturgeon, 32
  trout, 108
  whitefish, 32, 108
  your own catch, 32
fish, whole on ice, 5, 30, 32, 151,
  220, 254
five spice powder. See Chinese five-
  spice powder
flank steak, 91, 241
flanken, 72
flat cabbage (tatsoi). See tai goo
  choy
flatbreads
  Indian, 185, 191
  Middle Eastern, 152, 164, 258.
    See also pita
  Scandinavian, 127, 128
flattened rice (poha), 186
flavoring pastes, 3
flavoring waters, 151, 167
  cumin, 167
  orange blossom, 147, 159, 167,
    187

peppermint, 167
rose, 147, 151, 158, 159, 167, 187, 194, 223
sweetbrier, 167
flax seed, 62
Flay, Bobby, products, 5
Fleur de Sel, 5, 12, 13
flounder, 202, 228, 240
flours, 64, 93, 182, 222, 251
"OO" very hard, 132
amaranth, 64
atta, 186, 194, 195
bajri, 186
barley, 93
bean, 93
beet, 251
besan, 186, 195
buckwheat, 64
carrot, 251
chestnut, 64, 132
chickpea (ceci), 132, 147, 159, 259
corn, 174, 186
purple, 91
cornmeal, 62, 174, 179
dokra, 186, 195
fava, 91
fu fu, 174, 177
gari (cassava), 173, 174, 177
Indian, 185, 186, 195
manioc (cassava), 89, 91, 93, 173
masa harina, 85, 97, 99
millet, 186
mugwort, 244
oat, 64
pea, 93
plantain, 86
potato starch, 205
raggi, 186
rice 174, 186, 205, 223, 243
glutinous, 205, 223, 243
rye, 64
semolina (pasta), 132, 186
tapioca, 64, 91, 206, 223
water chestnut, 206
wheat, 64

peeled, 91
starch, non glutinous, 206
flowering
cabbage. *See* choy sum
chives, 203, 260
flying fish roe. *See* tobikko
focacia, 132
foie gras, 5, 7, 21, 22
Hudson Valley, 22
Fontina, 133
food colors, paste, 15
Foodstuffs frozen appetizers, 4
forbidden rice, 7
fortune cookies, 209
foule mudammas (Egyptian fava beans), 160
freekah, 159
French ingredients and products. *See* specific items
fritter mixes, 93
frogs, live, 208
Frontera products, 3, 4. *See also* Bayless, Rick
fructose, 15, 62
fruit and vegetable drinks, boxed, 110, 114, 151, 214
fruit, by the case, 251
fruit, dried, 6, 65, 158, 165
apricots, 167
blueberries, wild, 6
carambola (star fruit), 215
guava, 215, 229
kumquats, 215
lemons, 147, 159
limes, 147, 159
persimmons, 207
fruit fillings, 113, 124
fruit pastes, 93
fruit syrups, 93, 110, 114, 124
Italian, 133
fu fu, 173
flour, 174, 177
fudge, Indian. *See* barfi
furikake, 242, 250, 255
fuzzy melon/squash, 221, 229, 262

gai choy (mustard cabbage), 204, 221
gai lan (Chinese broccoli), 204, 213, 217, 221, 260
galangal, 10, 221, 229
galletas, 88
game, 21, 23, 24, 25. *See also* buffalo; duck; geese; ostrich; quail; rabbit; venison; wild boar
gandules. *See* pigeon peas
garam masala, 185, 189, 197
garbanzos. *See* chickpeas
gardiniera, 140
gari (cassava flour, farinha), 173, 174, 177
garlic, 228, 252
  pickled, 244, 253
garlic-ginger paste, 184, 188, 189, 204
gau ma (slippery vegetable, Vietnamese spinach), 205, 222
geese, 112, 203, 211
gefilte fish, 69, 70
gelatin, kosher, 69, 70
Georgian breads, 196, 261
German ingredients and products, 23, 24, 126–127
Ghana yams, 173, 176
ghee (Indian clarified butter), 186, 199, 260
gigandes (giant limas), 147, 150, 151, 155, 190
ginger, 10, 87, 197, 204, 209, 213, 222, 247
  buds. *See* myoga
  candy, 207
  chocolate covered, 8
  crystallized, 10, 40, 206, 225
  pickled, 244
  stem, 222
  young, 191, 204, 222
ginkgo nuts, 206, 242
ginseng, 215, 244
glumse. *See* quark
glutinous (sticky) rice, 205, 223
  flour, 205, 223, 243

goat, 21, 22, 158, 183, 261
  feet, 172
    smoked, 176
  fresh, 172, 262
  smoked, 172
gobo. *See* burdock
gochujang (hot pepper paste), 243, 251
gold sheets, edible (varak), 187
goose, 25, 259
  fresh, 25
  smoked, 24
gooseberry jam, 109
Gorgonzola, 133
gouda, 127
gourmet foods, 2–8
grains, 7, 62, 64, 108, 112, 114, 151, 162, 164, 182, 251. *See also* barley; buckwheat; corn; flours; kamut; millet; oats; quinoa; rice; rye; spelt; teff; wheat
  bulk, 63, 64, 162, 164
grains of paradise, 10
Grana Padano, 133
grape
  leaves, 43, 147, 155, 160, 162, 164, 190, 193, 263
  molasses/syrup, 147, 150, 263
  vinegar, 243
grapefruit soda (Ting), 178, 214
grapeseed oil, 2, 139
grass jelly drink, 207
Greek ingredients and products, 42, 43, 146–155, 163, 164, 259, 261, 263
green
  beans, French-cut, 225
  choy sum. *See* yu choy
  coconuts, 83, 177
  lentils, 64
  mango chutney (kuchela), 173
  mangos, 42, 183, 191
  papayas, 42, 205, 222, 225, 226, 227, 232, 260
  shredded, 228
green bean

ice cream bars, 263
starch sheets, 244
greens, 36, 41, 167, 172, 191, 259,
  261. *See also* herbs; specific types
  of greens
  Asian, 151, 203, 204, 212, 216,
    217, 221, 226, 227, 228, 229,
    232, 242, 252, 259, 260
  organic, 8
grissini, 133
grits, 62, 173, 179
groats, 62
ground beef, 23
grouper, 32
guajes, 83, 92, 94, 97
guajillo peppers, 83, 95
  powdered, 89
guanábanas. *See* soursops
guaraná soft drinks, 89
guava (guayaba)
  dried, 215
    Malaysian, 229
  jam, 174, 175
  juice, 86, 175
  paste, 85, 89, 93, 93, 175
  pulp, frozen, 89
  puree, 85, 174, 175
  syrup, 93
guava shells, canned, 93
guavas, 42, 83, 91, 172, 176, 179
guayaba. *See* guava
guinea bananas, 262
gum arabic, 15
gumbo filé. *See* filé
gummy candies, 65
gungoo peas. *See* pigeon peas
gway tiaow. *See* rice noodles, fresh
gyoza skins, 222

habanero peppers, 83, 84, 100, 172,
  176, 177, 179, 204, 259
habas. *See* fava beans
hair vegetable (black moss), 206
Haitian ingredients and products,
  42, 176. *See also* Caribbean ingredients and products

Haitian mangos, 42
halal/zabiha meat, 68, 158, 162,
  165, 183, 190, 193, 272
haldi. *See* turmeric
hallah, 69
halloumi, 148, 152, 155
halo halo, 223, 229, 244, 254
halvah, 147, 160
ham. *See also* pig; pork
  Black Forest, 126
  fresh, 20, 108, 221
  pickled, 229
  prosciutto, 2, 4, 130, 137, 138,
    139, 143
  Smithfield, 211
  Westphalian, 126
hardo bread, 178
harissa, 159, 167
Harrison poultry and eggs, 22–23
harusame sai fun (potato starch
  noodles), 243
hasa-hasa (fish), 254
havarti, 127
Hawaiian black sea salt, 13
Hawaiian red sea salt, 13, 15
hazelnut
  oil, 2
  syrup, 132
hazelnuts, 121, 147
headcheese, 108, 229
health foods, 8, 62–65
hearts of palm, canned, 91
heirloom vegetables, 36
herbs, 10–18, 36, 42, 90, 94, 165,
  221, 222, 227, 228, 232, 252,
  260, 261, 262
  angelica root, 159, 211
  basil, 10, 16, 17, 130, 132, 134,
    135, 139, 143, 222, 228
  bay leaf, Indonesian (salam), 184
  bitterleaf, 177
  borage, 16
  bulk dried, 14–15
  cilantro, 17, 83, 84, 87, 93, 222,
    224, 231, 262
  dill, 42, 108, 167

herbs (continued)
epazote, 10, 83, 91, 92, 94, 96,
97, 177, 259
ginseng, 215, 244
huauzontle, 83, 91, 94
lavender, 16
lemon verbena, 16
lemongrass, 183, 205, 222, 232
medicinal, 94, 167, 211
Middle Eastern, 165, 167
mint, 83, 122
oregano, 10, 16, 85, 132, 149
parsley, 17, 132
pennywort (rau ma), 227
perilla (shiso), 242
radix, 211
rosemary, 16, 132
sage, 109, 132
saw-leaf herb, 228
screwpine leaves, 229
sorrel, 16, 108
verdolaga, 83, 94, 96, 100, 108,
177, 259
Vietnamese, 221, 222, 227, 229
herring, 108, 116, 126
paste, 127, 128, 173
tinned, 114
hibiscus. See jamaica
hijiki, 244
hilsa (fish), 183, 191
hing (powdered asafoetida), 184
hog casings, 263
hoisin sauce, 205
holy basil, 222
hominy, 85, 100
grits, 173, 174
honey, 62, 108, 109, 111, 118, 120,
124, 148, 151, 152, 160, 263
date, 148, 160
liquor, 118
tupelo, 62
unfiltered, 62
sage, 148, 160
hookah tobacco, 162, 165, 167
horned water chestnut (water caltrop), 204

horseradish, 42, 108, 109, 121, 124
with beets, 108
Japanese (wasabi), 228, 240, 242,
243, 249, 255
hot bean paste. See chile-bean paste
hot pepper paste. See gochujang
hot peppers. See chiles
hot sauces, 85, 91, 173, 176, 177,
179, 204, 216, 222, 224, 247,
253. See also specific types
HP sauce, 127
huauzontle, 83, 91, 94
Hudson Valley foie gras, 22
huitlacoche (corn smut), canned,
85
hulled wheat, 147
Hungarian ingredients and products, 108, 146, 151, 261. See also
Eastern European ingredients
and products

ice cream
gourmet, 3
green bean bars, 263
Indian. See kulfi
lychee, 229
ichimi togarachi (Japanese chile
powder), 242
ikra (eggplant dip), 148
Indian flours, 185, 186, 195
Indian/Pakistani ingredients and
products, 164, 167, 182–199,
213, 262, 263, 272. See also
breads, Indian; chutneys; dals;
masala; pickles, Indian; sauces,
Indian cooking; snack mixes, Indian; spices, Indian; bakery
goods, Indian
Indonesian bay leaf. See salam leaf
injera, freshly made, 176
intestines, 162, 211, 244
Iranian ingredients and products,
164. See also Middle Eastern ingredients and products
Irish ingredients and products, 127
Irish oats, 127

Irish soda bread, 127
Israeli couscous, 147, 159
Israeli ingredients and products, 69, 70, 71. *See also* kosher foods
Israeli crushed tomatoes, 71
Italian bread, 8, 142, 258, 261
  whole wheat, 142
Italian ingredients and products, 32, 43, 130–143, 258, 261, 262, 273
Italian sausage, 24, 111, 130, 138, 138, 139, 140, 141

jackfruit, 206, 223, 244
jaggery, 187
jahlab syrup, 162
jalapeño peppers, 83, 87, 95, 100, 261
jamaica (dried hibiscus), 83, 87, 90, 159
Jamaica plums. *See* June plums
Jamaican grapefruit soda (Ting), 178, 214
Jamaican ingredients and products, 176, 177, 178, 214. *See also* Caribbean ingredients and products
Jamaican patties, 178
jams, jellies, and preserves, 38–39, 43, 91, 109, 111, 112, 114, 116, 118, 118, 119, 120, 124, 127, 148, 149, 151, 152, 160, 162, 163, 164, 207, 225, 259, 261, 263. *See also* specific flavors
jantaboon noodles. *See* rice sticks, wide
Japanese ingredients and products, 214, 226, 227, 228. 240, 241–246, 249–250, 251, 256, 253, 272. *See also* Asian ingredients and products
japonica rice, 62
Jarritos sodas, 86, 214
jasmine rice, 205
  sweet brown, 223
jellies. *See* jams, jellies, and pre-

serves
jellyfish, 203, 220
  dried, 203, 206, 241
jerk sauces and seasonings, 173, 176, 177, 179
Jew's mallow. *See* molukhia
jícama, 42, 43, 83, 94, 204
Jordan (candy-coated) almonds, 148, 160
Jordan (candy-coated) chickpeas, 160
Jordanian ingredients and products, 163. *See also* Middle Eastern ingredients and products
juice drinks, boxed, 110, 114, 151, 214, 262
jujube (Chinese red dates). *See* zizyphus
June plums (Jamaica plums), 172, 176
juniper berries, 10, 14
jute leaves, 242, 254
  frozen, 174, 177

kabocha squash, 204, 242
kaffir lime leaves, 222
kajmak, 148
kala jeera (black cumin, royal cumin), 10, 184
kala namak (black salt), 13, 184
kalbi (Korean beef ribs), 241
kalonji. *See* charnuska
kamut, 62
kangkong (water spinach). *See* ong choy
karela. *See* bitter melon
kasha (buckwheat groats), 62, 70, 109, 118
kashkaval, 148, 155
kasseri, 148, 149, 152, 155, 160
kataifa (shredded phyllo), 148, 160
katsuobushi (bonito flakes), 244
kecap manis, 243
kefalotiri, 148
kefir, 110, 114, 118, 148, 152, 160, 259

kefir (continued)
    chocolate, 118
kenkey, 174, 176
khakhara, 185
kibbeh, 165
kidney beans, 85
kidneys, 162, 213, 221
kimchee, 240, 244, 251, 252, 253, 255
King David bakery goods, 71
kingfish (surmai), 183, 191, 220
kishke, 69, 71
knackwurst, 24, 126
kohlrabi, 204
    preserved, 207
kokum, 184
kola nuts, 176
kolackys, 110, 120
kombu, 244
kona coffee extract, 15
konyaku, 244. *See also* shirataki
Korean bamboo salt, 13
Korean buckwheat noodles (naengmyon), 234
Korean drinks, 245, 253
Korean ingredients and products, 240–245, 251–253, 256. *See also* Asian ingredients and products
Korean melons, 242, 252, 255
Korean pancake mix, 229
korma (Indian cooking sauce), 187
kosher foods, 68–72, 272
    bakery goods, 69, 71
    cheese, 70, 71
    dairy, 70
    fish, 31, 33, 69, 71
    gelatin, 69, 70
    meats, 68, 69, 71
    poultry, 68, 69, 71
    prepared foods, 69, 71
    salt, 13, 70
    sausage, 71
    wine, 70
kouambeithes (Greek butter cookies), 154
kri-kri peanuts, 162

kuchela (green mango chutney), 173
kugel, 70
    low-carb, 71
kugelis, 111, 120
kulfi (Indian ice cream), 188
kumquat preserves, 148
kumquats, 44, 204
    dried, 215
kun choy (Chinese celery), 204
kvas, 110

La Guadalupana products, 91, 92, 98
labna, 42, 148, 152, 160, 162, 164, 165, 169
lactose, 62
ladoos, 188
lamb, 20, 21, 130, 146, 149, 158, 169, 183, 190, 193
    Australian, 6
    baby, 21, 22, 167, 261
    barbecued, 152
    ground, 146
    halal/zabiha, 190
    hearts, 82, 90
    leg, 167
    liver, 82, 90, 261
    stuffed, 164
    tripe, 162, 259
lard, 85, 90, 108
Latin American ingredients and products, 42, 82–105, 138, 151, 167, 177, 214, 260, 261, 263, 266, 272. *See also* specific ethnicities
lavender, 16
lavosh, 148, 160
lefse, 127, 128, 272
legumes, dried, 41, 64, 91. *See also* beans; chickpeas; lentils
lektc, 164
lemon
    sauce, 205
    vinegar, 222
lemon verbena, 16

lemongrass, 183, 205, 222, 232
lemons
    dried, 147, 159
    pickled, 187
lentils, 64, 147, 159, 161, 165, 182,
    185, 263. *See also* masoor dal;
    toor dal; urad dal
    beluga, 64
    black, 185
    brown, 147, 159
    bulk, 15
    French, 64
    green, 64
    red, 64, 147, 159, 161, 185, 199
    Spanish, 64
    yellow, 147, 159, 185
lily buds, 206, 222
lily bulbs, edible, 229
limas, giant (gigandes), 147, 150,
    151, 155, 190
Limburger cheese, 126
limes
    dried, 147, 159
    pickled, 187
Limonata, 133
limoncello, 133, 138
lingonberries, 127, 128, 272
liqueurs/liquors, 3, 5, 116, 262,
    272, 273
    cognac, 300-year-old, 3
    honey, 118
    Eastern European, 114, 117, 118,
        273
    German, 127
    Greek, 149
    Italian, 133, 138
    Japanese, 249, 272
    Korean, 251
    kvas, 110
    Latin American, 94
    ouzo, 149
    peach, French, 116
    rum, 3
    tequila, 3
    vodka, 114, 116, 118
lita squash, 83, 100

litchees, litchis. *See* lychees
Lithuanian ingredients and prod-
    ucts, 109, 111, 114, 117, 118,
    120, 263. *See also* Eastern Euro-
    pean ingredients and products
liver
    beef, 23, 71, 221
    calf, 108
    chopped, 70
    lamb, 82, 90, 261
    pig, 213
liver sausage/wurst, 24, 108, 126
ljutenitza (tomato-pepper dip), 148
lobster, 202, 263
    live, 33, 215, 259
locally-grown produce, 36–37, 42
long beans (asparagus beans, snake
    beans, yard beans), 183, 204,
    211, 222, 242, 254, 263
longan, 206, 222, 223
longaniza, 241, 254
loquat, 223
lotus root, 183, 204, 206, 211, 222,
    242, 260
lotus seeds, 206
lox, 69
luffa (silk squash, sinqua), 183,
    204, 215, 222, 242
lumpfish caviar, 34
lumpia, 244, 254
    wrappers, 244
lunch meats. *See* deli meats
lupini beans, 132
lutefisk, 127, 128
lychee
    ice cream, 229
    jelly, 207, 225
    juice drinks, 214
lychees, 42, 204, 206, 212, 215,
    223, 260

macadamia butter, 62
mace, 10, 184
mackerel, 202, 220, 240, 263
    dried, 221
    smoked and seasoned, 220

maftoul. *See* Israeli couscous
mahlab, mahlebi (sour cherry pits), 10, 159
makaneh, 162
malanga (amarilla, cocoyam, yautia), 42, 83, 91, 101, 102, 103, 138, 173, 176, 177, 259, 262
    blanca, 88, 105
    lila, 88, 104
Malaysian dried guava, 229
Malden sea salt, 5, 13
malt extract, 49
maltose-sesame candy, 252
mamemiso (soybean miso), 244
mamey, 42, 172, 176, 177, 262
    frozen, 262
    puree, 94, 262
mamoncillos. *See* quenepas
mamones. *See* quenepas
Manchego cheese, 137
mango
    chutney, 187. *See also* kuchela
    juice, 86
    paste, 85
    pickles, 187
    powder. *See* amchoor
    pulp, frozen, 89
    puree, 85, 174
mangos, 83, 87, 100, 183
    green, 42, 183, 191
    Haitian, 42
    Philippine, 42
manioc. *See* yucca
manouri cheese, 148
maraschino, 133
marcona almonds, 2, 7
marinades
    Chinese, 213
    seafood, 31
marinara sauce, 140
marmite, 127
marrofat peas, 127
marshmallows
    exotic flavors, 215
    mango-flavored, 99
masa, 91, 92, 97, 99, 100

fresh, 85, 97
harina, 85, 97, 99
prepared for tamales, 85, 92, 97, 98, 99
prepared for tortillas, 85, 92, 97
masala
    chaat, 185, 188, 189
    garam, 185, 189, 197
    panch phoron, 185
    tandoori, 185
    tikka, 185
mascarpone, 133
masoor dal (red lentils), 185
mastic, 43, 147, 159, 260
    Turkish delight, 154
matambre, 91
maté. *See* yerba maté
matzo, 69, 70
meats, 20–25, 108, 117, 221, 263. *See also* beef; buffalo; butcher shops; choice-grade meats; deli meats; game; goat; lamb; pork; poultry; prime meats; sausage; veal
    African/Caribbean, 172
    Chinese, 203, 209, 212, 213, 215
    choice-grade, 20, 21, 22, 23, 82, 88, 89, 259, 263
    Filipino, 254
    German, 23, 24
    halal/zabiha, 68, 158, 162, 165, 183, 190, 193, 272
    Indian/Pakistani, 190
    Italian, 20, 130, 137
    Japanese, 249
    Korean, 251, 253
    kosher, 68, 69, 71
    Latin American, 20, 88, 89, 91, 94
    naturally-raised, 22, 64
    offal, 20, 172, 241
    organ, 221. *See also* specific organs
    organic, 37
    primal cuts, 24, 89
    prime, 5, 21, 22, 111

sustainable agriculture, 36
meats, cured. *See* cured meats
meats, dry-aging in-house, 5, 8, 22, 23, 24
meats, preserved, 146
meats, seasoned and breaded, 4
meats, smoked, 23, 24, 24, 108, 151, 152, 172, 176
in-house, 5, 119
mecos. *See* chipotle peppers, brown
medicinal herbs, 94, 167, 211
medicinal teas, 94, 110, 114, 117, 207, 225, 245, 266
medicinals, Korean, 251
mein (Cantonese egg noodles), 205, 234, 236
melon seeds, 160
melons, Korean, 242, 252, 255
memmi, 242
merquez, 162
methi, methi leaves. *See* fenugreek
Mexican chocolate, 86, 100
Mexican ingredients and products, 3, 43, 82–86, 90, 94, 96, 190, 259, 261, 262, 272, 273. *See also* Frontera products; Latin American ingredients and products
Mexican oregano, 85
Middle Eastern ingredients and products, 4, 21, 22, 42, 43, 138, 151, 152, 158–169, 190, 193, 258, 259, 260, 261, 263, 272. *See also* specific ethnicities
milk, cultured, 110
milkfish, 241
millet, 62, 151, 174
flours (bajri and raggi), 186
mineral waters, Italian, 133, 137
mint, 83, 222
chutney, 187, 199
mirasol peppers, 95
mirin, 242
mirlitons (christophenes). *See* chayotes
miso, 244, 245, 249, 250, 255
mitsuba (trefoil), 242

Mitzva Farms, 71
mochiko. *See* rice flour, glutinous
mock duck (wheat gluten), 206
molasses
blackstrap, 62
carob, 147, 160, 167
date, 160
grape, 147, 150, 263
pomegranate. *See* pomegranate concentrate
mole pastes, 85, 92
molukhia (Jew's mallow), 147, 159
monkfish, 28, 31, 32
montasio, 131, 133
mooli. *See* daikon
moong dal. *See* mung beans
morello cherry syrup, 110
morels, 42
moritas. *See* chipotle peppers, red
Morning Rice drink, 245
morro (moro), puree, 94, 262
mote blanco (large white dried corn kernels), 85
mother of vinegar, 49, 267
mountain yams. *See* naga-imo
mousses, 2
mozzarella
bocconcini, 134
buffalo milk, 133
fresh, 133, 137, 139, 143
smoked, 133
MSG, 15, 223
mudfish, pickled, 205
mugwort flour, 244
mulberry
drink, 245
syrup, 147, 159
mung bean
noodles, 233
starch, 229
mung beans, 185, 207
mushroom
powder, 116
soy sauce, 202, 205, 209, 216, 217, 242

mushrooms, 108, 109, 118, 204, 212, 242, 242, 249, 259
  beech, 249
  black, 207
  chanterelles, 7, 42, 109
  enoki, 204, 242, 249
  morels, 42
  nametake, 242
  oyster, 42, 204, 212, 242, 249, 259, 260
  porcini, 109, 132, 139
  portobello, 259, 260
  shiitake, 204, 207, 242, 259, 260
  wood ear, 207
mushrooms, dried, 5, 109, 109, 207, 214, 244
mushrooms, pickled, 109, 112, 118, 259
mussels, 32, 82, 130
  live, 220
  tinned, 93
mustard
  cabbage. *See* gai choy
  greens, 136
  oil, 187
  seed, 184, 189
mustards, 2
  Dijon, 37
  gourmet, 2, 4
myoga (ginger buds), 242, 249
myzithra (cheese), 148

naan, 185, 191
naengmyon. *See* Korean buckwheat noodles
naga-imo (mountain yams), 242
ñames (white yams), 42, 83, 173, 176
nametake, 242
napa (Chinese cabbage), 204
natto (fermented soybeans), 244
Natural Ovens products, 71
nigari, 244
nigella. *See* charnuska
Nigerian ingredients and products, 176. *See also* African ingredients
and products
Niman Ranch pork, 7
nipa sap (coconut palm vinegar), 243
noodle dipping sauce (memmi), 242
noodles, 209, 210, 212, 214, 217, 222, 223, 228, 233–238, 249, 272. *See also* pasta
  bean thread (cellophane), 205, 206, 217, 243
  chow mein (fried), 210
  cornstarch, 233
  harusame sai fun (potato starch), 243
  Korean buckwheat (naengmyon), 234
  mein (Cantonese egg), 205, 234, 236
  mung bean, 233
  pancit (Filipino noodles), 243, 254
  potato, 233
  ramen (chuka soba), 205, 234, 243
  rice, 205, 223, 233, 235, 236, 238, 243
    fresh (chow fun, gway tiaow), 205, 211, 216, 217, 223, 235, 236, 243
    rice sticks, 205, 223, 235, 238, 243
    wide (jantaboon), 223
  vermicelli, 205, 223, 238, 243
  shirataki (noodles for sukiyaki), 243
  soba (Japanese buckwheat), 205, 222, 223, 234, 237, 243, 255
  organic, 7
  somen (wheat), 205, 223, 234, 237, 243
  sweet potato, 223, 253
  tapioca starch, 223
  tofu, 233
  udon, 206, 223, 234
  vermicelli, 237

wheat, 205, 210, 233, 234, 236, 237, 243
yacamein, 237
yam noodles (Korean), 223, 233, 243, 253
nopales (cactus paddles), 83, 97, 177
nori, 31, 225, 240, 244
nut butters, 62
nut oils, 2, 138
nutmeg, 10, 40, 122, 135, 184
  whole, 10, 12
nuts, 6, 64, 147, 158, 160, 164, 165, 192
  acorn starch, 244
  almonds, 2, 7, 65, 147, 148, 160
  bulk, 15, 63, 65, 162, 163, 167, 192, 259
  cashews, 147, 160, 182
  chestnuts, 132, 138, 206
  flavored with chiles and lime, 86
  ginkgo, 206, 242
  hazelnuts, 121, 147
  peanuts, 86, 162, 172, 182, 225
  pine nuts, 37, 130, 136, 147
  pistachios, 18, 147, 160
  soy nuts, 62, 65
  walnuts, 40, 147, 163, 168

oat
  bran, 62, 109
  flour, 64
oats, 109
  Irish, 127
obgono, 176
Ochos Rios products, 176
octopus, 32, 139, 202, 220, 240, 241, 249, 259, 262, 273
  baby, 241
  dried, 203
  tinned, 93
offal, 20, 172, 241
oil beans, 177
oils, 2, 4, 5, 50, 62, 63, 138, 268
  avocado, 62
  dende (palm), 174, 177, 179

  grapeseed, 2, 139
  hazelnut, 2
  mustard, 187
  nut, 2, 138
  olive, 2, 4, 138, 141, 149, 154, 155, 209
    organic, 63
  peanut, 209, 216
  perilla (shiso), 243
  pine nut, 4
  pistachio, 2, 4
  restaurant size, 214
  sesame, 209, 216, 247
  truffle, 2, 3, 138
  walnut, 2
  zomi (spiced palm), 174, 177
okra, 172
olive
  oil, 2, 4, 138, 141, 149, 209
    citrus, 4, 138
    Greek, 154, 144
  paste, green and black, 132
  tapenade, 2
olives, 5, 93, 138, 147, 158, 164, 169
  fresh, 259
  uncured, 132, 138
ong choy (kangkong, water spinach), 222, 227, 260, 263
opo squash, 222
orange blossom water, 147, 159, 167, 187
oranges
  bitter, 177
  blood, 8
  sour, 42, 173, 176, 179
Orangina, 133
orchietti, 132
oregano, 10, 16, 132
  Greek, 149
  Mexican, 85
organ meats, 221. *See also* specific organs
organic foods, 8, 43, 63–64
  noodles, 7

organic foods (continued)
  produce, 6, 8, 36, 37, 41, 43,
    63–64
osso bucco, 20, 130
ostrich, 21
oxtails, 241
ouzo, 149
oyster
  meat, 241
  mushrooms, 42, 204, 212, 242,
    249, 259, 260
  sauce, 202, 205, 209, 216, 217
oysters, 32, 202, 208, 220, 240
  fresh, 28
  frozen, 203
  live, 33, 220, 228

paan, pan leaves. *See* betel leaves
paczki, 120
Pakistani ingredients and products,
    190, 191, 193, 272. *See also* In-
    dian ingredients and products
Palestinian ingredients and prod-
    ucts, 163. *See also* Middle Eastern
    ingredients and products
palm
  fruit, 223, 244
  hearts, frozen, 177
  oil. *See* dende
    spiced. *See* zomi
  vinegar, 215, 255
pampana (Filipino sausage), 241
pancetta, 3, 130
panch phoron (Bengali five-spice
    blend), 185, 189
pancit (Filipino) noodles, 243, 254
pandan leaves, 222
pandanus (bai toey), 223
paneer, 187, 197
panela (loaf-shaped brown sugar),
    85
panforté, 262
panettone, 263
panko (Japanese) bread crumbs,
    223, 228, 244, 250, 255
pao de quijo mixes, 89, 91

papaya, pickled (atchara), 254
papaya-habanero hot sauce, 176,
    177, 179, 204
papayas, 83, 228, 260
  green papayas, 42, 205, 222, 225,
    226, 227, 232, 260
  shredded, 228
pappadams, 186, 192, 195, 196,
    199
paprika, 147
  hot, 147
  Hungarian, 108
  smoked, 5, 10
papusas, 94
paratha, 186
Parmesan, 37, 136
  Reggiano, 133, 135, 139, 140,
    143, 259
parsley, 17
  Italian, 132
parval, 183
pasilla peppers, 83, 95
passion fruit, 42
  frozen, 262
  jam, 174
  juice, boxed, 114
  paste, 85
  puree, 85, 174, 262
pasta, 4, 7, 132, 138, 140, 141, 152,
    273
  cannoli shells, 132
  gourmet, 138, 139
  orchietti, 132
  ravioli, 139
  rishta, 159
  rottoli, 139
  squid ink, 4, 132
  tagliatelle, salmon, 138
  trahana, 43, 147, 152
pasta, fresh/homemade, 140
pasta flour (semolina), 132, 186
pasta sauces, 137, 140
paste food colors, 15
pastrami, 69
pastries. *See* bakery goods
pâtés, 2, 3, 5, 108, 270

Patna basmati rice, 186
pea
    flour, 93
    shoots, 204, 242
    tips, 262
peanut oil, 209, 216
peanuts, 182
    green, 172
    kri-kri, 162
    roasted, 225
    spicy, 86
pears, wet white, 252
peas, 197
    marrofat, 127
Pecorino Romano, 133
Peking duck, 203
pelmeni, 114
    Siberian, 151
pennywort (rau ma), 227
pepicha, 94
pepper dips. *See* ajvar; ljutenitza
pepper puree, 148
peppercorns, 10, 11, 14, 184
    green, 11
    pink, 11, 248
    Sarawak, 11
    Szechuan (fagara), 11, 205
    Tellicherry, 11
    white, 11, 248
peppermint flavoring water, 167
peppers, 82, 89, 146, 151, 172, 260.
    See also chiles; red peppers
    cabbage-stuffed, 151
    pickled, 109, 152, 174, 177, 223
    roasted, 132
    stuffed, 148, 152
perilla (shiso), 242
    oil, 243
periwinkles, 208, 220
peron peppers, 83, 84
Persian ingredients and products,
    163. *See also* Middle Eastern in-
    gredients and products
Peruvian ingredients and products,
    91. *See also* Latin American in-
    gredients and products

persimmon vinegar, 243
persimmons, 40, 138, 242
    dried, 207
pesto, 17, 132, 141
Philippine mangos, 42
phyllo (filo) dough, phyllo sheets,
    148, 151, 153, 155, 158, 160
phyllo, shredded (kataifa), 148, 160
pick-your-own farms, 37
pickles, pickled foods, 43, 109, 114,
    116, 118, 223, 244, 249
    banana buds, 223
    burdock, 249
    carrots, 249
    cornichons, 2, 3
    cucumbers, wild, 162
    daikon (mooli), 223, 244, 249
    eggplant, 249
    fish, 116, 244
    garlic, 244, 253
    ginger, 244
    ham, 229
    Hungarian, 151
    Indian, 187, 193
    lemon, 187
    lime, 187
    mango, 187
    mudfish, 205
    mushrooms, 109, 112, 118, 259
    peppers, 109, 152, 177, 223
    hot, 174
    Polish, 42, 43, 116
    tamarind, 187
    turnips, 165
    ume (umeboshi), 244
pico de gallo, 97. *See also* salsas
pierogis, 110, 112, 113, 116, 124
pig. *See also* pork
    blood, 211
    casings, 263
    ears, 82
    heads, 82, 93
    hearts, 221
    intestines, 211
    kidneys, 213, 221
    liver, 213

pig (continued)
snouts, 172, 177, 203
spine, 82, 151, 203
spleens, 221
tails, 82, 90, 172, 176, 177, 203
tongue, 221
trotters, 20, 23, 82, 108, 114, 221
uterus, 221
whole, 23
pigeon peas (gandules, gungoo
peas), 85, 86, 174, 185. *See also*
toor dal
pigs, roast, 91
pilaf, bulgur, 149
piloncillo (cone-shaped brown
sugar), 86, 173
pine bud drink, 245
pine nut oil, 4
pine nuts, 37, 130, 136, 147
pink beans, 85
pink Peruvian salt, 13
pinto beans, 85
pistachio
barfi (Indian fudge), 196
oil, 2, 4
preserves, 160
Turkish delight, 154
pistachios, 18, 147, 160
pita bread, 148, 151, 152, 158, 160,
162, 164, 165, 168, 169, 191
Al-Khyam's best whole wheat,
162
pithaya. *See* dragon fruit
pitter, 176
pizza crusts, 132
pizza dough, 132, 139, 143
pizza puffs, 23
pizzas, 139, 262
pizzelle, 133
plantain
chips, 93, 192
flour, 86
plantains, 42, 48, 83, 90, 173, 177,
178, 179, 183
plantains, fried (tostones), 97, 151,
262

plum
jams/preserves, 148, 259
sauce, 205
wine, 229, 249
plums, 38
June (Jamaica), 172, 176
preserved, 207, 215
ume (Japanese plum), 242, 249
poa (fish), 191
poblano peppers, 43, 83, 95
poha (flattened rice), 186
Poky cookies, 225, 245
polenta, 130, 132, 136, 143, 173
Polish ingredients and products,
43, 90, 96, 110, 111, 114, 116,
117, 118, 120, 138, 167, 259,
260, 261, 262, 263, 273. *See also*
Eastern European ingredients
and products
Polish sausage, 111, 116
pollack, 241
roe, 241
pomegranate
concentrate (molasses), 43, 147,
159, 162, 163, 164, 167, 168,
169, 190
juice, 160
seeds (anardana), 184
wine, Armenian, 114
pomegranates, 183
pomelos, 42, 222, 231, 263
pomfret. *See* butterfish
ponzu (citrus soy sauce), 242
poppy seeds, 10, 108
white, 184
porcini, 109, 132, 139
dried (cèpes, boletus), 109, 132
paste, 3
pickled, 109
pork, 23, 93, 108, 112, 116, 124,
141, 203, 211, 215, 221, 262. *See
also* bacon; ham; pig; smoked
butt
barbecued, 152, 203, 212, 215
belly, 20, 108, 114, 213, 254
sliced, 241

carnitas, 20, 82, 88, 89, 94, 96, 97, 100, 262, 273
chicharrónes (fried pork skins), 82, 86, 93, 95, 96, 172
chitterlings, 23
chops, 23
fat, 117
hocks, 221
loin, 108
Niman Ranch, 7
pickled, 127
ribs, 23, 213
shoulder, skin-on, 221, 228
smoked, 108
sukiyaki, 241
tenderloin, 221, 224
pork fu (pork floss), 207
portobello mushrooms, 259, 260
pot stickers, frozen, 213
potato noodles, 233
potato starch (flour), 205
noodles. *See* harusame sai fun
poultry, 21–25, 112, 203, 211. *See also* capons; chicken; duck; geese; poussin; quail; squabs
fresh, 21, 22
grain-raised without antibiotics or hormones, 22
kosher, 68, 69, 71
live, 25
organic, 37
seasonings, 22
stuffed, 164
sustainable agriculture, 36
poussin, 21
prawns, 183, 203
head-on, 220
prepared/deli foods, 5, 94, 114, 116, 127, 259, 261, 262, 268, 270, 272. *See also* bakery goods
antipasti, 139
Asian, 6
Balkan, 261
barbacoa, 20, 88, 89, 100
calzones, 132
carnitas, 20, 82, 88, 89, 94, 96,

97, 100, 262, 273
Eastern European, 112, 114, 116, 117, 118, 261, 273
empanadas, 91
German, 126–127
gourmet, 5, 7, 268
Indian/Pakistani, 6, 192
Italian, 137, 138, 139
Korean, 251, 252, 253
kosher, 69, 71
Latin American, 91, 94, 97, 262
Middle Eastern, 261
papusas, 94
pâtés, 2, 3, 5, 108, 270
Peking duck, 203
pierogis, 110, 112
pizzas, 139, 262
salads, 3, 112, 116, 117, 138, 229
Scandinavian, 127–128
seafood, 30, 31, 32
salads, 31
shish kebabs, 261
soups, 31, 112
sushi/sashimi, 4, 33, 272
tamales, 23, 92, 96, 99, 262, 273
terrines, 2, 3
Thai, 227
tostones (fried plantains), 97, 151, 262
Vietnamese, 229
preserved (1,000-year-old) eggs, 202, 223
preserved plums, 207, 215
preserved thinking milk plum, 215
preserved vegetables, 207
preserves. *See* jams, jellies, and preserves
prickly pear (cactus fruit). *See* tuna
primal cuts (meat), 24, 89
prime meats, 5, 21, 22, 111
produce, 5, 36–44, 92, 93, 94, 96, 97, 132, 137, 152, 167, 172, 176, 177, 183, 191, 195, 203, 204, 212, 215, 221–222, 228, 241–242, 249, 253, 259, 260, 261, 262, 272 *See also* specific types

produce (continued)
  by the case, 138
  locally-grown, 36–37, 42
  organic, 6, 8, 36, 37, 41, 43,
    63–64
prosciutto, 2, 4, 130, 137, 138, 139,
  143
  cotto, 130
puddings (Irish breakfast sausages),
  black and white, 127
Puerto Rican ingredients and products, 262. See also Caribbean;
  Latin American ingredients and
  products
puffed rice, 186, 188
pumpernickel bread, 109
pumpkin
  gruel (Korean drink), 245
  jam, 91
  pick-your-own, 37
  ravioli, 139
  seeds, flavored with chiles and
    lime, 86
puntarella, 262
puri, 186
purple yam (ratalu), 183, 263
  grated, 263
  jam, 229, 244, 254
  powder, 244
purslane. See verdolaga

quail, 25, 203, 260
  eggs, 203, 221
  live, 25
quark (glumse), 126
quenepas (mamoncillos, mamones,
  Spanish limes), 173, 176
queso (cheese)
  añejo, 86
  asadero, 86, 96
  blanco, 86
  Chihuahua, 86
  cotija, 86 96
  criollo, 86
  enchilado, 86
  fresco, 86, 197

Oaxaca, 86, 96
  ranchero, 86
quince
  paste, 93
  preserves, 148
quinces, 91, 183
quinoa, 62

rabbit, 23, 130, 139
  live, 25
radicchio, 132
radishes, preserved, 207
radix, 211
raggi (Indian millet flour), 186
rahat loukoum. See Turkish delight
rambutans, 204
ramen (chuka soba) noodles, 205,
  234, 243
rapini. See broccoli raab
ras el hanout, 159
raspberries, 38
ratalu. See purple yam
rau ma. See pennywort
ravioli, 139
  pumpkin, 139
red
  bean paste, 244
  beans. See adzuki
  eggs, preserved, 244
  lentils (masoor dal), 185
  pepper (spice), 240
  powder, 243
  peppers (vegetable), 84
  roasted, 168
  tapenade, 2
  rice, 205
  wine vinegar, 209
refried beans, 85
Reggiano Parmesan, 133, 135, 139,
  140, 143, 259
relishes, 118, 229
restaurant sizes, quantities, 49, 54
  canned goods, 49
  chocolate sauce, 52
  condiments, 54
  oil, 214

salad dressings, 49
soups, 54
spices, 49, 54
restaurants' lines of products. *See*
chefs'/restaurants' lines of products
rex sole, 241
rhubarb, 38, 40
ribs, 23. *See also* beef ribs; pork ribs
barbecued, 203
rice, 62, 132, 185, 192, 223, 229,
243, 249, 251
Arborio, 132, 135, 139, 140, 143
basmati, 62, 147, 159, 186, 194,
199
brown, 186
Dehraduni, 186
Patna, 186
black, 205
brown, 62, 186, 223
Carnaroli, 132, 139
cooked in aseptic packs, 253
flattened (poha), 186
forbidden, 7
glutinous (sticky), 205, 223
japonica, 62
jasmine, 205, 223
long grain, 85, 243
medium grain, 85, 243
pearl, 85
puffed, 186, 188
red, 205
risotto, 130, 132, 139
short grain, 85, 243, 255
sweet, 243
Valencia, 85
Vialone Nano, 132, 139
wehani, 62
rice cake mix (bibinka), 229
rice candies (edible wrappers), 207
rice cracker snack mixes, 245
rice flour, 174, 186, 205, 223, 243
glutinous, 205, 223, 243
rice noodles, 205, 223, 233, 235,
236, 238, 243. *See also* rice sticks;
rice vermicelli

fresh (chow fun, gway tiaow),
205, 211, 216, 217, 223, 235,
235, 236, 243
rice papers, 207, 222, 223, 228,
231, 232
rice powder, roasted, 223
rice, puffed (chivda), 188
rice vermicelli, 205, 223, 238, 243
rice vinegar, 205, 207, 224, 242,
247
brown, 62, 243
rice wine vinegar, 248
ricotta, 133, 137, 139, 153
salata, 133
rishta (pasta), 159
risotto rice, 130, 132, 139
rock salt, 13
rock sugar, 205, 225
roe. *See* caviar
rogan josh (Indian cooking sauce),
187
Romanian wine, 261
rose
kulfi, 188
preserves, 148, 160
Turkish delight, 154
water, 147, 151, 158, 159, 167,
187, 194, 223
rose hip
jam, 109
syrup, 110
rose petal spread, 151, 190
rosemary, 16, 132
rosogollas, 188
rottoli, 139
royal cumin (black cumin). *See* kala
jeera
ruhu (fish), 183, 191
rum, 3
extract, 15
Russian ingredients and products,
114, 118, 151, 272. *See also* Eastern European ingredients and
products
rutabagas, 262
Ryazenka, 114

rye, 62
  breads, 109, 111, 120, 152
  flour, 64

sable, smoked, 32
saffron, 10, 18, 182, 184, 199
  kulfi, 188
sage, 109, 132
  honey, 148, 160
sake, 247, 249
salad cream, 127
salad dressings, restaurant size, 49
salam leaf (Indonesian bay leaf),
  184
salmon
  lox, 69
  roe, 3, 28, 34, 241
  smoked, 32, 108, 122, 151
  salsas, 3, 6, 85, 92, 93, 98
salt cod, 146
salt fish, 172
salt pork, 172
saltpeter, 117
salts, 12–13
  black salt (kala namak), 13, 184
  Danish smoked, 13
  Fleur de Sel, 5, 12, 13
  gourmet, 5, 12–13
  Hawaiian black sea, 13
  Hawaiian red sea, 13, 15
  Korean bamboo, 13
  kosher, 13, 70
  Malden sea salt, 5, 13
  pink Peruvian, 13
  rock, 13
  sea, 5, 13, 15, 242
  sel gris, 13
  Sicilian Trapani, 13
Salvadoran ingredients and products, 94. See also Central American; Latin American ingredients
  and products
sambuca, 133
San Marzano tomatoes, canned, 5,
  132, 139
sand dab, 241

sanding sugar, 15
sansho (Japanese pepper), 242
sap-sap (fish), 254
Sarawak peppercorns, 11
sardines, 130
  dried, 241
  smoked and seasoned, 220
  tinned, 114
sassafras. See filé
sata-imo. See taro
sauces. See also condiments; marinades; oyster sauce; salsas; soy
  sauce
  Asian cooking, 69, 205, 213, 228,
    250, 252
  banana, 229, 243, 254, 255
  bean, 205
  bulgogi, 243, 251
  char siu sauce (barbecue paste),
    205
  Chinese cooking, 213
  chocolate, restaurant size, 52
  criolla (Jamaican), 177
  duck, 69
  escabèche (Jamaican), 177
  fish, 205, 214, 222, 224, 225,
    226, 229, 231, 232, 243
  gourmet, 3, 6, 7, 31
  hoisin, 205
  hot, 85, 91, 173, 176, 177
    adobo, 83
    chile-bean, 216, 253
    chile-garlic, 217, 222, 224, 247
    harissa, 159, 167
    papaya-habanero, 176, 177,
      179, 204
    Sriracha, 205, 222, 223, 226,
      230, 232, 242
  HP, 127
  Indian cooking, 184, 185, 187
    balti, 185
    korma, 187
    rogan josh, 187
    tandoori, 185, 187, 192, 199
    vindaloo, 185
  jerk, 173, 176, 177, 179

lemon, 205
marinara, 140
mole, 85, 92
noodle dipping (memmi), 242
pasta, 137, 140
pesto, 17, 132, 141
plum, 205
seafood, 30, 31, 33
shabu shabu, 242
sofrito, 173
tonkatsu, 243
XO, 205
YR, 127
sauerkraut, 109, 118
saunf. *See* anise seed
sausages, 5, 23, 108, 111, 112, 117,
  118, 126, 146, 259, 261, 270, 273
  bangers, 127
  basturma, 146, 149, 158, 261
  blood, 126
  bratwurst, 24, 126
    Sheboygan, 126
    veal, 126
  chorizo, 24, 82, 89, 259, 260
  homemade, 21, 23, 24, 71, 111,
    112, 114, 116, 117, 130, 138,
    139, 151, 152, 259, 260
  house-cured/smoked, 124
  Hungarian, 146, 261
  Italian, 24, 111, 130, 138, 139,
    140, 141
  kishke, 69, 71
  knackwurst, 24, 126
  kosher, 71
  Latin American, 91
  Lithuanian, 111
  liver, 24, 108, 126
  longaniza, 241, 254
  makaneh, 162
  merquez, 162
  pampana, 241
  Polish, 111, 116
  Russian, 114
  puddings (black and white), 127
  soujouk, 146, 149, 158, 162
  sremska ljuta, 152

thuringer, 24
wieners, 126
saw-leaf herb, 228
scallops, 32
  dried, 203, 211
  in the shell, 31, 32, 241
  tinned, 93
scamorza, 133
Scandinavian ingredients and products, 110, 118, 127–128, 272
Scotch bonnet chiles, 172
screwpine leaves, 229
sea bass, 82, 220
sea cucumber, 221, 228, 241
  dried, 203
sea salt, 5, 13, 242
sea snails, 241
sea squirt, 220, 241
sea urchin, 221
  roe. *See* uni
sea vegetables, 62
seafood, 28–34, 202, 208, 220–221,
  252, 273. *See also* fish; caviar;
  shellfish
  baitop shell, 244
  clams, 32, 33, 82, 130, 202, 215,
    220, 228, 229, 240, 241, 249
  conch, 172
  crabs, 28, 202, 203, 208, 212,
    215, 220, 228, 231, 240, 241,
    259
  cuttlefish, 220, 241, 259
  eel, 202, 220, 221, 241, 249, 259
  jellyfish, 203, 206, 220, 241
  lobster, 33, 202, 215, 259, 263
  mussels, 32, 82, 93, 130, 200
  octopus, 32, 93, 139, 202, 203,
    220, 240, 241, 249, 259, 262,
    273
  oysters, 28, 32, 33, 202, 203,
    208, 220, 228, 240, 241
  periwinkles, 208, 220
  prawns, 183, 203, 220
  scallops, 31, 32, 93, 203, 211,
    241
  sea cucumber, 203, 221, 228, 241

seafood (continued)
  sea squirt, 220, 241
  sea urchin, 221
  seahorse, 211
  shark fin, 202, 207
  shrimp, 23, 32, 33, 82, 151, 183,
      172, 176, 191, 202, 211, 221,
      241, 259, 262
  snails, 202, 212, 215, 220, 229,
      241
  squid (calamari), 32, 93, 130,
      202, 203, 212, 220, 221, 241,
      254, 262, 263, 273
  turtles, 210, 212
  whelks, 208
seafood breading, 30, 33
seafood, canned, tinned, or jarred,
    93, 244
seafood, dried, 172, 176, 203, 211,
    212, 221, 241. *See also* fish, dried
seafood, fresh, 28–34, 220, 240, 252
seafood, frozen, 6, 32, 213,
    220–221, 252
seafood, live, 215, 229, 259
  clams, 33, 215, 228, 229
  crabs, 202, 208, 209, 215, 220,
      240, 259
  eel, 259
  lobster, 33, 215, 259
  mussels, 220
  oysters, 33, 220, 228
  snails, 212, 215, 229
  turtles, 210, 212
seafood sauces, 30, 31, 33
seafood, smoked, 2, 32
seahorse, dried, 211
seasonings. *See also* herbs; sauces;
  spices
  adobo, 83
  criolla, 173
  furikake, 242, 250, 255
  jerk, 173, 176, 177, 179
  Latin American, 89
  Middle Eastern, 159
  Polish, 108, 114, 117
  poultry, 22

  Vegeta, 108, 114, 117, 123
seaweed, 223, 225, 240, 249–250,
    251, 252
  hair vegetable (black moss), 206
  hijiki, 244
  kombu, 244
  nori, 31, 225, 240, 244
  wakame, 225, 244
seeds
  achiote, 10, 83
  alfalfa, 62
  black onion. *See* charnuska
  bulk, 167
  egusi (squash), 173
  lotus, 206
  melon, 160
  pomegranate. *See* anardana
  poppy, 10, 108, 184
  pumpkin, flavored with chiles
      and lime, 86
  sesame, 10, 147, 159, 184, 205
    black, 206
  watermelon, 207
sel gris (gray salt), 13
semen euryales, 211
semolina, 139, 159, 174
semolina (pasta flour), 132, 186
serrano peppers, 83, 84, 100
sesame
  candy, 160, 252
  oil, 209, 216, 247
  paste, 205, 207. *See also* tahini
  seeds, 10, 147, 159, 184, 205
    black, 206
sev (Indian chickpea-noodle
    snack), 188, 195
seven-spice seasoning. *See* shichimi
"sexy" drinks, 245, 253
seyjid, 167
shabu shabu sauce, 242
shallots, 231, 247, 252
Shaoxing wine, 217
shark fin, 202, 207
  dried, 203
Sheboygan bratwurst, 126
shellfish, 28, 33, 220. *See also* spe-

cific types
live, 33, 220
smoked, 220
sherry vinegar, 2, 3, 5, 261
shichimi, shichimi togarashi, 243
shiitake, 204, 242, 259, 260
dried, 207
shirataki (noodles for sukiyaki), 243
shiromiso (white miso), 244
shiso. *See* perilla
shlisikai dumplings, 111
shrimp, 23, 32, 33, 183, 202, 211,
241, 262. *See also* prawns
dried, 172, 176, 211, 221
fried, 32
head-on, 82, 151, 151, 202, 221,
259
smoked, 32
tiger, 191
shrimp cakes, 229
shrimp chips/crackers, 207, 245
shrimp paste, 205
shungiku. *See* chrysanthemum
leaves
Siberian pelmeni, 151
Sicilian Trapani salt, 13
silk squash (sinqua). *See* luffa
silver fungus. *See* white fungus
silver sheets, edible (varak), 187
silverfish, 254
sinqua (silk squash). *See* luffa
skate, 31, 32, 220, 241, 262
skirt steak, 20, 23
slippery vegetable (Vietnamese
spinach). *See* gau ma
Smithfield hams, 211
smoked butt, 124, 127
smoked caviar, 34, 146
smoked fish. *See* fish, smoked
smoked meats. *See* meats, smoked
smoked seafood. *See* seafood,
smoked
snack mixes
bulk, 15, 163, 192, 259
Indian, 188, 192, 195
nuts, 160

rice cracker, 245
snails, 202, 220
live, 212, 215, 229
sea, 241
snake beans. *See* long beans
snapper, 82
soba (Japanese buckwheat noodles), 205, 222, 223, 234, 237,
243, 247, 250, 255
organic, 7
sofrito, 173
soft drinks/sodas
Coco Rico coconut, 214
guaraná, 89
Italian, 133, 262
Jarritos (Mexican), 214, 262
Ting (Jamaican grapefruit), 178,
214
sole, 28, 220
solomon gundy. *See* herring paste
somen, 205, 223, 234, 237, 243
soprasetta, 3
sorrel, 16, 108
soujouk, 146, 149, 158, 162
soup mixes, 4
soups
borscht, 112, 117, 118
dashi, 244
restaurant size, 54
sour cactus fruit. *See* xoconostle
sour cherry
juice, boxed, 114
pits (mahlab, mahlebi), 10, 159
sour oranges, 42, 173, 176, 179
sour yogurt, 165
sourdough bread, 111
Lithuanian, 109
soursop (guanábana), puree, 94
South American ingredients and
products, 91, 94, 220–238, 266.
See also Latin American ingredients and products
Southeast Asian ingredients and
products, 219–232, 272. *See also*
Asian ingredients and products

soy foods, 62, 64, 207, 225, 244. *See also* tempeh; tofu; TVP
soy cheese, 62
soy milk, 62, 225, 244
soy nuts, 62, 65
   butter, 62
soy powder, 62
   fermented, 244
   roasted, 244
soy sauce, 64, 136, 209, 214, 216, 222, 224, 229, 242, 247, 255
   citrus (ponzu, yuzu), 222, 242, 255
   dark, 205, 222, 242
   light, 205, 222, 242
   mushroom, 202, 205, 209, 216, 217, 242
   tamari, 64, 243
   toyomansi, 243, 254
soybean
   miso (mamemiso), 244
   paste (denjang), 242, 243
soybeans
   dried, 207
   edamame, 225, 242
   fermented. *See* natto
Spanish
   lentils, 64
   limes. *See* quenepas
spelt (farro), 62, 109, 117, 132
spice blends, 158, 159, 163, 165. *See also* seasonings
   adobo, 83
   baharat, 159
   Chicago ethnic, 15
   Chinese five-spice powder, 40, 205, 210, 217
   curry powder, West Indian, 173, 176
   panch phoron (Bengali five-spice), 185, 189
   ras el hanout, 159
   shichimi, shichimi togarashi (seven-spice seasoning), 243
   tabil, 159
   zaatar, 159, 161, 162, 165

spiced buns (Caribbean), 178
spices, 10–18, 50, 64, 88, 117, 132, 137, 159, 162, 163, 164, 165, 176, 177, 182, 272. *See also* herbs
ajowan (carom), 10, 184, 196
Aleppo pepper, 10, 15
allspice, 10, 173, 184
anise seed (saunf), 184
angelica root, 159, 211
annatto seeds (achiote), 173, 244
asafoetida, powdered (hing), 184
bay leaf, Indonesian (salam leaf), 184
bulk, 14–15, 162
canela (Mexican/soft-stick cinnamon), 83, 173
caraway, 184
cardamom, 10, 12, 147, 159, 182, 184, 189, 194, 199
cayenne, 10
celery seed, 184
charnuska (black onion seed, kalonji, nigella), 10, 14, 184, 189
chiles, 10, 83, 87, 89, 90, 92, 93, 94, 95, 96, 100, 172, 184, 231
cinnamon (cassia), 10, 12, 14, 182, 184, 194
cloves, 184
coriander, 166, 184, 197
cumin, 166, 168, 184, 197
cumin seed, 189
dill seed, 184
fennel (finocchio), 132
fennel pollen, 15
fennel seed, 184, 189
fenugreek, 10, 147, 159, 167, 183, 184, 191, 195, 260, 262, 263
filé (gumbo filé, sassafras), 10, 173
galangal, 10, 222, 229
garlic, 228, 252
ginger, 10, 87, 191, 197, 204, 209, 213, 222, 247
grains of paradise, 10

Indian/Pakistani, 182, 184, 185, 191, 192, 193, 194, 195
juniper berries, 10, 14
kala jeera (black cumin, royal cumin), 10, 184
Latin American, 83, 85, 88, 89
mace, 10, 184
mahlab, mahlebi (sour cherry pits), 10, 159
mango powder (amchoor), 159, 184
mustard seed, 184, 189
nutmeg, 10, 12, 40, 122, 135, 184
obgono, 176
paprika, 5, 10, 108, 147
pepper, peppercorns, 10, 11, 14, 184, 205, 248
pitter, 176
poppy seed, 10, 108, 184
red pepper, 240, 243
saffron, 10, 18, 182, 184, 199
sansho (Japanese pepper), 242
sesame seed, 10, 147, 159, 184, 205
  black, 206
star anise, 10, 184, 205
sumac, 10, 147, 159, 161, 162, 165, 169, 193, 194
suya pepper, 176
Szechuan pepper (fagara), 11, 205
turmeric (haldi), 10, 184, 191
ukazi, 176
vanilla beans, 10, 12, 15
spices, restaurant quantities, 49, 54
spinach, 135, 136, 153, 246
  Vietnamese (gau ma, slippery vegetable), 205, 222
sprats, tinned, 114
spring roll wrappers, 207
sprouting seeds, 62
sprouts, 204, 242. See also bean sprouts
squabs, 203
squash, exotic varieties, 36

squid (calamari), 32, 130, 202, 220, 221, 241, 254, 262, 263, 273
  dried, 203, 212, 241
  fried, 32
  rings, frozen, 32
  tinned, in its own ink, 93
squid ink pasta, 4, 132
sremska ljuta, 152
Sriracha sauce, 205, 222, 223, 226, 230, 232, 242
star anise, 10, 184, 205
star fruit. See carambola
Starapolski bread, 119
steaks. See beef
stevia, 62
sticky rice. See glutinous rice
stomach, 254
Stracchino, 133
strawberries, 38, 138
  pick-your-own, 37
Strega, 133
sturgeon
  caviar, 3, 34
  smoked, 32
subscription farming, 36–37
sugar
  brown
    panela (loaf-shaped), 85
    piloncillo (cone-shaped), 86, 173
  cane, 173
  syrup/juice, 174
  decorative, 15
  fructose, 15, 62
  jaggery, 187
  lactose, 62
  rock, 205, 225
  sanding, 15
  turbinado, 173
sukiyaki
  beef, 241
  noodles (shirataki), 243
  pork, 241
sumac, 10, 147, 159, 161, 162, 165, 169, 193, 194
sun-dried tomatoes, 132

sun-dried tomatoes (continued)
    tapenade, 2
surmai. *See* kingfish
sushi, 4, 31, 33, 241, 249, 250, 272
sustainable agriculture, 36–37, 41
suya pepper, 176
Swedish brown beans, 128
sweet potato
    noodles, 223, 253
    paste, 91
squash. *See* delicata
sweet potatoes, 48
sweetbreads, 108
sweetbrier flavoring water, 167
sweets. *See* bakery goods
Swiss chard. *See* chard
syrups, 108, 116, 132, 147, 151,
    159
    almond, 132, 147, 159
    cane, 174
    fruit, 93, 110, 114, 124, 133, 147,
        159
    hazelnut, 132
    jahlab, 162
    Torani, 132
Szechuan peppercorns (fagara), 11,
    205

tabil, 159
tagliatelle, salmon, 138
tahini, 4, 62, 147, 155, 159, 164,
    259
Tahitian vanilla beans, 15
tai goo choy (tatsoi, flat cabbage),
    204
Taleggio, 133
Tam Tam crackers, 70
tamales, 23, 92, 96, 99, 262, 273
tamari, 64, 243
tamarillo, 83, 183
    puree, 94
tamarind, 83, 90, 167, 173
    candy, 99
    concentrate, 198, 199, 222
    juice drinks, 214
    paste, 85, 147, 159, 184, 263

pickled, 187
syrup, 93, 147, 159
tandoori
    cooking sauce, 187
    masala, 185
    paste, 192, 199
tapenades, 2, 4
tapioca
    flour, 64, 91
    pearls, 206, 223, 229, 244, 266
    starch (flour), 206, 223
    noodles, 223
taramasalata, 146
tarelli, 133
taro (dasheen, eddo, sata-imo), 42,
    48, 101, 102, 103, 172, 183, 203,
    204, 242, 254, 259
    chips, 93
    greens, 174
    leaves, 254, 262
    stems, dried, 244
tatsoi (flat cabbage). *See* tai goo
    choy
T-bone steaks, 23
teas, 50, 110, 117, 152, 245, 251,
    266–267, 272. *See also* yerba
    maté
    "bubble", 266
    bulk, 15, 164
    canned drinks, 207, 214, 245,
        266
    chamomile, 10
    Chinese, 117
    herbal, 110, 117, 266
    Indian, 117
    medicinal, 94, 110, 114, 117,
        207, 225, 245, 266
    Turkish, 149
    whole leaf, 164, 267
teff, 62
Tellicherry peppercorns, 11
tempeh, 62. *See also* soy foods
tempura mix, 244, 250
tendons, beef, 221, 241
tequila, 3
terrines, 2, 3

Thai (anise) basil, 222, 262
Thai ingredients and products, 4, 191, 214, 226, 227, 262. *See also* Asian; Southeast Asian ingredients and products
thuringer, 24
tiger nuts (earth chestnuts). *See* chufas
tiger shrimp, 191
tikka masala, 185
tilapia, 202
  live, 151, 215, 228, 241, 259
tilefish, 220
  dried, 241
tindora, 183, 195, 260
Ting (Jamaican grapefruit soda), 178, 214
tobacco (for hookahs), 162, 165, 167
tobikko (flying fish roe), 3, 34, 241, 249
  wasabi, 34
tocino (Filipino bacon), 254
tofu (bean curd), 62, 225, 244, 249, 250. *See also* soy foods
  baked, 62
  fermented (preserved), 207, 225
  natto, 244
  flavored, 62
  fried, 207
    atsuage, 244
  noodles, 233
  "pockets", 207, 244
  pressed, 207
  sheets, 207
tomatillos, 42, 83, 90, 94, 173, 177, 260
tomatoes. *See also* sun-dried tomatoes
  heirloom, 36
  Israeli crushed, 71
  San Marzano canned, 5, 132, 139
tongue, 91, 108
  cow, 82
  pig, 221
  veal, 263

tonkatsu sauce, 243
toor dal (yellow lentils), 185. *See also* pigeon peas
Torani syrups, 132
tort wafers, 114
tortillas, 85, 258, 262
  fresh, 82
tostones (fried plantains), 97, 151, 262
totoes (coconut cakes), 178
touloum, 160
toyomansi, 243, 254
trahana (Greek pasta), 43, 147, 152
tree fungus (black fungus). *See* cloud ear fungus
trefoil. *See* mitsuba
tripe, 91, 108, 211, 241
  beef, 221
  lamb, 162, 259
tropical fruit. *See also* specific types
  jams, 174, 175
  juices, 86, 175
  pastes, 175
  pulps, frozen, 89, 176, 262
  purees, 94, 100, 174, 175, 262
  sodas, 86
tropical fruit, canned, 93, 223, 254
tropical tubers, 88, 91, 101–105, 167, 172, 176, 260. *See also* boniato; malanga; taro; yucca
Trotter, Charlie, products, 7
trout, 28
  smoked, 108
truffle
  cream, 3
  oil, 2, 3, 138
  paste, 2
  powder, 2
truffles, 2, 3
tsu goo (Chinese arrowhead), 204
tubers. *See* specific types
tuna (cactus fruit, prickly pear), 42, 42, 83, 259, 261, 262
tuna (fish), 241
  canned with red pepper, 244
  Italian in oil, 261

Tunisian chili sauce (harissa), 159, 167
tupelo honey, 62
turbinado sugar, 173
turkey, 25
    live, 25
    smoked, 71
    wild, 23
Turkish delight (rahat loukoum), 148, 149, 154, 155, 160, 162
Turkish ingredients and products, 146–155, 163. *See also* Greek; Middle Eastern ingredients and products
turmeric (haldi), 10, 184
    white (zedoary), fresh, 184, 191
    yellow, fresh, 184, 191
turnips, 48, 248
    pickled, 165
turtles, live, 210, 212
tuvar beans, 184, 195
TVP (texturized vegetable protein), 15, 62. *See also* soy foods

udon, 206, 223, 234
ukazi, 176
Ukrainian ingredients and products, 111, 117, 152. *See also* Eastern European ingredients and products
ume (Japanese plum), 242, 249
umeboshi (pickled Japanese plum), 244
    vinegar, 62, 64, 248
umeshi plum wine, 229
unagi (grilled eel for sushi), 249
unfiltered honey, 62
uni (sea urchin roe), 220, 241
urad dal (black lentils), 185
Utenos beer (Lithuanian), 117

Valencia rice, 85
valor beans, 184, 195
vanilla
    beans, 10, 12
        Tahitian, 15

extract, 15
    powder, 159
varak (edible gold or silver sheets), 187
variety meats. *See* offal
veal, 20, 130
    bologna, 126
    bones, 108
    brains, 263
    bratwurst, 126
    breast, 130
    cutlets, 130
    shanks, 20, 130
    tongue, 263
Vegeta, 108, 114, 117, 123
vegetables, dried, 223. *See also* mushrooms, dried
vegetables, frozen, 7
venison, 21
verdolaga (purslane), 83, 94, 96, 100, 108, 177, 259
verjus, 159
vermicelli
    rice, 205, 223, 238, 243
    wheat, 237
Vialone Nano rice, 132, 139
Vietnamese cilantro, 222
Vietnamese ingredients and products, 215, 226, 229. *See also* herbs, Vietnamese; Southeast Asian ingredients and products
Vietnamese spinach (slippery vegetable). *See* gau ma
Vietnamese table salad, 221, 227, 229
vindaloo (masala, paste, sauce), 185
vinegar mothers, 49, 267
vinegars, 2, 3, 4, 5, 6, 50, 62, 62, 63, 222
    aged, 2, 5, 7, 134, 138
    balsamic, 2, 4, 5, 132, 134, 136, 138, 139, 143
    black (Chinkiang), 205, 222
    cane, 243, 255
    cider, 62
    coconut, 215, 222

grape, 243
lemon, 222
nipa sap (coconut palm), 243
organic, 63
palm, 215, 255
persimmon, 243
rice, 205, 207, 224, 242, 247
  brown, 62, 243
  wine, 248
sherry, 2, 3, 5, 261
ume/umeboshi, 62, 64, 248
wine, 2, 37, 132, 209
vodka, 114, 116, 118
  chocolate, 116
  Georgian black currant, 114
  Polish, 116, 118
  Russian, 118
  Scandinavian, 118
Vong products, 4, 5

wakame, 225, 244
Walker's Wood products, 176, 177
walnut
  oil, 2
  preserves, 148
walnuts, 40, 147, 163, 168
wasabi, 228, 240, 242, 243, 255
  fresh, 249
wasabi peas, 245
water caltrop. *See* horned water
  chestnut
water chestnut flour, 206
water chestnuts, fresh, 205, 207,
  212, 214, 222, 263
water spinach (kangkong). *See* ong
  choy
watermelon seeds, 207
waters
  Italian mineral, 133, 137
  Middle Eastern flavoring. *See* fla-
    voring waters
wehani rice, 62
Westphalian ham, 126
wet white pears, 252
wheat. *See also* bulgur; freekah
  berries, 109, 152

couscous, 64
flour, 64
  peeled, 91
germ, 62
gluten, 225
mock duck, 206
noodles, 205, 210, 233, 234, 236,
  237, 243. *See also* soba; somen;
  and udon
starch (non-glutinous flour), 206
wheat, cracked, 151, 159, 190, 259
wheat, hulled, 147
wheat, whole, 62, 159, 190
whelks, 208
white
  beans, 85
  fungus (silver fungus), 207
  miso (shiromiso), 244
  turmeric (zedoary), 184, 191
  yams (ñames), 42, 83, 173, 176
whitefish, 28
  roe, 3, 28, 34
  flavored, 3
  smoked, 32, 108
wieners, 126
wild blackberry jam, 114
wild boar, 21
wild turkey, 23
wine, 3, 5, 6, 114, 116, 261,
  268–270
  Alsatian, 127
  Armenian pomegranate, 114
  champagne, 268
  Croatian, 261
  German, 127
  Japanese
    mirin, 242
    sake, 247, 249
  kosher, 70
  plum wine, 229, 249
  Polish, 116
  Romanian, 261
  Shaoxing wine, 217
wine vinegar, 2, 37, 132, 209
wine yeast, 49
winemaking supplies, 49, 267

wing beans, 222
winter melons, 184, 205
winter storage vegetables, 36
wonton wrappers, 207, 211, 213, 217
wood ear mushrooms, dried, 207
wrappers, wraps, 211, 213, 222
  for egg rolls, 211
  for empanadas, 85, 97
  gyoza skins, 222
  for lumpia, 244
  rice papers, 207, 222, 223, 228, 231, 232
  for spring rolls, 207
  for wonton, 207, 211, 213, 217

XO sauce, 205
xoconostle (sour cactus fruit), 96, 262

yacamein noodles, 237
yam noodles, 223, 233, 243, 253. *See also* shirataki; sweet potato noodles
yams, 172, 173, 177
  cush-cush (yampi), 260
  Ghana, 173, 176
  naga-imo (mountain), 242
  white (ñames), 42, 83, 173, 176
  purple (ratalu), 183, 263
  jam, 229
  yellow, 173, 176
yard beans. *See* long beans
yautia. *See* malanga
yeast, wine, 49
yellow
  chives, 203
  lentils, 147, 159, 185
  turmeric, fresh, 184, 191
  yams, 173, 176
yerba maté, 91, 93, 139
yogurt, 148
  Eastern European, 118
  Greek, 155, 259
  Indian, 187
  Mexican, 96

Middle Eastern, 152, 160, 162, 162, 164
  sour, 165
YR sauce, 127
yu choy (green choy sum), 214, 222
yuba (bean curd skin), 244
yucca (cassava, manioc), 42, 43, 83, 84, 88, 90, 91, 101, 102, 105, 151, 173, 176, 177, 179, 260, 262
  chips, 93
  couscous (attiéké, de manioc), 174
  flour, 89, 91, 93, 173
  juice. *See* cassareep
  leaves, frozen, 174
  meal, 174, 229
yuzu (citrus soy sauce), 255

zaatar, 159, 161, 162, 165
zabiha. *See* halal/zabiha
zedoary. *See* turmeric, white
zeppelinis (mix for), 120
zizyphus (Chinese red dates, jujube), 205
zomi (spiced palm oil), 174, 177

334

About the Author

photo by
Tamara Bell

Marilyn Pocius has been writing, cooking, and eating weird things all her life.

Growing up on the Southwest Side, Pocius learned that Chicago is a collection of ethnic neighborhoods (hers was Lithuanian). Her earliest culinary memories are Lithuanian black bread, which she still loves, and pickled herring, which she still hates.

At the University of Wisconsin, she studied French, Chinese, and Russian and graduated with a B.A. in linguistics. She is also a chef graduate of the Cooking and Hospitality Institute of Chicago. Her career as an advertising agency creative director gave her an opportunity to write television commercials for national accounts, like Kraft, Kellogg's, and M&M Mars.

Pocius does market tours, food demos, and consulting for a variety of organizations, including Edible Chicago, her business venture with partner Julie Gibson-Lay. As a freelance writer, she has contributed to the *Chicago Tribune*, Pioneer Press suburban papers, and others. Pocius currently works as a cookbook editor for Publications International in Lincolnwood.

She lives with her daughter, Genevieve, her calico cat, Sophie, and her mutt, Purdie. She is an amateur herbalist and organic gardener and likes to grow unusual vegetables and exotic herbs. She is also active in the local food scene and a member of the International Association of Culinary Professionals, Culinary Historians of Chicago, and Slow Food USA.

Lake Claremont Press

Founded in 1994, Lake Claremont Press specializes in books on the Chicago area and its history, focusing on preserving the city's past, exploring its present environment, and helping to cultivate a strong sense of place for the future. Visit us on the Web at www.lakeclaremont.com, and contact us for a catalog at 773/583-7800 or lcp@lakeclaremont.com.

Booklist

The Politics of Place: A History of Zoning in Chicago

Finding Your Chicago Ancestors

Wrigley Field's Last World Series

The Golden Age of Chicago Children's Television

Chicago's Midway Airport

The Hoofs & Guns of the Storm: Chicago's Civil War Connections

Great Chicago Fires

The Firefighter's Best Friend: Lives and Legends of Chicago Firehouse Dogs

Graveyards of Chicago

Chicago Haunts: Ghostlore of the Windy City

More Chicago Haunts

Muldoon: A True Chicago Ghost Story: Tales of a Forgotten Rectory

Creepy Chicago (for kids 8–12)

Literary Chicago

A Native's Guide to Chicago, 4th Edition

A Native's Guide to Northwest Indiana

Award-winners

The Chicago River: A Natural and Unnatural History

Near West Side Stories: Struggles for Community in Chicago's Maxwell Street Neighborhood

Hollywood on Lake Michigan: 100 Years of Chicago and the Movies

The Streets & San Man's Guide to Chicago Eats

Coming in 2006

A Field Guide to Gay and Lesbian Chicago

Today's Chicago Blues

A Chicago Tavern: A Goat, A Curse, and the American Dream

Chicago's Business and Social Clubs

From Lumber Hookers to the Hooligan Fleet: A Treasury of Chicago Maritime History